Comprehensive Schools:
Past, Present and Future

Comprehensive Schools:
Past, Present and Future

Alan Weeks

Methuen   London

First published in 1986 by
Methuen & Co. Ltd
11 New Fetter Lane,
London EC4P 4EE

© 1986 Alan Weeks

Typeset by
Scarborough Typesetting Services
and printed in Great Britain by
Richard Clay (The Chaucer Press) Ltd,
Bungay, Suffolk

*British Library Cataloguing in
Publication Data*

Weeks, Alan
Comprehensive schools: past, present
and future.
1. Comprehensive high schools –
Great Britain
I. Title
373.2'5'0941   LA635

ISBN 0–416–40690–4
ISBN 0–416–40700–5 Pbk

To Pam

Contents

List of tables and graphs

Acknowledgements

The author and publishers would like to thank the ILEA for their kind permission to use the photograph of the Elizabeth Garrett Anderson School formerly the site of both Starcross and Rising-hill Schools on the cover.

Cover photograph taken by Brooke Calverley

1
Why comprehensive reorganization?

Politics and practicalities

In July, 1965 the then Secretary of State for Education, Anthony Crosland, sent out Circular 10/65 to local education authorities and other bodies informing them that Government policy was in favour of non-selective secondary schools and asking them to submit reorganization plans which would create such schools in their areas. A detailed account of this Circular is provided in Chapter 2. Why was the Government confident that comprehensive schools were acceptable to the electorate, to local education authorities and to teachers? Of course the Labour election manifesto had indicated that the Party leadership would accelerate secondary school reorganization, and thus the Secretary of State's justification for Circular 10/65 could have been that 'the people had spoken'. But why had Labour been confident enough to include reorganization in the manifesto? Robin Pedley (1963) provided an answer by quoting Victor Hugo: 'Nothing is so powerful as an idea whose time has come.'

This was meant to indicate that there was an ideology of comprehensiveness in secondary education and that this had become politically powerful by 1965. Since politics may be the art of the possible it is interesting to try to trace why the comprehensive idea had become possible. Julienne Ford (1969) is most illuminating on this. The post-war population bulge started to move into secondary schools in 1957 with a consequent increase in the demand for scarce grammar school places. The social group most disappointed in this objective was the one which straddled working-class and middle-class distinctions, a marginal group with inconsistent status rankings. Clear evidence of this was the increasing numbers of secondary modern schools offering General Certificate of Education (GCE) O level courses (357 schools in 1954 rising to 1350 schools in 1959). The staying-on rate in secondary modern fifth years rose from 7 per cent in 1959 to 10 per cent in 1964. The fact that the 11-plus selection procedures became increasingly unpopular was not so much an objection to selection *per se* as an objection to a particular selection procedure which chose so few children for grammar schools. In the poll reported in *New Society* (Donnison 1967), 37 per cent of social class AB were against comprehensive schools but the corresponding figure for class C1 was 20 per cent, for C2 15 per cent and for DE 11 per cent. The largest support for comprehensive schools came from class C2 (58 per cent). If politicians such as Harold Wilson saw comprehensive schools as grammar schools for all, his view was shared by a growing number of aspiring parents who regarded themselves as middle class or wanted their children to be regarded as such.

A closer look at the *New Society* poll reveals that only 16 per cent of the parents surveyed would have chosen a comprehensive school for their children and 76 per cent wanted to keep grammar schools. It was a vote against the secondary modern school rather than anything else, a clear revelation that it was a grammar school education which parents sought for their children. But if the comprehensive school could provide this, a rose by any other name . . . In a Plowden Commission survey, 51 per cent of the parents of children in their last year of primary education hoped these children would go to grammar schools, but grammar schools were never designed for more than the top 20 per cent of the ability range.

Evidence of an aspiring and prosperous working-cum-middle-class existed in Leicestershire in the 1950s and 1960s (Mason 1970). The county went comprehensive between 1957 and 1969. Stewart Mason, the Chief Education Officer at the time, described a new population, working in new industries, eager for education. He met this demand by engineering secondary school reorganization.

It may have been the dawning of this surging demand for more grammar school education that attracted many rank and file members of the Labour Party long before its leaders were awakened to its existence, but it is even more likely that early support for comprehensive schools was made on ideological or practical grounds. Secondary reorganization was not a political issue before 1960, and early comprehensive schools were as likely to evolve in Tory areas as in Labour ones (see Chapter 3). By 1960, however, the attention of Labour leaders was engaged by the need to acquire the votes of an aspiring working-class. Comprehensive schools seemed a very neat way of providing this group with the prestigious education they desired. Harold Wilson adopted reorganization as part of what he called the 'white-hot technological revolution' – the modernization of society and the economy in order to preserve support for Labour.

Before all this, however, the ideology of the comprehensive school drifted in a political vacuum, probably kept alive by the National Association of Labour Teachers (NALT) more than any other group, although there was minority support in the National Union of Teachers (NUT) (Fenwick 1976), the odd local authority became keen on reorganization, and a Conservative Government sometimes allowed it. Comprehensive schools were seen as a practical and economical system in sparsely populated rural areas, or in new or reconstructed housing estates or in new towns such as Crawley, Harlow and Kirkby. A few experiments in these places hardly seemed to matter as long as established grammar schools were not affected.

An argument often used in favour of these early reorganizations was that comprehensive schools would tend to be larger and therefore able to offer a wider range of curricula and resources under one roof to a wider range of pupils within economies of scale. This was especially important in areas with scattered populations.

Another practical argument was that since the number of grammar school places varied dramatically from one area to another some sort of reorganization was necessary for the sake of fairness. No one would agree to any levelling down of places since the percentage of those available varied from 8 per cent to 40 per cent in England and Wales. Perhaps the best substitute for raising the overall number of grammar school places was to have comprehensive schools, a matter of expediency rather than ideology. The ideology only became politically important when it was used to provide convincing arguments for political ends. Strong evidence that the tripartite system was failing to provide equality of opportunity was available for ten years or more before leading politicians discovered it.

Perhaps the main stimulus for reorganization was the unpopularity of secondary modern schools. The schools, in general, can hardly be blamed since they were starved of resources. The 'parity of esteem' notion, which was a bedrock of tripartism, was just a dream. In the *Times Educational Supplement* *(TES)* of 19 March 1965, Cyril Hughes wrote that secondary modern schools had soldiered along on hard rations and a shortage of ammunition since 1944. Secondary moderns only hit the headlines when trouble brewed in them. But Hughes noticed that as the comprehensive debate developed it became apparent that grammar school supporters also loved secondary moderns. They took great pains to show how successful these schools were, proving the tripartite system worked. How strange this sudden affection, mused Cyril Hughes. If secondary moderns were so good why not make all schools secondary moderns (not such a bad idea)? The reality was that they were working under difficult conditions and false pretences, except for the showplaces which the grammar school pundits visited.

In 1967, 17 per cent of secondary modern teachers were graduates compared to 78 per cent of grammar school teachers. The pupil--teacher ratio in secondary moderns was 19:1 on average and 16.6:1 in grammar schools. Their so-called 'freedom' to experiment with new subjects and methods was the 'freedom' of a beggar (Griffiths 1971). The great bulk of secondary moderns were stern and formal places, like the senior elementary schools they succeeded, with an 'Old Testament' approach to discipline (Griffiths 1971). Small wonder they were delighted to concentrate new energies on emerging fifth year pupils, whose parents demanded success at O level, or at least in commercial and technical examinations.

Before considering the ideology and the fifteen years of upheaval in schools it heralded, it is intriguing to wonder how successful some positive discrimination (never mind parity) for secondary moderns would have been. With the local authority behind them, some secondary modern schools were very successful. By 1965, Bournemouth (where that prosperous *nouveau riche* working class must have been well in evidence) had a staying-on rate of more than 50 per cent in secondary modern schools, and in Surrey and the East Riding more than a quarter of all secondary modern pupils took O levels. A little Government money to help the local initiative would have gone a long way, and it might have saved a great deal of disruption. But perhaps it was not 'possible', whereas a surge of comprehensiveness and its available ideology was.

Ideology

The comprehensive school ideology centred on the principle of equality of opportunity, backed by research reports showing poor opportunities in secondary modern schools. For example, Hilde Himmelweit (1970) followed up a 1951 sample of secondary modern and grammar school pupils in 1961 and found that 79 per cent of the grammar school leavers had entered middle-class occupations whilst only 25 per cent of secondary modern leavers had done so. There has never been any doubt in people's minds that the comprehensive school was designed to ensure that all pupils had the best chance possible to do well at school in order to maximize their life chances. It was a naive view in that it may have led to the existence of a larger number of brain surgeons, many of whom would have become rubbish collectors because there would have been too many brain surgeons chasing too few jobs (Ford 1969). Those who hold to the principle of educational equality naively believe that increasing the economic 'pool of talent' can only have satisfying results for the economy and everybody concerned. Julienne Ford considered that it was social justice rather than economic efficiency that was being sought, although politicians may have settled for a situation in which brain surgeons were rubbish collectors as long as there were enough brain surgeons (a common enough situation in other occupations, e.g. teaching).

The ideology of comprehensive schools has been and is still saddled with these sorts of confusions. Indeed, in the 1960s (see the *TES* editorial, 11 December 1965) commentators complained about the failure of educational philosophers to tackle the loose thinking of the comprehensive debate. It was clear from many statements of 'the comprehensive principle' that their authors had much more in mind than simply good jobs. Pedley (1963), for example, wrote of the fullest development of everyone's talents. Everyone was of equal worth in the sense of being equally deserving of help towards 'personal growth'. This was about the potential which each child has, and the right of each child to develop that potential with the help of teachers. This was the 'quality' in the 'equality'. Pedley considered the achievements of individuals as incomparable, being based on uniqueness, and he particularly objected to orders of merit which compared the incomparable on unscientific scales. Margaret Miles (1968), head of Mayfield Comprehensive School in south London, wrote in a similar vein and the joint statement of the National Foundation for Educational Research (NFER) working party on comprehensive schools in the late 1960s called for equal prestige for a wide variety of achievements (Ross *et al.* 1972).

When Julienne Ford (1969) tried to make sense out of the 'comprehensive principle' and 'equality', she concentrated on the economic aspects of the problem, the 'equal chance' of becoming 'unequal', i.e. getting a good job. The final order of merit was to be based on the actual 'merit' of individuals, a sort of natural or just order. Too early selection could prevent the fullest development of talent, could inhibit equality of opportunity for those with talent, might prematurely confine pupils' occupational horizons and might prematurely segregate potential vocational 'successes' from 'failures'. Ford was criticized for this concentration on economic opportunity, e.g. by Peter Daunt (1975) who dubbed it the 'First View'. The 'Second View' had more to do with the notion of individual 'potential', that is the principle that the education of any individual is of intrinsically equal value to the education of any other individual. Far from dismantling social stratification, social mobility, through a meritocratic contest system, would intensify it (the theme of Michael Young's 1958 essay).

The persistence of elitism

Ford had every excuse for concentrating on the economic opportunity aspect, however, since this was what concerned the politicians of both major parties. Crosland (1962) wrote of the inappropriateness of a 'weak' equality, which was the so-called 'equality' of tripartism, an 'equal' start for those measured as such by tests given at 11 years old. He preferred a 'strong' equality in which this measurement had to take heed of possible environmental disadvantage and a school system had to be devised in which there was an equal chance to 'acquire intelligence'. This had to be the all-in school, avoiding early selection based on potentially unfair tests and providing opportunities for late developers and those retarded by environmental disadvantage who had been rejected in the tripartite system. Edward Boyle, from the other side of the political fence, used exactly the same sort of argument in the Foreword to the Newsom Report in 1964 (Griffiths 1971).

This 'strong' equality theme echoes through evidence given earlier in this chapter that this part of the 'comprehensive principle' referred to the spreading of grammar school education to more pupils rather than to any new concept of schooling, or to an individual 'potential' wider than a potential for a place in a pool of economic talent. As we have seen, both of the major political parties strongly supported the narrower view, as did parents and teachers. An article called 'A look at Leicestershire: progress of the plan' in the *TES* of 12 February 1965 related how teachers in the upper tier 14 to 18 schools believed that their schools were as good as grammar schools, if not better, largely because they did not suffer from the weakness of early selection. But it was obvious that they expected a 'good' (i.e. selective) intake at 13-plus from the 11 to 15 schools that fed them (Benn and Simon 1970). At this time, selection was ostensibly based on parental choice but to what extent this choice was 'guided' is not clear, except that the 11 to 15 schools in Leicestershire tended to be overloaded with disaffected working-class pupils. Parents had to promise to keep their children at the 14 to 18 schools until at least a year after the statutory leaving age of 15. Pedley (1978) noted that the tiered plan was more likely to persuade grammar school teachers to accept comprehensive reorganization. But he also noted that poorer parents may not have been able to keep their children at school and that this would leave a 'rump' at the junior comprehensive. But to be fair to Leicestershire, particularly Stewart Mason, there was concern here for a genuine and informed parental choice until all pupils could be taken into the same senior comprehensive. But to many minds (e.g. Benn and Simon 1970) 'guided' parental choice worked against working-class pupils and reproduced a selective system hardly different from the tripartite.

Pedley (1978) and Rubinstein and Simon (1973) discovered that early show-place comprehensives frequently developed around established grammar schools, stressed academic achievement, and were heavily streamed. From her prestigious school Margaret Miles (1968) wrote that 'levelling' had been upwards. In such circumstances, the 'rump' of junior comprehensives in tiered systems appeared in 11 to 18 schools in low fourth year streams, the prototype 4E or '4 Mafia'. In another show-place, Kidbrooke School, a music teacher complained in 1964 that there was no pulling up for girls from a poor home background and these formed the 'difficult element'. She believed that comprehensive schools helped those who might just have failed the 11-plus and late developers, but in practice it was very difficult to move girls from one stream to another. She dismissed the idea that clever pupils had beneficial effects on the less clever (see the *TES*, 1 January 1965).

This, then, is the setting for meritocracy in the comprehensive school; the grammar school broadened its base in the hope of squeezing out some extra talent, while politicians told the electorate that they now lived in a fairer society. Circular 10/65 stated baldly that the Government wanted to 'preserve all that is valuable in grammar school education for the children who now receive it and make it available for more children'. We must remember that Harold Wilson had pledged his torso and his mac to the grammar school. It had provided a trained workforce and it had helped the working-class child. More of the same was required, especially in science, mathematics and technology where the working-class was especially under-represented. As Griffiths (1971) pointed out, the grammar school ethos was simple and politically and socially attractive. It fully accepted the demands of external examinations and catered for modest vocational needs and entrance to red brick universities. It suited the middle class, and an extended version of it could satisfy those aspiring to become middle class. Especially attractive to those nervous about the effects of reorganization were systems which retained elements of selection, such as senior comprehensives or sixth form colleges, particularly if they were housed in ex-grammar schools. Such semi-comprehensives could run along-side grammar schools and direct grant schools in a mixed economy seeking a wider pool of economic talent without throwing successful practice overboard.

Better selection procedures

In the 'comprehensive' idea, then, selection had a secure place. Indeed, it was not selection *per se* which worried meritocrats but *early* selection and the particular efficiency of the 11-plus procedures. People began to wonder whether any system of selection at 11 years old could work. Pedley (1963) concluded that no selection at 11 could be accurate enough, and whatever system was tried there would still be 6 or 7 children out of 20 who would be placed in the wrong school. The Opinion Research Centre poll of 30 June 1967 (Donnison 1967) showed a large majority in a sample opposed to the 11-plus whilst only a minority (although a large one) favoured comprehensive schools. Denis Marsden (1971) believed that parents objected to the traditional procedures of the 11-plus and wanted new selection procedures based on verbal reasoning tests and teachers' reports. A committee appointed by the British Psychological Society in 1957 pronounced against the use of intelligence tests to select children because they measured their educational experiences (at school and at home) rather than anything else (Vernon 1957). The NFER report of the same year (Yates and Pidgeon 1957) indicated that intelligence tests would never eliminate a 10 per cent error in allocation. In the sample of 78,000 children studied 12 per cent had been misplaced. Christopher Hill (1972), looking at developments in selection procedures, reported that research showed that teachers' assessments were the best predictors of secondary school success. At that time only one local authority which had selection procedures did not use these assessments, whereas many more did not use intelligence tests.

Delayed selection was a way out of this problem because, in the comprehensive school, assessments by teachers could be used as the basis for movement between streams (although the evidence from early comprehensives suggests that this sort of flexibility did not exist). But the hope was that an evolving and continuous teacher assessment in the comprehensive school could discover the 'real ability' of the pupil far more efficiently than the 11-plus.

Not only did formal selection at 11 appear inefficient but also the more protracted selection in the primary school (sometimes from the age of 7 or 8) which resulted in rigid streaming by the third or fourth year. This very early selection could affect the formal selection at 11 because those in low streams were likely to be discouraged from taking the 11-plus or encouraged to believe that they would do badly at it, with the result that they did do badly at it. Placement in lower streams could indicate that failure was expected and the pessimism could spread to misplaced able pupils, especially those from a working-class background who, as Neave (1975) suggested, were potentially more susceptible to teacher judgements about them. To be accurate, there has never been any irrefutable evidence of the self-fulfilling prophecy but the work of Douglas (1964) in this field was extremely influential in the 1960s. Even if his conclusions could be refuted there is no doubt that he persuaded many people that streaming in the primary school was wrong and that selection at 11 was very unfair to children from a working-class background. Strangely enough, some of those who opposed streaming in the primary school saw no objection to it in the secondary school. Later, more of them saw the wisdom of mixing ability in the lower secondary years. It was a question of finding a balance between the necessary delay of selection and the fear of losing talent through not weeding it out early enough.

Social engineering

A major part of the 'comprehensive principle' is concerned with social engineering. The relationship of this to the opportunity argument was never clear, and to some extent there is a contradiction between a desire for more social mobility and a desire for social equality. This is a good reason why the politicians, apart from Crosland, did not dabble too much in various arguments about 'equality' but made the most of 'opportunity', which is more of a vote-catcher. Equality is fine as long as it refers to catching up with someone else, but few want to know about others catching them up. The ideology, however, contained within it the idea of social engineering. In the second NFER report (Monks 1970) the comprehensive was seen as a place for children of all abilities, who would all help one another. They would represent a cross-section of society, an integrated society within a school assisting the integration of society in general.

Ford (1969) closely examined the relationship of the comprehensive school and this 'Fairer Society'. Explicit statements about such a connection were hard to find, which is no wonder when we consider the philosophical complications involved. Ford had to construct an 'ideal type' theory by fusing together various statements about the supposed benefits of comprehensive schools. From this fusion she formulated a number of hypotheses, including the claim that a comprehensive school will enable pupils to see social stratification not as a fixed entity, but a flexible one. This change will widen the occupational horizons of pupils. In other words, the comprehensive school will encourage more to join the merit contest. But the hypothesis went further than this in suggesting that because of the change, social interaction limited to within boundaries of anticipated occupational destination declined. Ford did not delve into the inherent illogicality of having these two hypotheses supporting one another (hence Daunt's complaint from the 'Second View'). After all, if a pupil moves up in the contest this is in itself a confirmation of the whole stratification process. The conservatism of *nouveau riche* classes has happened too frequently in history to be an accident. How was increased opportunity likely to improve social integration? Jackson and Marsden (1962) found that success could take bright working-class children out of their class and into a sort of stratification limbo, and stratification is harnessed to opportunity. In any case, in her very small sample, Ford found no evidence of changed attitudes or social integration in a comprehensive school (see Chapter 6).

Opportunity not only refers to vocational opportunity at 16 or at 18 but also to opportunity after higher education. The Robbins Report of 1963 called for an increase in the number of 18 year olds going on to higher education from 8 to 17 per cent of the age group by 1980. This report, in fact, expressed little confidence in the notion of a 'pool of talent', yet only in the sense that it suggested restriction – a limit – rather than expansion. Robbins claimed that only 61 per cent of young people from the homes of manual workers who might be expected to go to grammar school actually went to one. This was the main reason why the percentage of working-class students at university was low (in the case of male students the figure had remained static between 1928 and 1960 at 6.5 times less than the number for the sons of nonmanual workers).

2
Policy from Westminster, 1965–85

Circular 10/65

In his pamphlet of 1963, *Educational Opportunity*, Edward Boyle opposed the sharp differentiation of pupils into types or levels of ability, and argued that tripartism should not be regarded as the right and normal way of organizing secondary education. In the Foreword to the Newsom Report, he wrote of equal opportunity of acquiring intelligence (Newsom 1963). At this time there was growing backbench support for comprehensive schools among Conservative Members of Parliament, especially from the Bow Group (from 1959). Their leader, Edward Heath, made no move to dissuade them, no doubt as conscious as Harold Wilson of the need to gain the votes of an aspiring working-class. Conservatives spoke of 'good' comprehensives, by which they meant a school like a grammar school. They wanted more children to enjoy the benefits of such an education, Harold Wilson's view exactly. In the election campaign of 1964 he promised that grammar schools would disappear only over his 'dead body'. He was to be reminded many times about this promise. A parent, protesting at the possible demise of grammar schools in Bristol in 1964, held a placard which read 'Wilson's pre-election pledge. ''Grammar schools will be abolished over my dead body.'' And now?'

If Wilson sounded like the Bow Group, Boyle sounded like Crosland, who had also written about equal opportunity to acquire intelligence (Crosland 1962). This solid support from growing sections of both major parties was a powerful factor in determining the sort of comprehensive schools which evolved. Briefly, they had to be very similar to the grammar schools they were supposed to replace. If anything, this was rather a vote of confidence in the concept of the grammar school. Pupils in them would be expected to engage in a meritocratic contest, with a bit more help for some. In any contest, of course, there are losers but this was something which the politicians could afford to ignore.

National Opinion Polls during the 1964 election campaign suggested that as an important election issue education was second only to the cost of living. It appeared that commitment to secondary school reorganization would not, at least, lose votes. In the new Labour Government, Michael Stewart, a firm champion of comprehensive schools, was Education Secretary. His caution, in November 1964, not to rush into any 'sham' version of a comprehensive system was a portent of back-sliding to come. Anthony Crosland, who replaced Stewart soon after, spoke of comprehensive schools as the normal pattern of secondary education within five years and also warned against makeshift schemes. The Conservative supporters of comprehensive schools, including Boyle, made it clear that they opposed any national reorganization. In their view, this was a matter for local education authorities.

But the Government soon forced through a Commons motion supporting national reorganization (21 January 1965) designed to preserve all that was valuable in grammar school education and to ensure that more pupils were provided with it. How this would be done and how long it would take in each area would vary, but it was time for a declaration of Government policy of support for the comprehensive idea.

Nearly six months went by before Crosland concluded lengthy consultations with local authorities and teacher unions and issued Circular 10/65, 'The Organisation of Secondary Education', to local authorities, governors of direct grant schools, and to voluntary aided and special agreement schools on 12 July (DES 1965). This referred to the Commons motion of 21 January and requested plans for reorganization from local authorities. It supported the principle of local variation based on the views of local authorities, the distribution of population and on the circumstances of existing schools. By building on present foundations and achievements each area could construct a comprehensive system from one or more of six patterns. Two of these were not fully comprehensive but for some areas it was hoped that they might prove a useful interim way of edging towards a fully comprehensive system.

The first pattern was the straight through 11 to 18 school. This was the best way to have comprehensive education, according to the Circular, but it might be impractical in some areas because many existing schools were too small for a viable all-in school. A school of about a thousand pupils (6- or 7-form entry) could make up a viable comprehensive (previous official calculations had suggested a much higher figure). Using buildings on more than one site was an idea which needed careful scrutiny in each case, especially if the sites were far apart and divided by busy roads.

If an 11 to 18 school was not feasible, the Circular suggested a two-tier system with transfer of all pupils at 13 or 14 from a junior to a senior comprehensive. A senior school might be fed by more than one junior school, demanding a high degree of collaboration between the schools, true of all tiered systems. The Circular mused on whether transfer should be at 13 or 14. Transfer at 14 gave the senior school a restricted time to prepare pupils for public examinations. A tiered pattern of schools could fit existing buildings and it could grow later into a fully-fledged 11 to 18 system.

The interim patterns suggested were also tiered, involving transfer at 13 or 14 to a school catering for sixth form work. This would be based on parental choice. In one pattern pupils could remain at the lower age school until leaving at 15, or transfer to the senior school. The Circular urged that 11 to 15 schools should develop GCE and Certificate of Secondary Education (CSE) courses – making them 11 to 16 schools – so that pupils could be transferred to the senior school for sixth-form work.

The other interim pattern was transfer at 13 or 14 to a 13/14 to 15/16 school, or to a 13/14 to 18 school, depending on parental choice. Parents from 'less educated homes' must have adequate guidance in making their choices and junior comprehensives must cover all ranges of ability and have a wide range of subjects, especially if the transfer was at 14. The Circular pointed out that interim schemes should only be planned for a limited period before full reorganization.

Another pattern discussed was 11 to 16 schools feeding 16 to 18 sixth form colleges or 11 to 18 (or 13/14 to 18) schools at sixth-form level. The Circular was doubtful about 11 to 16 schools because of the potential loss of contact between junior and senior pupils and the availability of specialist teachers to staff them. But the sixth form college and the 'mushroom' 11/13/14 to 18 school was potentially economic in the use of specialists. It was proposed that sixth form colleges should cater for the needs of all 16 to 18 year olds and could link their work with colleges of further education. But the number of sixth form colleges and mush-rooms should be limited. This also applied to the final pattern, a middle school pattern of 8/9 to 12/13 schools. The Circular pointed out that the Plowden Commission was investigating possible changes in the age of transfer to secondary education and perhaps it was better to await their verdict on this before giving wholehearted support for middle schools. However, it was possible that existing small secondary schools could be used to house new middle schools.

Local authorities were exhorted to use existing buildings because there was no guarantee of money for new buildings or for extra staff to meet the needs of reorganization plans. Teachers were in short supply and there would be an even greater strain on staffing when the school leaving age was raised to 16 in 1970. Specialist staff had to be used in the most economic ways. The Burnham Committee, meanwhile, was working on plans to safe-guard salaries.

Circular 10/65 looked forward to a good social mix of pupils in comprehensive schools, bringing about enhanced social toler-ation and understanding. Catchment areas should be intellectu-ally and socially comprehensive and districts could be linked if necessary in order to achieve this balance. Local plans were to include voluntary schools if possible, allowing variations in the pattern, if necessary, to embrace them. Negotiations with direct grant schools were to aim at a closer liaison with them (see Chapter 6).

Plans were to be submitted within a year, and after consultations with local teachers and parents. Extensions would be granted in special cases. The plans were required to contain detailed proposals for the following three years, starting by September, 1967, and to include mention of every single local school. The plans were also to be costed and current building projects re-adjusted to accommodate them. It was suggested that there might be some more money for building in 1967–8, but only 'might be'.

There are various ways of looking at Circular 10/65. It is possible to see it as a plan bogged down by the clogging realities of the economic situation or as a boon to the freedom of local authorities, or as a persuasive, restrained, reasonable and acceptable compromise in the circumstances and on a very sensitive issue. It was certainly no blue-print for the future because it under-estimated the usefulness of middle school and separate sixth form systems to local authorities seeking something to suit existing buildings and something inexpensive to run. However, it was particularly useful for Crosland to employ the vote-catching, and in this case cheap, principles of variety and local freedom. Margaret Thatcher also made full political use of these principles in 1970 when extolling the virtues of local freedom was also expedient in shifting the responsibility for reorganization to local authorities.

The immediate effects of the Circular was that it appeared to give strength to authorities committed to reorganization and it seemed to get others moving. However, the goodwill it sought was not very forthcoming because opponents of comprehensive schools treated 10/65 like an Act of Parliament and the comprehensive issue became a bitter struggle in many areas. Pro-comprehensive campaigners later looked back on the Circular with a certain amount of distaste, judging it as toothless, un-enlightened, contradictory and vague. Benn and Simon (1970) considered that a circular, which is an advisory rather than a statutory instrument, was inadequate for a major reform, and this led to inefficient local planning. Because it left the initiative to the authorities without much guidance many plans were hatched after little research or consultation had taken place. These were piecemeal plans, lacking in method and open to the dominance of Chief Education Officers and/or small groups of councillors.

Benn and Simon regarded 10/65 as a reflection of the conditions prevalent at the time and virtually useless as a policy document or as a guide to local authorities. It underplayed the potential of middle schools and separate sixth form arrangements. It appeared to ignore evidence (from Leicestershire and elsewhere) of the absence or mis-use of parental choice at 13 or 14 in some tiered schemes. In one place (Section 16) the Circular mentioned entry conditions to sixth form colleges and in another (Section 35) transfer at 16 as an automatic right. Its lack of teeth was nowhere more evident than in its failure to generate negotiations between local authorities and direct grant schools (only a handful of links were forged, see Chapter 6) with the result that reorganization was held up in many areas and the direct grant schools continued to 'cream' maintained schools of pupils with above average ability.

A number of authorities showed contempt for 10/65 by simply refusing to submit plans or to re-submit them after rejection or by sending in plans which retained selective schools (a useful survey of the responses of every local authority by 1970 is provided at the end of Tyrrell Burgess's book, 1970).

Paul Bellaby (1977) concluded that 10/65 was generally hazy about what 'selection' meant nor did it make any reference to internal selection which became one of the central issues in the comprehensive debate. While preaching economy it still championed the 11 to 18 school, which, on the whole, was not suited to existing buildings. James (1980), however, concluded that 10/65 gave a greater sense of urgency to those areas committed to reorganization, such as Tynemouth. Bath, Southampton and Birmingham, for example, might never have moved without the Circular, although in the case of Birmingham the plan submitted was clearly selective and heralded ten years of wrangling. None the less, 10/65 was an incentive to re-submit previously blocked and rather hasty schemes from Labour councils. The opportunity had been provided for the enthusiastic to work out with more precision the plans they wanted. But according to Benn and Simon, in the event the plans were inadequate.

If 10/65 represented the work of a nervous Cabinet this is easily explained by the acute financial crisis of 1965. There was no money for reorganization and if there was some to come this would have to be shared between expanding higher education and the costs of raising the school leaving age (not to mention what Plowden was about to recommend for primary schools and priority areas). Crosland was waving the banners of change, but for a bright tomorrow not a penny-pinching today. How much of a change he intended, in any case, is thrown into doubt by his regard, shared by his Cabinet colleagues, for meritocracy, and by the interesting fact that a month before 10/65 he agreed to the closure of Risinghill Comprehensive School in Islington, London, a school that had held a promise of the brighter things in English secondary education, a deeper appraisal of what comprehensive education could mean (see Berg 1968).

Policy, 1965-70

Labour went to the country again in 1966 and the election manifestos and campaigns provide interesting glimpses of party policy. The Conservative pamphlet 'Putting Britain Right Ahead' expressed a belief in educational diversity and suggested that forcing comprehensive reorganization on local authorities was a 'damaging irrelevance' to variety and local autonomy. The party conference also referred to the lack of experimental research into the effectiveness of comprehensive schools (and yet did nothing to remedy this situation while a Conservative government was in power between 1970 and 1974).

Labour won the election with an increased majority, indicated more official support for middle schools and in Circular 10/66 announced that money for major building projects would be restricted to comprehensive schools. Throughout the life of this Government until 1970, the Department of Education and Science

(DES) issued statistics on the national progress of reorganization which tended to exaggerate how well it was going (see Chapter 4). These figures included plans without completion dates and they always referred to how many areas were comprehensive or planning on becoming so rather than to the number of pupils still in selective schools. It was left to the Comprehensive Schools Committee, a pressure group for reorganization founded in 1965, to provide more realistic assessments of progress.

Not only was there a wild diversity in local plans (no one should object to comprehensive schools on the grounds of lack of variety) but there was also a certain inconsistency in ministerial judgements of what to let through and what to reject. The DES accepted Tynemouth's 1966 plan for sixth form colleges for 350 to 400 students but turned down Ealing's plan of 1967 because its planned colleges for 300 to 600 were too small; 34 per cent of 11 to 16 schools accepted by the DES were smaller than this. Other oddities were the receipt of public money for new grammar schools in Plymouth and Sutton after Circular 10/66 had expressly disallowed this type of expenditure and the fact that Surrey costed the six patterns of the Circular for their area (discovering they would all cost too much) while Merton was allowed to reorganize in 1969 using the most expensive pattern for Surrey.

In 1967 there appeared to be some hardening of conflicting views in the Tory ranks. While the Conservative Conference still opposed hasty and ill-considered imposition and Government pressure on local authorities Boyle reiterated support for the comprehensive idea and gave general backing to the idea of a comprehensive system. But Margaret Thatcher supported those, the majority, who supported a binary system of selective and non-selective schools. Boyle thought that a new Conservative Government would maintain Circular 10/65 and 10/66, but by 1969 Heath was saying that they would both have to go. At the 1967 Labour Conference motions for compulsory reorganization and the compulsory integration of independent schools were lost by only a few votes. The parties were polarizing on the comprehensive school debate. In January, 1968 the Government announced the postponement of the raising of the school leaving age to 16 from 1970 to 1972 due to financial problems. Thus comprehensives, struggling to become established, were denied for two years the 20,000 or so extra teachers this measure would have provided.

Following the swing to the Right in the local elections of 1968 and 1969 the Labour leadership made a move towards compulsion in reorganization, by that time Party policy. Edward Short, the Education Secretary, introduced a Bill in February, 1970 to compel local authorities to have regard for the comprehensive principle. The Bill allowed some selectivity in sixth forms and some commentators referred to it as a 'bulldog without teeth' (Griffiths 1971). In the event, Labour members were missing from vital Committee stage meetings, and the Bill was lost and not recoverable before Labour was thrown out of office.

Policy 1970-4

The new Tory Education Secretary, Margaret Thatcher, issued Circular 10/70 in June, 1970, a month after the General Election. The new Circular cancelled Circulars 10/65 and 10/66 and recommended a binary system of comprehensive schools and tripartite schools. It based this on the principles of local freedom and variety in education. In order to follow these principles reorganization schemes were to be viewed school by school under Section 13 of the 1944 Act (the section requiring sanction by the Government of any change in the type of a school). General criteria for this scrutiny would be based on good educational practices, local wishes and the wise use of resources. Schemes already at the DES could be returned for possible reconsideration, but by June, 1971, only two local authorities had taken advantage of this. Circular 10/70 made it clear that local authorities were free to determine the shape of educational provision in their own areas.

By 1972, Margaret Thatcher had 'saved' 92 grammar schools, mainly 'famous or well-known' (rather like Sir Keith Joseph's 'schools of proven worth' – see later in this chapter). According to Caroline Benn in her sixth annual review (1972) reorganization plans for 200 schools were held up as a result of local indecision following Circular 10/70 and another 400 were held up because of lack of money. In 1971 in Surrey, parts of which were reorganized, the local authority wanted to stop parents in these areas sending their children to grammar schools in unreorganized areas but Margaret Thatcher blocked this move under the terms of Section 68 of the 1944 Act about parental rights in education, another useful political weapon which was used with increasing frequency in the 1970s. Parents in Harrow were allowed to send children to grammar schools in other districts of the local authority. Yet Margaret Thatcher presided over the demise of more grammar schools than any other Secretary of State for Education, not something she would like to be reminded of (see Chapter 4). The momentum of reorganization was so strong that she could only restrain it slightly.

After 1969, a special fund for meeting the costs of raising the school leaving age had operated, providing £125 millions over three years. This was meted out to local authorities according to the current staying-on rate into fifth years. The north of England, with a lower rate than the south, did well out of this, although the total grants were pitifully small. Moreover, some of this money was clawed back by the Government freeze on new secondary school building in 1970, a 'roofs over heads' policy giving priority to existing buildings. At the same time the Government increased aid to direct grant schools, totally ignoring the recommendations of the Public School Report of 1970 (Donnison 1970) for integration of these schools into the maintained (comprehensive) system. In addition, the 1972 Government White Paper, *A Framework for Expansion*, gave priority to the primary sector (DES 1972). Yet, despite all this, reorganization accelerated and would have been even faster with greater Government blessing and more money. The main effect of Tory and financial restrictions was to encourage only partial reorganization and the increased adoption of tiered, middle school and separate sixth form systems (see Chapter 5).

Policy, 1974–9

The war of the circulars continued with the return of Labour to office in 1974. Reg Prentice's 4/74 withdrew Margaret Thatcher's

10/70. Local authorities still practising selection over part of their area or all of it, were asked to submit reorganization plans by the end of the year. No selective school would be included in any building programme. But there was no extra money for new comprehensives. The only common element in all the circulars, Labour and Tory, was a plea for the wise use of resources, or comprehensives on the cheap. The Government managed to scrape together an extra £25 million in 1975, but this was a drop in the ocean.

Circular 4/74 took a tough line over voluntary schools which blocked reorganization, but virtually ignored direct grant schools. Voluntary schools which did not get on with the job might lose their grant (although such a threat could only be carried out where local authorities could manage without voluntary schools). Whereas 10/65 had looked forward to co-operation with direct grant schools in pursuit of mutual reorganization, 4/74 threw them a crumb. They might fit into some local schemes, but the Government had other plans for these schools.

One complaint about 10/65 was that it it made a plea for the wise use of resources yet stuck out for the 11 to 18 school, probably the most expensive overall reorganization plan given the size of existing schools. Local authorities had to take the initiative on middle schools and sixth form colleges or mush-room schools. But Labour had hardly learnt from this enterprise. Circular 4/74, still anxious for the wise use of resources, was just as keen on the 11 to 18 school, or, failing that, tiered schools. A school, it suggested, need not be too large. From this one might deduce that for ideological and vote-catching reasons the Labour administration had to support the 11 to 18 school but secretly hoped for the adoption of cheaper tiered arrangements. As in Circular 10/65 there was an absence of arguments for the middle school or separate sixth form provision, which were readily available (see Chapter 5).

Circular 4/74 recognized that the reorganization of local government in April, 1974 would affect local systems of schools where the policies of former authorities, now joined, had dif-fered, or where reorganization had brought about a change in party control. (Details of some of the areas affected in this way are given in Chapter 3.)

The Labour Government went on the offensive against the direct grant schools, offering them a place in the comprehensive system or nothing if they remained selective. In 1975 about 122,000 pupils attended the 171 direct grant schools, about 3 per cent of all secondary pupils (maintained and independent). Two of these schools were already comprehensive. The Government plan was to phase these either out altogether or into the maintained comprehensive system, allowing maintained pupils already at these schools to finish their courses. A few local authorities, such as Manchester and Leicestershire, had already stopped using direct grant schools. The cost to the Government in allowing maintained pupils to finish their courses continued at about £23 million a year (about equal to the special fund for comprehensive reorganization set up in 1975).

In the event, 119 of the schools decided to go independent. Of the 52 schools which went comprehensive 48 of them were Catholic (out of 56 Catholic direct grant schools). The Government agreed to meet the heavy debts which these schools had incurred. By 1977, the Government had saved about £15 million (the cost of financing existing direct grant schools was about £13 million in 1976–7) and they had lost a vast source of sixth form expertise for the state system.

By 1977, moreover, the Government was under increasing pressure to make comprehensive education statutory, both from within its own party ranks and from pressure groups, now including the NUT. The 1976 Act, which received its Royal Assent in November, empowered the Secretary of State for Education to require local authorities and voluntary organizations to submit proposals for comprehensive reorganization which could be realized within five years of such proposals. The Secretary of State could reject proposals on educational grounds and call for fresh ones. No state education could be on selective lines, effectively confirming the end of the direct grant system. Even if local authorities took up places in non-maintained schools for special cases (e.g. a need for boarding education) the schools chosen had to be non-selective.

From 1977 to 1979 was the period of the 'rebel' authorities, now beleaguered by law. By the time of the 1976 Act a handful of authorities had said they might not or would not ever have a completely comprehensive system. The swing to the Right in the local elections of 1977 encouraged the 'rebels' to hold out in the hope that a new General Election would return the Tories to power. The Conservative Central Office overtly backed local resistance, even setting a panel of twelve Queen's Counsels to supply it with legal advice and help if required.

The Secretary of State, Shirley Williams, chased up 'rebels' and laggards but they were able to procrastinate in a number of ways (see Chapter 3). It seemed that only High Court action would bring some of them to heel. By the time of the General Election in 1979 the case of the two schools in Ripon had been decided in the Secretary of State's favour (the local authority hoped to keep open an ex-grammar school and an ex-secondary modern as two new comprehensive schools) but the appeal on this verdict had not been heard and there were four other cases pending. The grounds for litigation were concerned with the extent to which the Government could determine the details of any local plan under the terms of the 1976 Act and also an uncertainty among lawyers as to whether the Act could compel completion of any plan by a fixed date. The Act ordered completion within five years of acceptance of a plan but if local authorities persisted in submitting plans which the Secretary of State found unsuitable the lack of a final date showed up a weakness in the Act. In the Ripon case, the Act had stood the test but the appeal might have gone differently and cases based on controversy over completion dates had not been heard.

Policy, 1979–85

The fun and games ended with the General Election. Margaret Thatcher quickly repealed the 1976 Act. There the pendulum has rested because it has been proved very difficult and daunting to re-convert reorganized schools back to tripartite schools. To re-create the vast majority of grammar schools would also mean the re-creation of large numbers of secondary modern schools. There would be thousands echoing Harold Wilson's old threat, 'over my dead body'. Indeed, only Sutton Coldfield School has reverted. This school became comprehensive in 1974. In 1980 the then Secretary of State, Mark Carlisle, agreed with Birmingham City Council that it should revert to grammar school status. Shortly after this Labour gained control in the city and pressed Mark Carlisle to change his mind but he refused to do so.

In 1984 there were plans for partial reversion in Solihull and Redbridge, but in both places there was extensive local opposition to the plans. In Redbridge, 53 per cent of the parents replying to a poll favoured the abolition of the remaining grammar schools in the area even though the questions on the poll paper did not invite them to make any comment on these schools.

In any case, by 1981 the most serious consideration for many local authorities was not the reorganizing of tripartite schools but the impact of falling rolls. The last Labour Government set up an NFER research project into the effects and implications of falling rolls and this reported in 1980 that the Government would be best advised to pursue a policy of school closures in order to concentrate resources in remaining schools (Briault and Smith). The Conservative Government adopted this policy and a 1981 Circular announced that there would be a surplus of over a million school places by 1986. It asked for local plans to reduce accommodation.

One of the perennial problems of comprehensive reorganization has been the need to produce sixth forms large enough to make economic use of scarce resources (see Chapter 7). This was also the most pressing problem generated by falling rolls. The solution in many areas to the problem of unviable sixth forms has been the sixth form college or the mushroom school, or at least some form of consortium or linked work. These are all potential solutions to the problems of falling rolls along with the idea of the tertiary college housing all local full-time and part-time 16 to 19 education. The first tertiary college opened in Exeter in 1970. After all, this does represent a natural growth of the comprehensive principle of housing all types of education under one roof.

A number of local authorities have now submitted plans for reorganization in response to falling rolls but it has been obvious that the Secretary of State, Sir Keith Joseph, is strongly in favour of retaining 'schools of proven worth'. In the case of Manchester he insisted that they retain three of the city's 11 to 18 comprehensive schools with strong academic records: Burnage, Parrs Wood and Whalley High. Eric Briault, one of the authors of the 1980 NFER report, expressed his 'disquiet' over this retention of uneconomic sixth forms. But later the Secretary of State refused Durham's plan to close sixth forms in three 11 to 18 schools (August, 1982). DES figures in 1977 showed that the average size of sixth forms was 79, and the figure for 1981 was 84. The DES considered that a sixth form under 100 was uneconomic (Briault said 150). Yet in 1977, 40 per cent of comprehensive sixth forms had less than 50 pupils.

In February, 1983 Sir Keith Joseph turned down Gloucestershire's plan for converting two grammar schools and three secondary moderns into comprehensive schools sharing sixth forms, an interesting solution to the dual demands of comprehensiveness and falling rolls. A similar plan for Salisbury was also rejected (April 1983) because the Secretary of State wanted to keep two grammar schools, and he also wanted to follow the wishes of a 'substantial number of local people'. There is another neat combination of comprehensive reorganization and a response to falling rolls in Worcester (1983). Here, eight secondary modern schools will be replaced by six 11 to 16 comprehensive schools with sixth form colleges in the ex-grammar schools, the old end-on scheme mooted for the country as a whole in the mid-1960s (see Chapter 5). Sir Keith Joseph accepted this plan.

The role of the Department of Education and Science in secondary reorganization

The political merry-go-round of circulars seems to indicate that the civil servants at the DES had very little part to play, first in formulation of pro-comprehensive policies and later their opposite, and, later still, another pro-comprehensive programme. After all, they are now at Waterloo Station and not Westminster. The DES developed a reputation for being unwilling to invite participation in policy-making from sources outside the Government and for being rather secretive. Yet this was hardly the case with the negotiations which preceded Circulars 10/65 and 4/74. Local authorities, the teacher unions and other bodies were fully consulted. Possibly the DES's real problem has been a lack of enthusiasm for innovation rather than stand-offishness or secretiveness. A fear of innovation could have sent the permanent secretaries into talks with a view to getting help and sharing blame in uncharted seas.

No such talks preceded Circular 10/70, which was strictly non-innovatory, pointing to the conclusion that the DES feared innovation, not participation. In 1975, the Organization for Economic Co-operation and Development issued a report on policy-making at the DES (see Dickson 1975) which concluded that the DES preferred steady change on well-established lines rather than rapid transformation. Barry MacDonald (1979) thought he detected pressure on the DES in the 1970s to be not only less secretive but also more commanding. Philip Venning (1980a) in a brief sketch of political advisers for the Permanent Secretary at the DES, an office originating with Labour in power in 1974, suggested that the DES had to be pushed into a positive role in education. But this positive role, when it came, and renewed Her Majesty's Inspectorate (HMI) activity, concerned itself with control of the curriculum rather than with secondary organization. Secondary reorganization was very much the result of social and economic demand for more extensive meritocratic education, backed, with considerable delay and nervousness, by political leaders of the two major parties and by a politically manipulated and muddled ideology.

3
Local and interest group policies

Local authority initiative and resistance

The creation of comprehensive schools before 1965 tended not to
be a political issue. They were mostly purpose-built 11 to 18
schools and tended to be show-places, that is isolated examples
of an educational ideology practised by a few zealot teachers
(although the case of the music teacher at Kidbrooke, see p. 8,
indicated that not all teachers in them were happy). Otherwise,
the existence of comprehensive schools in scattered rural populations or in new towns or housing estates raised few political eye-
brows. By 1962, 25 of 46 counties had some comprehensive
schools but in only 4 of them had Labour held office at any time
since 1945. In 2 predominantly Labour counties there were no
comprehensives. Seventeen of 76 county boroughs had comprehensives, but of the 20 county boroughs in constant Labour
control only 2 had comprehensives. Studies of early reorganization, for example, Donnison on Croydon (1966) and Peschek
and Brand (1966) on West Ham and Reading, found that the paid
professionals in the education office were the main initiators of
change rather than the councillors. This fact is also well-
illustrated by the work of Alec Clegg in the West Riding and
Stewart Mason in Leicestershire.

After 1945, in the West Riding, the local Conservatives opposed
tripartism and opened their first comprehensive in 1956. Chief

Education Officer, Alec Clegg (later Sir Alec) supervised the evolution of numerous reorganization plans division by division (he supported divisional autonomy). The county was the first to experiment with middle schools (see Clegg 1965).

In Leicestershire, Stewart Mason played a similar leading role (Mason 1970). Mason wrote that his county was conveniently small and round (except for one area) with the city of Leicester in the middle, connected to all parts of the county. Teachers from all over the county could easily attend meetings in the city. There were many new urban and industrial areas with a new population eager for education. There was a strong consensus for doing away with the 11-plus. There were no serious big city problems and only a small number of pupils from ethnic minorities.

The changeover was slow, taking over twelve years (1957–69) but it was a planned progression. Mason adopted the tiered system of transfer at 14 because it suited existing buildings. But selectivity was slowly eased out, with partial transfer at 14 based on parental choice phased into complete transfer when the staying-on rate beyond 15 reached an average of 80 per cent for any area. The system which had evolved by the early 1970s was 5 to 10 schools, followed by 10 to 14 schools and then 14 to 18 schools. So Clegg and Mason were notable members of a small band of professionals who pioneered comprehensive schools, with other examples in Reading (Percy Taylor, see Peschek and Brand 1966) and Darlington (where the reorganization plan was named after the Chief Education Officer, the Peter Plan, see Batley *et al*. 1970) and perhaps the three Chief Education Officers (CEOs) interviewed by Kogan and Van der Eyken (1973).

In comparing the relative powers of central and local government in reorganization it thus appears that before 1965 much depended on local initiative and the CEO in particular. A sudden rush of reorganization in large urban areas in the north in 1963 may have been influential in getting other areas moving. Liverpool, Manchester, Lancashire, Preston, Rochdale, Blackburn, St Helens, Bolton, Wigan, Bradford and Sheffield all reorganized around this time. Perhaps the prospect that Labour would win in 1964 had something to do with this mini avalanche. Rubinstein and Simon (1973) also thought that the planned raising of the school leaving age encouraged local authorities to get moving on reorganization.

In framing Circular 10/65, Crosland consulted the national body of the local education authorities, the Association of Education Committees (AEC), and the teachers unions. After the event, these bodies all asked where the money for change was. Finance must have been a major factor in shaping local authorities' action on reorganization, both in terms of speed, in terms of whether to reorganize parts of their areas or all of them and in terms of the type of comprehensive schools envisaged. But increasingly after 1965, the political hue of the party in local control mattered. Reorganization most certainly became a political hot potato after 1965. Bellaby (1977) considers this to be the crucial factor in reorganization in the period under review. Sixty-five per cent of county boroughs under Labour control between 1962 and 1972 had 25 per cent or more of their pupils in comprehensive schools by 1972 compared to 14 per cent of other county boroughs. When the deadline for 10/65 arrived in July, 1966 54 per cent of Labour boroughs were on time with their plans compared to 32 per cent of other boroughs. Seven of 10 authorities which never replied to 10/65 were Conservative and the 5 which submitted plans too late for consideration before the 1970 election were all Conservative.

The advent of comprehensive reorganization was a red letter day in the development of the art of procrastination or prevarication. The predominantly Conservative authorities, intent on this in the 1960s and 1970s, have on the whole got away with it. Much has been made in recent years of a supposed increase in central political power, but this could indicate the increase of a power already severely limited. It is unlikely that Labour Governments could have acted on reorganization without a general mandate from education authorities, and they relied heavily on local initiative. The pace of change most certainly rested with the localities. The dislike of rapid innovation on the part of the DES, discussed in Chapter 2, was hardly evidence of a strong central influence in reorganization.

Philip James (1980) cited the wide variety of local plans as evidence against the existence of central domination. He referred to an article by D. E. Ashford which concluded that the increase of central funding between 1949 and 1967 led to no reduction of local diversity (Ashford 1974). The block grant system of local funding from the Government after 1958 meant that it had little control over how the money was spent. What control there was was negative. The three CEOs interviewed by Kogan and Van der Eyken (1973) believed that central control worked within tentative guidelines rather than on strong prescriptions.

But James (1980) while subscribing to the thesis of a limited central influence, admitted that the potential for more control was there in the 1944 Act (particularly Sections 13, 68 and 99). A newer block grant system started in 1981 sought to have closer oversight of what central money was spent on in the localities, couched in terms of local educational needs and resources. Some educational commentators have seized on this move by the Conservative Government as evidence of an intended takeover (e.g. Burgess and Travers 1980). Moreover, Ashford's (1974) conclusions are challenged by other research, such as Eileen Byrne's into spending in Lincoln, Nottingham and Northumberland between 1945 and 1965 and beyond (Byrne 1974).

The editorial in the *TES* of 18 March 1966 commented on the growing art of delaying tactics by local authorities, a 'cultivated haziness' in their plans (this publication was not well-disposed to comprehensives then but a later change of editor also meant a change in tune). Marsden (1971) picked out Birmingham as a large and influential authority sitting it out after sending in a plan which retained selection. Benn and Simon (1970) detected stalling or slow resubmission in the cases of Bexley, Halifax, Southend and Reading. Benn (1968) noted that if a plan was rejected a local authority committed to reorganization would quickly resubmit but others either refused to do this or sent in a new plan hardly different from the old one.

In areas which switched to Tory control before 1970 there was a possibility of reversing reorganization, as happened in Leeds in 1967. From 1967 to 1969, 16 authorities withdrew or reconsidered plans. It was reported in the *TES* of 10 November 1971 that 'Political swings create hot-potch of systems', a survey of the twenty outer London boroughs. Conservatives had blocked plans put up by Labour and already accepted for Bexley and Brent. A political swing could result in a compromise, as in inner London, where Christopher Chataway's plan to leave forty grammar schools (catering for 10 per cent of the area's secondary pupils) was the price of the reorganization of the rest. In Darlington, however, the attempt by the Tories to go completely into reverse was unsuccessful (Batley *et al.* 1970). The swing to the Right had not stopped reorganization in Enfield, Haringay and Waltham Forest, and the Chairman of the London Boroughs Association of Education Committees considered that new Tory councils in these areas had basically resisted the temptation to unscramble comprehensives acting on responsible educational motives. According to him, it would have been a relatively simple matter to reverse plans. Of the 20 outer boroughs 5 were fully comprehensive, apart from 'creaming' by direct grant and independent schools; 3 were to start reorganization in September, 1971; 4 in 1972; and 5 'after' 1973. The 3 remaining boroughs became 'rebels' against the 1976 Act (see Chapter 2). These were Bexley, Redbridge and Sutton, all of whom wanted to keep some of their grammar schools. In no outer London borough could they hope to avoid creaming and some of them had a very deliberate policy of using local direct grant schools, for example, Richmond and Croydon (in the latter borough, 7 per cent of pupils were annually creamed off in this way).

In the outer boroughs there were still 37 grammar schools in 1977 (DES 1978). The 40 in the ILEA were phased out only between 1975 and 1978 (a handful went independent). Most of the direct grant schools in the London region became independent schools.

By 1969 Labour had lost almost every city and county borough. Had not reorganization accelerated between 1965 and 1968 the chance may have gone. The momentum garnered in these years carried over the swing to the Right locally and nationally. Like Leicestershire (see p. 30) many counties steadily reorganized over a long period. In Essex the new towns of Harlow and Basildon went over first, then the rural divisions, then the old towns, but some of them with venerable grammar schools, such as Chelmsford and Colchester, only partially reorganized during the period. In Hampshire reorganization was based on historical accident and the sort of schools which were in existence, according to its Chief Education Officer (see DES 1978). Thus Southampton and Portsmouth went for middle school systems with the former having sixth form colleges as well, an unusual combination with middle schools. The old county council area had started with sixth form colleges or mushroom schools but by 1978 the CEO was hoping to bring in middle schools. But falling rolls have made this virtually impossible.

Changes in local government in 1974 potentially favoured comprehensive reorganization because many new Labour committees inherited unreorganized areas and it was easier for them to set the ball rolling than for Tories to kick it backwards. A handful of the 25 authorities promising to complete reorganization by 1980 in 1975 plans in fact completed in advance of that date because of acceleration by Labour councils.

The most famous case concerning local government reorganization and secondary school reorganization was Tameside, where a planned switch to comprehensive schools was reversed. This area was a group of small towns and suburbs scattered between Manchester and the moors, previously administered by Lancashire and Cheshire. Both counties had been in the middle of reorganization. Labour won the new area with a big majority and went ahead quickly towards complete reorganization. But in May 1976, the Tories came in on a political landslide and announced that reorganization, due for September of that year, was cancelled. Eleven-plus tests were hurriedly arranged for 3000 11 year olds but the three major teacher unions refused to administer them and asked the Secretary of State, Fred Mulley, to intervene under Section 68 of the 1944 Education Act. Under this the Secretary of State had powers if the local authority was acting 'unreasonably'. Mulley ruled that reorganization must go ahead but the local authority challenged his right to do this. He took them to the High Court, which ruled in his favour (12 July 1976). But on 26 July the Appeals Court reversed the judgement and on 2 August the Law Lords dismissed Mulley's appeal. On 9 August the education committee began selection procedures without the help of any 11-plus results, local headteachers, teachers or any of their own office staff. The work was organized by a retired primary school head. His team worked entirely from primary school record cards, of which there were four different varieties in the area. Many of the cards had information missing since many primary heads had not bothered with them in 1975 because of the imminent end of selection, although they had been clearly instructed to keep records going. Some cards had not been filled in since 1972.

The Law Lords based their judgement on the fact that the Tories had been voted in on a mandate for selective education. They further observed that by basing his case on the issue of selection the Secretary of State had 'fundamentally misconceived and misdirected himself'. Mulley might have had a better case if he had objected to the inadequate selection procedures being used, although the Lords thought them adequate enough for the relatively small number of grammar school places to be allocated (about 240 places: of these 224 were actually allocated). Thus, Tameside joined the 'rebels' when the 1976 Act was passed later in the year.

There were seven other 'rebels'. Three of these were Buckinghamshire, Trafford and Kingston (which had no comprehensive schools at all, and still does not have any). All categorically refused to end all selection. The others were Essex, Bexley, Redbridge and Sutton, these four wanting to retain named grammar schools. There were also a much larger number of 'sometime' authorities (refusing to put up a date for the completion of reorganization). Some of them made the plea that they could not afford complete reorganization within the immediate future.

In Redbridge, 9 per cent of 11 year olds in 1969 had verbal reasoning (VR) scores of over 130 (5 per cent in 1971 when the national average was 2 per cent). In view of this special situation the local authority wanted to retain two three-form entry grammar schools and also places at direct grant schools (thus making provision for about 7 per cent of secondary pupils). In 1975, 90 per cent of the area's 11 year olds sat selection examinations. Those who passed well, but not well enough for a grammar school place, were able to select the comprehensive school they preferred. In this way some of the other comprehensives were said to have been 'double-creamed' (e.g. Loxford School).

'Rebel' and 'sometime' authorities, and the fact that in some areas the percentage of pupils in comprehensive schools actually fell between 1975 and 1977 (Trafford, Dorset and Gloucestershire), induced pro-comprehensive pressure groups to denounce the Secretary of State for not enforcing the 1976 Act more forcibly. In 1977, more swings to the Right occurred in local elections. Shirley Williams sent for new proposals from the 'rebel' eight in May. In response, Bexley promised full reorganization in fifteen years, Sutton ten while Kingston suggested 1982 as a completion date. Buckinghamshire offered nothing because its education committee could not decide on a plan. Redbridge still wanted to keep its grammar schools. Tameside said they needed more time to think, and when its plans finally emerged (in September) the request was for £2.5 million to finance the reorganization of grammar schools into 11 to 18 schools and their secondary modern schools into 11 to 16 schools, the mushroom pattern, which Bexley and Buckinghamshire also favoured.

There were particular problems in some areas, such as the case of the Ripon schools described in Chapter 2. Kirklees in the West Riding was won by the Tories in 1977. Finding one area (Heckmondwike, Liversedge and Batley) unreorganized they pressed on with plans which included the retention of Batley Grammar School. The local authority said it had parental support for this but a local Labour councillor retorted that such support had been assessed from a meeting attended only by parents who sought grammar school places for their children (Tameside had also cited parental pressure in its campaign to keep grammar schools).

The position at the end of 1978 showed that thirty-eight authorities had resisted the DES's attempt to get definite plans and time schedules. Thirty-four had been in touch with the Secretary of State. In the cases of the other four (Birmingham, Kirklees, neither of them 'rebels', Sutton and Redbridge) court cases were pending. Victory over Ripon no doubt encouraged Shirley Williams to think that she could hurry up others. But new proposals from Tameside in March, 1978 (two months late) only differed from the first in minor details (certainly not the £2.5 million they wanted) and the Secretary of State ordered a third version. Legal advisers for Sutton were of the opinion that the Secretary of State could not compel an authority to complete reorganization by any specific year under the powers given to her in the Act. Birmingham was saying that she could not refer to particular schools in responding to plans. The General Election came before any of these interesting cases could be heard.

Power balances in the local education authorities

If power to initiate or resist rested in local authorities, who wielded this influence? In the case of education officers such as Clegg and Mason there was little doubt about who took the initiative but elsewhere the issue is more clouded. Saran (1973) produced a useful survey of local studies of reorganization policies as well as presenting his own analysis of them in Middle-sex. Many of these researches confirmed the strong influence of the Chief Education Officer, e.g. Donnison and Chapman (1965), Peschek and Brand (1966). But very often there had to be negoti-ations with a 'magic circle' of councillors, especially the Chair-man of the Education Committee (Peschek and Brand 1966). Indeed, Brand concluded that the CEO only had dominance if the local parties were relatively disinterested in reorganization. In both West Ham and Reading a permanent Labour majority left a vacuum of initiative which was filled by the CEO.

In contrast, Batley *et al.* (1970) noted initiative on the part of councillors and a working relationship between them and the paid officers, a relationship which either could dominate. Saran's analysis tended to confirm this conclusion, although he pointed out that there was no guarantee that a particular relationship would remain static. Roles and strengths changed over time. James (1980) noted the advantage that professionals had in their contact with the DES and with local teachers. They monopolized the local channels of communication; they were information gate-keepers. But their potential dominance rests in matters of resource allocation rather than in ideological issues, and, as reorganization became more and more a political matter, there was likelihood of the local parties assuming more influence in decision-making. After 1970 there is evidence of the polarization of the Parties in local education, connected with the concept of 'corporate management'. This was a watchword of the reorganization of local government, in which senior planning teams sought to have more control over education committees and CEOs, ostensibly in pursuit of greater efficiency and accountability through centralized planning. This has led some CEOs to support the removal of education from local administration. George Cooke, a former CEO, suggested that the reorganization of local government, whilst invested with the good purpose of unitary, all-purpose authorities sharing out the national economic cake more fairly than before, had turned out to be an opportunity for the new political masters to attack education committees and CEOs and savage the education service (Cooke 1980). The new local councils set up the Council of Local Education Authorities (CLEA) in 1974 and this has superseded the previous national body of education committees (the Association of Education Committees) and this change also reflected a growing representation of non-education interests in local education, a tendency which could only increase the politicization of local government. Robert Jennings (1977) also traced an evolving preponderance of party politics in the educational administration of three outer London boroughs and in three counties in 1973–4, although the CEOs here retained enormous influence. Nevertheless, each of the six chairmen of the education committees saw vast potential for interference in educational policy-making by central planning committees of local councils, but it all came too late really to affect the passage of secondary school reorganization. By 1974 the die was cast, except for a number of redoubtable areas. However, current solutions to problems of falling rolls (see Chapter 2) are potentially going to be more the work of local parties than was the case with secondary reorganization.

Cabals of education officers and senior councillors were a natural result of the fact that political engineering is a full-time and a rather obsessive occupation, and only a few people could commit themselves to this type of activity since local politics is largely a matter of voluntary, part-time work. Very often less than six people were closely involved in the formulation of local reorganization plans. James (1980) concluded that many councillors were content to accept this situation since they did not consider that voting was affected by the reorganization issue. Only a few of them were interested generally in policy-making while the rest regarded themselves as unpaid social workers and no more. Probably only the younger councillors had any regard for consultations with other vested interests in education, such as teachers and parents, so this again made it unlikely that many of them would interest themselves too closely in reorganization. Observers such as Marsden (1971) and Benn and Simon (1970) considered that, in any case, there was a great deal of ignorance about secondary school organization on the part of councillors in general.

Teacher unions

Fenwick (1976) has made a useful study of teacher union attitudes towards reorganization. There was some support in the NUT in the 1950s from grammar school teachers disenchanted with their schools, but this was strictly a minority element and generally the membership sought to preserve its own interests in the tripartite schools. The leadership of the union sought unity above all. They were not strongly opposed to a few experiments as long as members' status and salaries were protected. The other unions were generally antagonistic towards comprehensive reorganization, especially those representing grammar school teachers.

All the unions wrote lengthy comments on Crosland's drafts of Circular 10/65 and James (1980) thought that these induced the Secretary of State to adopt a more conciliatory tone than he might otherwise have done. But in local battles unions seldom seemed to have much influence. They appeared unable to block reorganization in the four areas studied by Parkinson (1980). In Middlesex, Darlington, West Ham and Bath the unions were listened to, but it was a question of lending support rather than taking independent action. Branches could obviously afford to be more partisan than the national executive. Younger teachers tended to support reorganization more than older NUT members.

It was the perennial desire of the NUT to be the sole union that probably prompted its change of heart during the Labour administration of 1966 to 1970. If the majority of its members were going to be working in comprehensives, whether they liked it or not, then it was in the general interests of the NUT to become a pro-comprehensive union. It was a slow process. Although the union delegates were strongly in favour of comprehensive schools in evidence given to the Plowden Committee, their general public image was more neutral. But the 1969 NUT Conference called upon the Government to abolish selection by law and in 1970 it showed open hostility to Margaret Thatcher's Circular 10/70, especially as she had not bothered to consult them about it. The National Association of Schoolmasters (NAS) and the Union of Women Teachers (UWT) followed in the NUT's wake a bit later.

By the time of the 1974 Labour Government, the NUT had become severely critical of Conservative education policy and was one of the pressure groups seeking the banning of secondary selection by law. The NAS position at this time was that it supported comprehensive schools but not 'botched-up' schemes on the cheap. This union has maintained a long and continuous campaign against disruption in large comprehensive schools, especially in respect of physical assaults on teachers.

Parents

Circular 10/65 called on local authorities to consult with teachers and parents in drawing up reorganization plans. However, the most vociferous parents in the 1960s were those objecting to the demise of grammar schools. Thus parents and pupils from Bristol were marching with banners in London at the end of 1964 as something similar was happening in Liverpool. The National Educational Association (NEA), formed in October, 1965 to safeguard parents' freedom of choice in secondary education, had its origins in the Old Boys' Association of Hampton Grammar

School. The activities of the local branches of the association centred on grammar school premises, supported overwhelmingly, sometimes passionately, by the national and local media. There was plenty of financial and legal backing for the NEA and its power and influence are well illustrated by the famous battles in Ealing and Enfield.

In Ealing, parents sought a High Court injunction to prevent reorganization, taking their stand under Section 76 of the 1944 Act, which was about education in accordance with parental wishes. The decision went against them, on the grounds that Section 76 was about matters such as religious education or the curriculum but not about the conditions of entry to a school, or its size, or local development plans for the pattern of schools.

Enfield parents also failed in 1967 because the High Court decided on the point of 'balance of convenience' that there would be chaos if reorganization was reversed (strange that this prospect was not decisive in the Tameside case nine years later). An appeal led to an injunction against 8 out of 16 schools being altered, but only because of a technical violation of the 1944 Act which the Secretary of State, Patrick Gordon Walker, soon corrected.

As was seen earlier in this chapter, local authorities locked in battle with Shirley Williams often cited parental support for their action. On the opposite side of the fence the Campaign for the Advancement of State Education (CASE) was associated with pressure for comprehensive schools by parents, and its recent decline in membership may well be connected with the achievement of four-fifths comprehensivization in this country. Only a fifth of local areas had CASE groups in 1980, a third of which were in London. Perhaps the Assisted Places Scheme and other Tory inventions will restore its vitality. According to Rick Rogers (1980) members tended to be Labour, middle-aged and middle class. Their finest hours were probably in 'rebel' areas as a minority group fighting for reorganization in a hostile climate, for instance the Stop the 11-Plus Campaign in Redbridge and the Kingston Parents' Association for Comprehensive Schools. In 1980, CASE joined with other pro-comprehensive groups to form the Right to Comprehensive Education (RICE, see p. 44).

But parental and communal pressures have had only marginal influences, although James (1980) listed places where they were certainly listened to and they may have had some moderating influence (Brighton, Leeds, Brent, Haringay, Hounslow, Newham, Sheffield, Chesterfield, Middlesex and Liverpool). But there was no consultation in Darlington and Gateshead (Batley *et al.* 1970) and only in Hounslow did a public meeting have any impact on a plan of reorganization. Recently, however, parents joined teachers in Bexley, along with representatives from pro-comprehensive groups, in preventing the re-conversion of Erith School to grammar school status. Again, in 1982 and 1983 parents in Salisbury were influential in saving two single-sex grammar schools (on this we have the word of Sir Keith Joseph himself).

Parents have had more influence on comprehensive schools after reorganization than before through the medium of choice of school. Schools with strong records of success at O and A levels attracted parental favour in areas where parental choice was given priority. Since this right to choose is now statutory under the 1980 Education Act the effect of parental choice in creating hierarchies of schools, and a new partism in secondary education, is likely to grow (see Chapter 7).

Voluntary bodies

Voluntary organizations had less effect in holding up reorganization before 1970 than afterwards. Then they became very sticky in some areas. In certain cities the Catholics in particular had many schools, and they very effectively held up the completion of reorganization in Liverpool and London. In Liverpool they educated 40 per cent of secondary pupils at the start of this period. The retention of 40 voluntary grammar schools in the inner London plan meant that 10 per cent of pupils there were in these selective schools (another 5 per cent were in other selective schools in the area). Voluntary schools were left out in a growing number of local plans but before 1970 the more impecunious Catholic authorities were glad to go comprehensive because of the need for more state financial aid. It was the more financially stable Catholic schools which were able to hold out, sure in the knowledge that in most cases local authorities could not manage without them.

Voluntary schools were generally small, and thus basically unsuited for use as 11 to 18 schools, and the voluntary bodies could not afford new building (despite a 75 per cent grant aid, increased to 80 per cent in 1966, for this). Often a tiered arrangement was used for them, and sometimes a middle school pattern. But voluntary organizations could easily procrastinate because they were needed, despite the threat in Circular 4/74 to cut off their inheritance.

Governors of schools

Just a brief note here on school governors. Their limited role and influence in secondary schools is nowhere better illustrated than in secondary reorganization. Governors of voluntary schools generally held more sway because of their special bargaining position. In any case, representatives of voluntary bodies on governing bodies of voluntary schools always out-voted other interests. Their affiliation in London, the Association of Governing Bodies of Greater London Aided Grammar Schools, forged the compromise with the Inner London Education Authority (ILEA) in 1967.

Perhaps the most publicized case of lay governors holding up proceedings was in Shropshire where governors at Adam's Boys' Grammar School, Newport objected to a plan which put a new comprehensive school on two sites and involved expensive building alterations, and refused to issue a Section 13 notice (a notice of significant change in the use of school buildings obligatory under Section 13 of the 1944 Act). They successfully delayed matters until the return of a Conservative Government in 1979.

Comprehensive school pressure groups

From 1965 a series of pro-comprehensive school pressure groups operated. The Comprehensive Schools Committee (CSC) issued statistical information between 1965 and 1970, spearheaded by its information officer, Caroline Benn, who wrote its annual reviews and other pamphlets. She constantly criticized DES assessments of the progress of reorganization which referred to the number of local authorities which had comprehensive schools or had submitted plans for them rather than referring to the percentages of schools which were comprehensive and the percentages of secondary pupils in them. As far as the plans were concerned, dates for completion were seldom realized, in a few cases, never. The Comprehensive Schools Committee tried to fill in the gaps with necessary information, referring also to delayed plans and the extent to which comprehensive schools were creamed of bright pupils by selective schools.

Because of exasperation with slow progress, and with the advent of Margaret Thatcher, the CSC converted to the Campaign for Comprehensive Education (CCE) in 1970, continuing its statistical flow but making more specific and biting attacks on Government inaction. When Labour returned in 1974, the CCE pressed them to outlaw selection.

Growing dissatisfaction with internal selection in comprehensive schools led to the formation of a further group in 1975, seeking to remove differential class grouping and curriculum provision based on ability. This was the Programme for Reform in Secondary Education (PRISE). The return of the Tories in 1979, followed by their promotion of the Assisted Places Scheme for maintained pupils at selective independent schools (a new type of direct grant system) produced a further notch in pro-comprehensive pressure, the Right to Comprehensive Education (RICE), uniting the older pressure groups under one banner in 1980, including CASE (see p. 41).

4
The pace of reorganization

As discussed in Chapter 3, the Comprehensive Schools Committee criticized the DES for publishing statistics of the number of local authorities which were reorganizing or planning to reorganize. This gave a rosier picture of the progress of change than if figures of schools and pupils were given. Using the number of local authorities as a historical guide to reorganization is complicated because of the reorganization of local government in 1974, reducing the number of authorities from 163 to 104. Thus comparing 1973 and 1975 by referring to the number of authorities is impossible because many of the new areas were amalgamations across old local boundaries. The *TES* analysis of March, 1975 (Vaughan) provides a profile of progress up to that year in terms of the numbers of authorities, and this can be compared to the DES figures for 1981. The *TES* in 1975 reported that 20 local authorities out of 104 had become fully comprehensive. In 1981, the DES figures showed that 63 authorities out of 97 (this excluded the Welsh authorities) were fully reorganized, 33 operated a mixed economy of comprehensive and tripartite schools and one, Kingston-on-Thames, had no comprehensive schools (DES 1981a).

Table 1 below, compiled from Vaughan (1975), shows the percentages of pupils in comprehensive schools in each of the local education authorities (there were 104 authorities in 1975). This table seems to indicate that the 70th percentile in 1975

Table 1 Percentages of pupils in the maintained system attending comprehensive schools, 1975

Percentage of pupils	Number of local educational authorities
over 90	33
over 80	51
over 70	65
over 60	74
over 50	81
over 40	86
over 30	91
over 20	93
over 10	100

One hundred and three authorities had some comprehensive pupils and one (Kingston-on-Thames) had none.

Source: Vaughan 1975.

(65 local authorities) became the 100th percentile in 1981 (DES 1981a). This does not mean that all authorities with over 70 per cent of their pupils in comprehensives in 1975 completed reorganization by 1981 nor does it mean that some authorities with less than 70 per cent in comprehensives in 1975 did not complete reorganization by 1981. Reorganization was more complicated than that.

The 33 authorities with grammar schools in 1981 included 7 London boroughs, 9 metropolitan districts and 17 counties. Kent led the way with 19 grammar schools, followed by Lincolnshire (16), Buckinghamshire (14), Devon (11), Gloucestershire (11), Dorset (9), Liverpool (9), and Trafford (8). In this year there were 3300 comprehensive schools, 200 grammar schools and 380 secondary modern schools (DES 1981a).

Thirty post-1974 authorities (nearly a third) never had an approved date for completion of reorganization despite the fact that 129 schemes (110 for the greater part of the areas involved) were approved by the DES by 1970, when there were 163 local authorities. The trends by 1970 indicated a rapid acceleration of reorganization which would complete the process within a few years. This never materialized, perhaps owing to four years of

Tory control. Margaret Thatcher's inability to stem the tide can alternatively be regarded in another light as the prevention of complete inundation. It is also possible to view central political policies as rather irrelevant to the pace of reorganization (see later in this chapter). Benn and Simon (1970) calculated that had the 1967–8 rate of acceleration been maintained full reorganization would have been achieved by 1980, but on the reduced 1968–9 rate (nothing to do with Margaret Thatcher) only 80 per cent of pupils would be in comprehensive schools by 1980. In fact, there were 88 per cent.

One clear change after 1970 was that authorities tended to opt for reorganization of only parts of their areas, and this accounts for the failure of full reorganization as much as 'rebel' or 'some-time' authorities (all of whom did reorganize partially except Kingston). This indicated massive local political support for the binary system of tripartite schools and comprehensive schools, certainly encouraged by Margaret Thatcher's pursuit of this between 1970 and 1974. The effect is perhaps best illustrated by the fact that in 1972 141 new comprehensive schools were planned for 1973, 55 for 1974 and 20 for 1975 (Benn 1972).

On the number of pupils undergoing tests of selection at 11 at various times Hill (1972) is a useful source. In 1964 only 2 authorities had no selection procedures but this number had increased to 26 in 1968 (16 per cent) and 51 (31 per cent) in 1972. In 1980, the figure was 65 per cent (68 out of 104 authorities). The figure for pupils tends to show a quicker demise for selection tests since the *TES* survey of March, 1975 showed 75 per cent of them not doing tests, higher than the figure for authorities in 1980 (Vaughan 1975).

Graph A shows a very regular line for the incidence of the abolition of selection tests. It is a neat history of reorganization. But its validity can be tested alongside graphs of the percentages of pupils in comprehensive schools and the percentages of these schools in the whole secondary system using the DES (1978b) report and later DES press releases.

The Graph B line is almost as steady as the first. The steepest rise is between 1972 and 1974, particularly 1973–4, confirming the effect of the momentum generated by 1970, but it was only

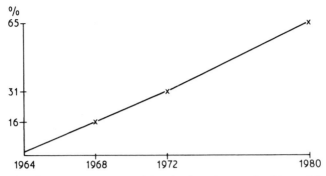

Graph A Percentages of local education authorities with no selection procedures, 1964–80

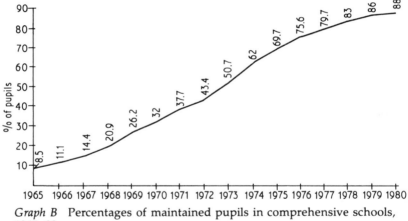

Graph B Percentages of maintained pupils in comprehensive schools, 1965–80

a slightly increased tempo; it could have been much faster. Yet it did not pick up with Labour in control, but fell off. By 1980, however, only 4 per cent of maintained secondary pupils were in grammar schools compared to 19 per cent in 1970 and 25 per cent in 1965.

Graph C concerns the number of comprehensive schools shown as a percentage of the total maintained secondary system.

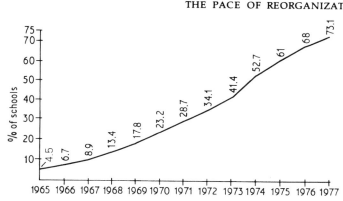

Graph C Percentages of comprehensive schools in the maintained system, 1965–77

The only serious upturn in the graph line is again for 1973–4, but it is a very minor upturn. The total impression, as with the other two graphs, is one of regularity. This regularity seems to bear little relation to the political see-saws of the period because the slightly enhanced rate in the 1970s came seven to nine years after Circular 10/65 and immediately after the attempt to slow down change in Circular 10/70. The comparatively regular rate of change over fifteen years could be more closely associated with a solid social and economic demand rather than ideological switches. The 1976 Act came at a time when perhaps the original surge of demand for equality of educational opportunity was abating, aborting Labour's move to enforce reorganization. But it was not only Government that appeared somewhat irrelevant to social and economic demand. The NUT, for instance, was rather neutral about comprehensive schools during the first surge in support of them but later argued for compulsory reorganization when the main surge was over. Then again, pro-comprehensive pressure groups grew impatient at the failure of the Labour Government to sweep aside the last bastions of tripartism, but neither they nor the Government seemed able to do very much about it. By this time the popular demand for reform had diminished, leaving the field to the strident minority of elitists and to more pressing concerns of contracting budgets and school rolls.

5
Patterns of reorganization

Early reorganization was dominated by the 11 to 18 school, clearly relating to the ideology of the all-embracing school. As mentioned earlier, before 1965 most comprehensives were purpose built, somewhat special, tending to be show-places, but with mass reorganization such luxuries had to go. Many existing buildings were too small for viable 11 to 18 schools and the immediate solution to this in many places seemed to be tiered junior and senior comprehensive schools, especially as this offered something of a compromise to supporters of selection. This could shift from 11-plus to 13- or 14-plus in the interim systems suggested by Circular 10/65. Elsewhere, local initiative in the main brought forth separate sixth form systems or middle-school systems. The Circulars of 1965 and 1974 gave a nod to these ideas, but little more.

The declining portion of the reorganized system devoted to 11 to 18 schools should not, however, be over-estimated. New schools built after 1965 still tended to be 11 to 18 schools (in 1970 42 per cent of 11 to 18 schools had been purpose built compared to 12 per cent of 11 to 16 schools). The use of split sites to construct 11 to 18 schools was as common as the use of tiered schools. Moreover, the rise of middle school involved the creation of many 8 to 12 schools with transfer to 12 to 18 schools, which made up 4 per cent of the comprehensive system in 1976. If in 1963 68 per cent of comprehensive schools were 11 to 18 schools this figure had only declined to 56 per cent in 1972 (including the 12 to 18 schools) and to 52.3 per cent in 1976 (including 12 to 18 schools). This is a figure which is likely to decline further in the present era of falling rolls as 11 to 18 schools tend to become uneconomic, especially in their sixth forms.

Earlier, the impact of separate sixth form systems and middle schools fell on the use of tiered schools rather than on the all-through school. By 1972 the pattern was that 91 local authorities had 11 or 12 to 18 schools, 30 had tiered schools, 19 had middle schools and 12 had separate sixth-form provision. By 1976 tiered schools took up only 15.8 per cent of the total of comprehensive schools whereas 25 per cent of them were 11 to 16 schools feeding some type of separate sixth form and 10 per cent were middle schools deemed secondary schools. A larger number of middle schools were deemed primary. If 11 and 12 year olds in 8 to 12 schools are added to this picture, middle schools can be seen as rivalling tiered schools as a secondary school system. Both these types of school are now under pressure from falling rolls, perhaps the middle school more than the tiered school because it tends to be smaller. Their present death rate (see p. 56) now makes them the fourth and least popular pattern of compre-hensive schools behind 11 or 12 to 18 schools, 11 to 16 schools with separate sixth form provision, and tiered schools.

The movement towards separate sixth-form provision and middle schools in the late 1960s and the early 1970s is indicated by the fact that only a fifth of all local schemes in 1967–8 were for these types of provision but by 1971 this proportion increased to a third. In 1970, a fifth of all plans included 9 to 13 middle schools. In September, 1971, of 230 new schools opened in that month which had sixth-form provision 35 per cent of them offered it in sixth form colleges or mushroom schools compared to 17 per cent in tiered senior comprehensives (48 per cent in 11 or 12 to 18 schools).

Analysis of the patterns in 1976 (DES 1978b), including only schools deemed as secondary (2878 schools), was as shown in Table 2 below.

Table 2 Percentages of types of schools in the total maintained secondary school system, 1976

Type of school	%
11 to 18	48.3
11 to 16	25.1
13 to 18	8.7
12 to 16	4.3
11 to 14	4.0
12 to 18	4.0
16 to 18	2.4
14 to 18	2.3
11 to 13	0.7
13 to 16	0.1
10 to 16	0.1

Source: DES 1978b.

At the same time there were 509 9 to 13 middle schools (i.e. twice as many as the 13 to 18 schools they were feeding) plus about 40 10 to 13 or 14 schools, and about 645 middle schools deemed as primary schools. Middle schools at this time fed all-through schools and tiered schools equally but as 8 to 12 schools began to outstrip 9 to 13 schools (see p. 55) they tended not to feed tiered schools. In this way, middle schools became more tied to the all-through school and tiered systems fell behind in the total pattern of comprehensive education.

The mosaic of patterns is now bewildering. By 1977 there were 47 different LEA patterns of post-10 education (a detailed list of areas and patterns is given on pages 165, 166 and 167 of the DES report of 1978). Table 3 shows the variety of schools in Humberside. By 1972 23 per cent of local authorities had two distinct types of provision within their areas, 7 per cent had three types and 3 per cent had four. In 1981 (Passmore 1981) just over half the English local authorities had the same age of transfer to secondary education for all their pupils, 27 had two ages of transfer and 14 had three or more. By 1980, Hereford and Worcester had five different types of comprehensive education within its boundaries. The term 'comprehensive' has become misleading. From the original rather simple system of 11 to 15 or 16 or 11 to 18 schools,

Table 3 Types of comprehensive schools in Humberside, 1977

Type of school	Number in area
11 to 18	24
13 to 18	19
11 to 16	12
12 to 18	4
12 to 16	4
16 to 18	1

Source: DES 1978b.

there are now 47 LEA patterns. Perhaps the lack of selection in the new 'system' justifies the use of the term 'comprehensive' because very little else does, and when the extent of internal selection in comprehensive schools is considered (see Chapter 7) this sort of justification is further weakened.

Middle schools

The Plowden Report of 1967 gave a boost to a middle-school ideology by supporting the idea of an extension of a primary school approach beyond 11 years of age, referring to a teaching situation which continued to stress the basics, had more teachers who would teach a group of subjects rather than narrow special-isms, and emphasized a strong pastoral relationship between particular teachers and particular groups of pupils (although how all this is supposed to be exclusively 'primary education' is elusive. It is very much a part of the Countesthorpe philosophy – see Chapter 8).

It was expediency rather than ideology which set the middle-school movement rolling. The DES imagined that existing primary schools would be used for middle schools (e.g. DES 1966) but overlooked the use of ex-small secondary schools as 9 to 13 schools (another example of how the civil servants in West-minster were out of touch with local circumstances). The early surge was in 9 to 13 schools, and only later did the more ideo-logically supported 8 to 12 schools take over from them. In many places, the use of the 9 to 13 idea avoided the use of split sites for comprehensive schools. Later, there was a growing tendency to dislike transfer at 13 because secondary schools wanted four clear years to prepare pupils for their external examinations. The same argument had been used more forcibly against transfer at 14.

Academic support for middle schools in addition to that from Plowden came from Nisbet and Entwistle's study in Aberdeen (1966). They concluded that there was no 'correct age' of transfer; throughout Europe a variety of ages applied. Moreover, puberty could not be fixed at any particular age and, in any case, puberty did not necessarily bring marked changes in mind and personality. The authors believed that there should be a gradual transition from one stage of education to another between the ages of 10 and 13. Local conditions and constraints could determine an age of transfer in any locality but an alternative was to have a school bridging these years.

There was also the formidable support given to the middle-school idea by Alec Clegg, Chief Examination Officer in the West Riding, who expressed strong opposition to transfer at 14, which he considered too late for secondary education (Clegg 1965). The patterns of comprehensive schools which developed in the West Riding were very varied because Clegg supported divisional autonomy and appreciated the vastly differing conditions in different areas. He was happy to see transfer from the primary stage anywhere between 8 and 10 and transfer to secondary education between 11 and 13, although he did personally support the extension of a 'primary' approach to 12.

Support for a new type of school based on the ideology of an existing type of school (that is, the primary school), or based on a sort of psychological limbo and depending on expediency, did not have fair prospects. After all, the middle school was obliged to offer some of the specialist work of the early years of secondary schooling. It was noted in the DES report of 1978 that secondary schools in middle-school systems grumbled about having to remedy the lack of in-depth subject study in middle schools feeding them.

Mervyn Taylor and Yvonne Garson (1982), looking at 800 middle schools in a national survey, concluded that 8 to 12 schools remained essentially primary schools while 9 to 13 schools were under-established in terms of specialist teachers and resources. They had not been able to forge effective links with secondary schools. An 8 to 12 school falling below a two-form entry and a 9 to 13 school falling below a three-form entry had extreme difficulty in providing specialists in mathematics, science and languages. Maureen O'Connor, writing in *The Guardian*, pointed out that there had been no detailed research to substantiate the suggestion that middle schools had bridged a junior–secondary divide, by producing better results at 16, for instance (O'Connor 1982). Within middle schools there was often a sharp transition from primary to secondary education. Yet John Burrows (1978) argued that middle schools had been centres of curriculum innovation and organizational flexibility. Leicestershire's 10 to 14 schools still claim to provide specialist teaching for younger children and child-centred work into the secondary age range (see Doe 1983). On middle schools, see also Hargreaves and Tickle (1980) and Blyth and Derricott (1977)). The Her Majesty's Inspectorate's (HMI) recent study of 9 to 13 schools (DES 1983) concluded that falling rolls and declining resources were having a detrimental effect on schooling standards. The following HMI report on 5 to 12 and 8 to 12 schools was no more favourable (1985b).

There were only 15 middle schools in 1969, only one of which was an 8 to 12 school (DES 1978b). Within the next year, 125 more were opened including 31 which were deemed primary, and 4 first and middle schools combined. By 1973 there were 687 middle schools (303 deemed secondary, i.e. 9 to 13, although the DES deemed 9 9 to 13 schools in 1977 as primary schools, 242 deemed primary and 143 first-middle schools). In 1977 the total was 1632 with the number of 8 to 12 schools outstripping the 9 to 13 schools from 1974 on (in 1973–4, 263 8 to 12 schools were opened). In 1979 there were 1764 middle schools (390 were combined first-middle schools, 754 were deemed primary and 620 were deemed secondary). In 1981 there were 1412 8 to 12 and 9 to 13 schools compared to 1374 in 1979.

This, however, was the high-water mark. The small size of middle schools, which had made them expedient, was now their undoing. The desired 3-form entry produced about 500 pupils in a fully-grown 9 to 13 school but of 522 of them in 1977 only 174 were of this size (227 of them had fewer than 400 pupils and 104 less than 300). By November 1981, 11 of 48 local authorities with middle schools were considering scrapping them and, in the summer of 1982, the decision was made to close 44 middle schools in Wirral and Birkenhead. In 1983 79 schools in Stoke disappeared, and similar policies are being pursued in Brighton, Cheshire, Devon, Hull, Kirklees, Oxford, Rochdale, Lincolnshire, Suffolk, Staffordshire and Wigan. Thus expediency, the architect of middle schools, may also become the demolisher.

Separate sixth-form provision

As in the cases of middle schools and tiered schools, the evolution of a system based on mushroom schools or sixth form colleges was based on expediency. Many existing schools were too small for reorganization into 11 to 18 schools because they would waste scarce resources such as teachers of mathematics and science, especially at sixth form level. There was an urgent need for economy where there was pressure for a wide range of subjects to be made available to a few students. There was a rapidly expanding number of sixth formers after 1960, a growth which only levelled off in the mid-1970s (the percentage of pupils in maintained schools remaining at school till 17, as a percentage of the number of 14 year old pupils three years earlier, was 8 in 1960, 16 in 1969, 18 in 1973, where it remained, strangely enough, after the raising of the school leaving age). The expansion was the result of post-war birth bulges and an improved staying-on rate, and may have solved the problem of small sixth forms, but the new sixth forms of comprehensive schools demanded a greater range of courses and approaches than ever. Comprehensive schools, meanwhile, remained obstinately small. The 1000-pupil school which Circular 10/65 considered essential was achieved by under a half of them in 1977 (1341 schools out of the 2977 taking pupils up to 16 or 18 years of age). Thus, finding economic use of sixth form resources remained a serious problem throughout the period, and falling rolls has now made the situation critical, forcing a new wave of reorganization.

Grouping sixth-form provision was the solution for many local authorities, and the various ways of doing this were all in use by 1970. Informal or formal links between sixth forms of adjacent schools were sometimes extended to consortia of groups of schools, as in Birmingham. There were also sixth form centres used by the schools of a locality, as in Tower Hamlets. The mushroom 11, or 13, or 14 to 18 school received sixth formers from its own fifth form as well as from feeding 11 to 16 schools. Finally, there was the area sixth form college receiving from local 11 to 16 schools, and these colleges could embrace all the full-time and part-time 16 to 19 education of the area (tertiary colleges).

Separating sixth-form work into colleges or gathering it into mushrooms were new departures for English education, requiring something of an ideology to support it. But the foundation for the new types of sixth form organization was expediency. One of the embarassments of arguing for sixth form colleges or mushrooms was that convincing arguments for 11 to 16 schools also had to be produced in the same way that the supporters of grammar schools had to defend secondary modern schools.

Sixth formers in separate colleges, it was argued, would feel more like 'students' than 'pupils', and would not be distracted by rather annoying prefect duties (Pedley 1978). The social mix with students from other 11 to 16 schools (in colleges or mushrooms) would be a bonus. A prevailing early idea, one appealing to crypto-elitists, was to house sixth form colleges or mushrooms in ex-grammar schools. The outcome of this was often the mushroom school since there was usually no reason to cut out 11 to 16 education from the ex-grammar school. In the large number of schemes including 11 to 16 schools in 1968 only half envisaged colleges. At that time 21 per cent of comprehensive schools were 11 to 16 but there were only 3 sixth form colleges in the entire country. But when the plans of 1968 came to fruition their number increased rapidly, from 21 in 1973 to 38 a year later and 59 by 1975 (DES 1978b) and by 1981 there were over a hundred colleges (Watkins 1983).

The arguments for the system continued to accumulate in these years, a triumph of rationalization. The 11 to 16 school would avoid the weakness of tiered schools in splitting secondary education at 13 or 14. Pedley (1978) reported some elitists as saying that it was silly to pretend that grammar schools and secondary moderns could ever be equal and that the best means of achieving equality of opportunity was transfer of able pupils at 16 to mushrooms or colleges provided by grammar schools, an 'end-on' system for linking tripartite schools without destroying the established grammar school sixth form (also in Benn and Simon 1970). It was an interesting rationalization, another of those educational reforms which could have promoted equality of opportunity without wholesale reorganization. This is the solution to falling rolls used in Worcester in 1983 where it is intended that ex-grammar schools become sixth form colleges. How comprehensive would these mushrooms or colleges have been? Even Benn and Simon (1970) agreed that mushrooms could be comprehensive if they were not selective. Since the late 1960s, the raising of the school leaving age and the development of the CSE examination have become ways of potentially diluting selectivity for an 'end-on' system. These were two of the methods used by comprehensive schools to swell their sixth forms. It is possible to visualize grammar school sixth forms or colleges with open entry for ex-secondary modern pupils, but if anyone doubts the progress equality could have made in an 'end-on' system they must also remember the uphill struggle it has had in many comprehensive schools.

It is a matter of fact that sixth form colleges have a good record of open entry policies. One of the earliest colleges, Luton, asked entrants for 4 O levels (with the result that local 11 to 16 schools developed sixth forms for extra O levels and CSEs) (Marsden 1971). Of the schools in the Benn and Simon (1970) survey of sixth forms 31.5 per cent asked entrants for only 1 O level and other early colleges, such as Mexborough, Stoke and Rotherham, began with an open door policy (Macfarlane 1978). In Brent it was their potential for selectivity that prompted the Labour council to abandon the Tory scheme for sixth form colleges. But, at a recent count (Watkins 1983), only three of more than a hundred colleges now claim a restricted entry policy.

From the start, however, there were doubts about the 11 to 16 school, a school without its own top. Would it attract well-qualified specialist staff? Would younger pupils lose the benefit of the presence of sixth formers? Would transfer at 16 to another school discourage some pupils? Comprehensives with sixth forms had a staying-on rate of 59 per cent compared to 37 per cent in 11 to 16 schools (Benn and Simon 1970). Neave (1975) found that transfer dissuaded many from doing extra O levels. The DES (1978b) suggested that 11 to 16 schools needed careful running and some positive discrimination in resources, not something they would have mentioned a year or two later. Like their secondary modern colleagues, teachers in 11 to 16 schools could easily be regarded as rather inferior creatures. In 1968, 11 to 16 schools had an average of only 13 per cent of pupils in the top 20 per cent ability range compared to the average of 15 per cent in all comprehensives and an even higher figure in mushroom schools (Benn and Simon 1970).

Yet the NFER study of 1974 to 1978 (Dean *et al.* 1979) analysed supposed advantages possessed by 11 to 16 schools. It revealed that some teachers liked to specialize in teaching younger age groups. Research showed that the absence of sixth formers could lift the performance of fifth formers. When it came to advising them about staying on teachers could be more impartial because they were not in the game of getting as many sixth formers as they could for their own schools.

The NFER questioned 4448 16-plus students in 45 institutions of all types, at the beginning and end of their courses. Students in colleges seemed more content with their courses than those in schools, especially if they had come from grammar schools. On the whole, they felt that they had been better prepared for higher education or employment. They had been offered a wider range of courses. As far as the teachers were concerned they saw more advantages in separate provision than disadvantages, although they reported occasional difficulties in recruiting staff for 11 to 16 schools.

A later study (Watkins 1983) reported that the hundred or more colleges contained 18 per cent of maintained sixth formers.

Watkins reported a 1981 survey of 7 colleges which found that three-quarters of their students thought they gained from not being housed with younger pupils and most of them were 'pleased' with their courses. Eric Briault, in his study of falling rolls, also found that students preferred a separate 16 to 19 school (Briault and Smith 1980).

Unfortunately, scientific research into 11 to 16 schools is not available. They represent something of a forgotten sector, with nothing in them for the politicians, who created them as part of a reorganization deal in harness with mushroom schools and sixth form colleges, something they were happy to boast about. (See Briault in the *TES* of 26 February 1982, which also has a series of short accounts of 11 to 16 schools in a variety of local circumstances.)

Linked sixth-form work was favoured as a way of retaining 11 to 18 schools. This was a very useful system where schools were close to one another in urban areas. The ILEA promoted the idea in 1970 because so many of its schools were small. As a result the Tower Hamlets Sixth Form Centre was housed in the old George Green Grammar School building while this school became a community comprehensive and moved from the East India Dock Road to a £2 million campus on the Isle of Dogs (see Patricia Rowan (1977)). Birmingham grouped its secondary schools into a handful of consortia, sharing not only sixth form facilities but those for earlier years as well. But Briault (Briault and Smith 1980) found that existing examples of linked work did not work very well, even when only two schools were involved. Much valuable time was wasted trying to administer workable arrangements.

The idea of separately grouped or linked sixth-form work has persisted strongly, however, throughout the period and is now much favoured, on new grounds of expediency, in an era of falling rolls. A quarter of the schools planned in 1968 were to have some form of separate sixth-form provision and the proportion was a third in 1970 (Benn and Simon 1970).

In 1976, 11, or 12, or 13 to 16 schools made up 29.4 per cent of all comprehensive schools, so the proportion in the plans of 1970 was virtually realized in the system of six years later. In 1980 there were 918 11 to 16 schools and 148 12 to 16 schools, a total of 1066 out of 3279 comprehensive schools (32.5 per cent compared to 29.4 per cent in 1976). In 1976 sixth form colleges made up 2.4 per cent of all comprehensive schools so that it was clear that mushroom schools took the majority of sixth form entrants from 11 or 12 to 16 schools.

As in the case of the sixth form college the tertiary college idea was based on an evolving ideology, perhaps even more so since it was an obvious extension of the comprehensive principle. In the same way as a comprehensive school would embrace all-comers at 11-plus the tertiary college would embrace all at 16-plus, from A level aspirants to part-time vocational trainees (Pedley 1978), using the old term 'county college' from the 1944 Act. The tertiary college represented a union of the traditional academic sixth form, the provision of extra O levels and CSEs and CEEs (Certificates of Extended Education), vocational training, full-time and part-time.

Early tertiary colleges developed in Exeter (1970) and Barnstaple, although many other schools had linked courses with further education colleges. By 1971 Exeter College had 1350 full-time and 3000 part-time students (Griffiths 1971). But grand plans like this, especially suited to an urban hub with spokes to semi-rural communities, were rare, and by 1977 there were only ten tertiary colleges. Now, however, it seems that there are likely to be many more because of a rapidly diminishing sixth form population. Grouping all 16 to 19 provision into one institution makes more economic sense than ever, adding to its existing egalitarian appeal. With this trend the 11 to 16 school seems to have an assured future (an ideology for them is desperately required). The number of sixth form colleges is also set to rise in an era of falling rolls.

In the Manchester scheme, to meet a tumbling secondary school population and despite Sir Keith Joseph's intervention and saving of three schools of 'proven worth', the modified plan retains the plan of sixth form colleges forming 'tertiary consortia' with further education colleges. The Croydon scheme has four sixth form colleges including a tertiary college (and this involved the closure of all middle schools in the area). In Bradford there is to be full integration of all young people on vocational training. Coventry's intended answer to falling rolls is to place all 16 to 19 education into its existing 11 to 18 community schools, with special vocational courses ranging over the 14 to 19 age range. They hope this will avoid closures and amalgamations. In 1982, Richmond-on-Thames concentrated all its 3000 16 to 19 students into one tertiary college and Wandsworth may soon adopt this plan.

Tiered schools

Like 11 to 18 schools some of their tiered counterparts might now have to amalgamate into 11 to 18 or 11 to 16 schools. The basic problem with tiered schools at the beginning of this period was whether they deserved the label 'comprehensive' by avoiding selection. In Leicestershire there was a clear intention to phase selection out but elsewhere this was done with less alacrity, and some authorities, e.g. Kent and Cumbria, still use the 'interim' systems suggested by Circular 10/65, with guided 'parental choice' as the selective principle. There was early evidence that pupils from working-class backgrounds tended to stay in or drift to the early leaving school (in 1964 the staying-on rate in middle-class Oadby was 84 per cent and in working-class Hinckley 43 per cent (Pedley 1978) although Eggleston gave the figures as 85 per cent and 39 per cent (Eggleston 1965)). Eggleston, in fact, found little evidence of selectivity in intakes to the upper schools in Leicestershire. He concluded that transfer did not increase the working-class drop-out rate at 15. G. E. Whalley (1970) found that upper schools were under-subscribed because parents either did not understand official information or accepted advice from teachers about the poor potential of their children because they were themselves diffident about what their children could do (Whalley used a sample of 130 parents).

One of the other problems for early plans for the introduction of tiered schools was the existence of large numbers of single-sex schools. Whereas two small mixed tripartite schools could be turned into two tiers this was not possible if they were single-sex and people wanted them to stay that way, as many did. In

Darlington, single-sex education was abandoned after a great row within the Labour ranks locally. Keeping single-sex education in the area meant that three junior comprehensives would have to feed five senior schools (Batley *et al.* 1970). In other places single-sex education was retained, especially in inner London, very often, by insisting on having 11 to 18 schools (i.e. very small ones). In my study of London comprehensive schools in 1982 (Weeks 1983) a half sample of ILEA schools (71 schools) contained 45 single-sex schools, many of them quite small. Many single-sex schools became upper tier schools (only 38 per cent of upper schools were mixed in 1970 compared to 81 per cent of all comprehensives). However, 94 per cent of 14 to 18 schools were mixed at that time, so that it was the 13 to 18 school which tended to be single-sex, great numbers of them housed in ex-single-sex grammar schools.

Tiered arrangements were approved in Circulars 10/65 and 4/74 because of their potential for economy of resources but in 10/65 the DES stressed the need for close collaboration between the tiers in order to produce continuity in the curriculum and in organization. Moreover, junior comprehensives had more potential problems than 11 to 16 schools in attracting specialist staff and resources. The DES report of 1978 had accounts of poor accommodation in junior comprehensives, and poor co-ordination between them and senior comprehensives.

In many instances, the tiered solution was turned down for the sort of reasons outlined above, in favour of split-site 11 to 18 schools. Again, evidence in favour of such an arrangement materialized, but many educators instinctively disliked the idea of split sites because of potential disruption. The head of Sir Richard of Chichester School in Camden Town admitted the administrative burden (although the sites are, in fact, only a few hundred yards apart) but he believed that because of its potential difficulties the school worked harder to overcome them and forged a strong sense of internal co-operation (O'Connell 1970). Benn and Simon (1970) discussed the pros and cons of split-site schools. In the first NFER survey (Monks 1968) 22 per cent of comprehensive schools had split sites and in the second, smaller sample (Monks 1970) this figure was 24 per cent. Compared to one-site schools, their public examination results were superior, although this was possibly related to the fact that they tended to be larger and larger schools achieved better results. Many 11 to 18 schools with a high intake of top ability range pupils were on split sites (41 per cent of them, compared to 27 per cent of schools without this icing on the cake), the explanation probably being that that these were ex-grammar school buildings housing comprehensives.

The NFER discovered that split-site schools basically organized themselves to prevent staff and pupils commuting between the sites. On average, 20 to 30 per cent of both of them moved between sites. Only one school moved more than a third of its pupils. Generally, the potential awkwardness of split sites made everyone in them work harder to iron out problems, as the head of Sir Richard of Chichester School had suggested; a victory for British muddling through. Secondary reorganization without it would have been impossible. The Rutter Report (Rutter *et al.* 1979) also discovered that split-site schools had fewer behaviour and delinquency problems.

By 1970 tiered schools tended to use transfer at 13 rather than at 14, which was regarded as giving the senior school too little time to prepare pupils for public examinations. Such insistence meant the continuation of some 11 to 13 schools, which many regarded as about as educationally rewarding as a transit camp. However, Bradford thought it achieved something in its 11 to 13 schools and received the support of Alec Clegg, who strongly opposed transfer at 14.

Whether transfer was at 13 or 14, by 1970 a fifth of all local reorganization plans were for tiered systems, double the 1965 figure (Benn and Simon 1970). In 1972 there were tiered schools in 39 local authorities. Out of 163, 91 had 11 or 12 to 18 systems and 19 had middle-school systems (Hill 1972). The decline of transfer at 14 is shown by the fact that there were 11 to 14 and 14 to 18 systems in 24 areas in 1970 (Donnison 1970) but only in 14 in 1972 (Hill 1972) whereas 11 to 13 and 13 to 18 systems were in 9 areas in 1972 compared to 2 in 1970. Also 11 to 15 or 16 schools, with potential transfer at 13 to 13 to 18 schools, existed in 14 areas in 1972 compared to 4 in 1970. This indicated, in the Thatcher period, a growth of tiered systems which were potentially selective. Two areas in 1970 and 1972 had transfer from 11 to 13 schools to 13 to 16 or 13 to 18 schools.

Conclusions

To sum up, the 11 or 12 to 18 school has maintained its supremacy between 1965 and 1985, making up about half the system. This proportion may fall because falling rolls favour separately grouped or shared sixth-form provision. All the other patterns of reorganized schools make up substantial minority patterns. In the early 1970s, tiered systems were the second most common pattern but by 1976 both separate/shared sixth form systems and middle school systems had superseded tiered schools. The special sixth-form systems, moreover, outstripped middle-school systems by 1980 and this tendency will increase because of falling rolls. Tiered systems may also decline further, but not at the rate of middle schools. The fastest expanding type of school may become the 11 to 16 school. This is the only sector of the comprehensive system without a mature ideology, but this does not usually hamper developments in secondary reorganization.

6
The meritocratic school

The meritocratic ideal type

In Chapter 1 the confusion surrounding the 'comprehensive principle' was discussed. Whereas there was acknowledgement from all quarters of the need to promote equality of educational opportunity some educators recognized aims beyond this. 'Opportunity' was about higher education and employment. This was a vital part of the 'comprehensive principle' but Pedley (1978) was concerned with the unique talents of individuals, and a number of writers referred to individual potential, the 'Second View', as Peter Daunt (1975) put it. Although Anthony Crosland referred to tripartism as supporting a 'weak' equality, that is one not really providing equality of opportunity, referring merely to opportunity could in turn be regarded as 'weak' because it allowed internal selection in schools and state support for selective independent schools. It allowed parents to buy selective education. Thus, the 'equality' was diluted by other considerations – of freedom, of elitism, of the needs of the national economy. A really 'strong' equality would be one adhered to steadfastly, excluding other principles and demands. Any form of selection, in the system of education and in the internal organization of comprehensive schools, would have to be confined within the terms of a newer and 'stronger' equality.

An excellent account of the dilemma over the 'comprehensive

principle' was provided in an article by Denis Marsden (1969). He had the same difficulty as Julienne Ford in that there were not many clear-cut statements of any 'principle'. From various sources, he constructed two ideal type 'principles' or profiles. The titles of his two profiles, 'meritocratic' and 'egalitarian', were not meant to indicate particular educators nor particular schools. Indeed, the point was that educators and schools exhibited a bewildering confusion of the ideal types.

According to Marsden, the 'meritocratic' school was traditional. It wanted to equalize educational opportunity by maximizing a pupil's academic attainment. It believed in a hierarchy of merit, in competition, in hard work and in a 'middle-class leaven' providing leadership and culture. Such a school aimed at producing trained manpower for the economy. Its intake would be balanced to ensure that it had a fair proportion of middle-class and high ability pupils. It had to be large in order to provide a variety of courses and the efficient use of specialist staff. Its sixth form would be selective and academic (the less able could go to sixth form colleges). It would be streamed, formal, with academic class teaching. There would be specialist teachers for 'high-fliers' and high emphasis on staff with science degrees. The curriculum would be varied. There would be much sorting-out of pupils through counselling and the discovery of individual skills. The school would be closed to the community but parental interest would be welcomed. O and A levels would have top priority along with university entrance and very high quality work in mathematics and science.

This type of school is most certainly the extended grammar school very much in the minds of Labour and Tory politicians. This would be the school to tap the 'pool of talent', the grammar school for all. It would delay selection (despite Marsden's analysis, meritocrats grudgingly accepted the use of mixed-ability grouping in the lower years of secondary schooling), but not for too long in case the talent was lost.

How successful have comprehensive schools been in being 'meritocratic' on these indices above, in being grammar schools for all? A major acid test is, of course, public examination results. Have comprehensives done better here than tripartite schools?

The answer to this, affirmative or negative, might be further explained by 'failure' in some of the preferred processes for meritocratic schools as outlined by Marsden.

Comparing meritocratic comprehensive schools and grammar schools

First of all, some account of the possible sources for information about meritocratic performance is needed. In the early days of the Labour Administration there were Tory calls for proper research into the efficiency of comprehensive schools before any whole-sale reorganization was ordered. In December 1964, following the revelations by a music teacher at Kidbrooke School mentioned earlier (p. 8), Geoffrey Lloyd asked in the House of Commons for a review of well-established comprehensive schools. At the same time, Sir John Lockwood, Master of Birkbeck College, called for an adequate assessment of all the consequences of radical recasting. Perhaps a few experimental schools could be examined because the comprehensive movement seemed to appeal to emotion rather than logic. He said that parents were more interested in educational quality than a classless society. Julienne Ford (1969) asked whether reform would bring a 'fairer society', and added that it was a gigantic experiment using millions of children. Little attempt had been made to examine it first. On the question of whether comprehensive schools would produce more meritocratic talent than tripartite schools, controlled longitudinal research was necessary.

Parents could have objected to experiments being performed on their children, experiments, moreover, which did not have the backing of scientific research. Perhaps Geoffrey Lloyd's idea of studying established comprehensives could have been tried. On the other hand, these were rather special places; predominantly 11 to 18 schools, often well-publicized show-places attracting heads and teachers keen on the comprehensive principle. Perhaps comprehensive schools would have shown up very well in 1965. Opponents in the examination statistics war (see pp. 74–81) overlook the possibility that performance in comprehensive schools could have seriously declined after 1965. Pedley

(1963) calculated that 14 per cent of pupils in twenty comprehensive schools passed in five O levels or more compared to a
national average of 10 per cent. Perhaps in 1962 the infant system
was vastly different from the mass kaleidoscopic system of ten
years later, which should have been compared with what was left
of tripartism. About this time the two systems were relatively
balanced numerically whereas before it would have been difficult
to assess a comprehensive system which had not matured.
Tripartism, however, was doomed except in its bed-rock areas,
and either suffering the pangs of imminent death or still
producing the best examination results in the land, as some of
these schools had always done. It would have been instructive to
show how varied grammar results were. At the inauguration of
the Programme for Reform in Secondary Education (PRISE) in
1975 Professor Peston pointed out that, given all their advantages, results in grammar schools had not been all that splendid.
But the remaining grammar schools in the late 1970s were probably not representative of the system in its heyday. The critical
years for comparing the two systems were probably between
1972 and 1975, when they were in harness, but the NFER finished
its research by 1972 (at that time, studying only 12 schools).
Margaret Thatcher blithely supported a binary system yet missed
a marvellous opportunity to compare the two parts of it.

Large-scale and longitudinal research would have cost a great
deal of money, but not in terms of the national education budget.
Many people who were happy to see comprehensive schools
given a try complained about reorganization on the cheap. That
was not giving them a fair trial, and it was essentially change on
the cheap not to spend money on research. How much would
large-scale research have cost, the equivalent of one or two new
schools? One gets the distinct impression that politicians were
ill-disposed towards effective research, fearful either that the
investigation would show the effectiveness of comprehensive
schools or vice versa. A massive educational reform based on so
little knowledge could only be either very daring or very
dangerous.

Academic research into comprehensive schools could have
been strictly comparative; in other words, it would have

compared examination results, entry to higher education and vocational achievements at reorganized and tripartite schools. Let us say the areas chosen could have been Greater London, Manchester, Sheffield and a rural area. I select Manchester and Sheffield because statistics in the mid-1970s seemed to suggest that comprehensives in Manchester were doing badly but in Sheffield they were doing well. The researchers could have gone deeply into the reasons for success or failure, especially on intake profiles, capitation, facilities, teaching ability, and so on. Michael Rutter's team had that sort of brief (Rutter *et al.* 1979) but were looking only at twelve London comprehensive schools and no tripartite schools.

We are working here strictly on meritocratic terms. Some commentators have explained that it was impossible to compare tripartite and comprehensive schools since they differed in their aims. This conclusion needs to be challenged. In the first place, as has been seen, there is considerable confusion over exactly what the aims of comprehensive schools are and, secondly, a closer investigation of possible aims of grammar schools may not uncover as many differences from comprehensive schools as imagined. It would be unwise to condemn all grammar schools for failure to pursue social cohesion or to adopt caring attitudes, or actively to support equality of opportunity. I cannot remember my small east London grammar school failing in these areas. Moreover, it is easy to forget that maintained grammar schools were set up on the basis of equality of opportunity and the basic rationale of secondary modern schools was to help less fortunate members of society. Perhaps the major difference between comprehensive schools and tripartite schools was in methods rather than in aims – they wanted the same things but one system believed in segregation and the other in integration. We might well ask how integrative comprehensive schools are when there is a great deal of evidence of segregation in them.

Egalitarian principles go much further than examination results and jobs. But politicians, many educators and a great many parents see education in these terms. Therefore, it is reasonable to ask whether comprehensive schools do well in these spheres. If not, they hardly suit the society they are supposed to serve. I think comprehensive schools have to achieve good meritocratic results and, then, because of all the other benefits attributed to them, they must achieve much more. It is thus perfectly legitimate to enquire into results at these schools.

Another major complaint about comparisons is that comprehensive schools are creamed of bright pupils by selective schools. But if research builds in intake profiles this can be taken into account. However, it is true that creaming can have wider adverse effects than simply removing bright pupils. It can also prevent the recruitment of teachers who like to work with bright pupils. The staff intake profile needs to be considered. And there are other effects. For instance, Young and Brandis (1971) found that schools starved of talent tended to stream on good behaviour rather than ability, with adverse effects on already struggling results. General morale can be low in such schools, further depressing performance in a welter of alienation and disruption. Good research, however, could discover and analyse all this. Results would then be lined up against all the other factors. Creaming must be regarded as a fact of life if one wishes to compare the two systems of schools because if it did not exist, by definition there would be no tripartite schools to use for comparison.

Thus, it appears very unfortunate that the only substantial large-scale official research project should have concluded that it was impractical to compare comprehensive schools with other types because their ideals differed, they were new, and many of them were still incomplete, and that pupils in different schools could not be matched up on the basis of, for example, parental interest or attitudes to school. These explanations sound like excuses. Did the ideals differ all that much, and did their meritocratic ideals differ, at all? Perhaps in 1971 comprehensive schools were relatively new and incomplete (although many were not) but subsequently this was less and less true. To say that it is impossible to match pupils in different schools is tantamount to saying that no two schools could ever be compared. This is plainly ridiculous, especially if it is items like examination results, jobs and entry to higher education which are being compared. There are obvious limitations to the comparison of any two schools but in no sense is it impossible or impracticable. It is a pity that the NFER team came out with its disclaimer in 1972, when education was on the threshold of that period when the best comparisons could have been made. Julienne Ford (1969) pointed out that researching into the success or failure of comprehensives was a complicated business because of the variety of confounding variables which were relevant. Because of this, she was not prepared to stake her life on any conclusions she made from the study of only three schools. Nevertheless, from this study she came up with a mass of statistical detail providing answers to specific questions about meritocratic success. Other researchers complained about her making judgements from such a small sample, but it was a pity that they did not try their hand at emulating her work, perhaps on more schools than she could.

As it is, the Labour Government had no mandate in 1976 to make reorganization compulsory. It is true that they had a manifesto about secondary reorganization and they had been elected to power. But the pattern in politics should be that social and economic policies depend on research to some extent. There has to be ideology but this cannot be entirely divorced from social and economic fact.

The NFER research, sponsored by the Government late in 1965, surveyed 331 comprehensive schools in 1966, practically all those then in existence (Monks 1968). What a wasted opportunity for comparative research. A second-stage report on 59 of these schools was issued in 1970 (Monks 1970), and a third was on 12 of the schools (Ross *et al.* 1972). As the need for large-scale research grew so the NFER sample became smaller and smaller. Since then, there has been no research of a general nature and with the tripartite system now in a corner the chance has gone to compare two mature systems. Gray *et al.* (1983) studied 20,000 pupils who left all types of school in Scotland in 1976 and found that comprehensive schools raised slightly fewer pupils to the top but helped more to progress beyond the minimum. They seemed to narrow down middle-class advantage but the authors of the report point out that this could possibly only apply to certain areas of Scotland.

Other research has been small scale, like Ford's. Her comprehensive was well-established, relatively uncreamed (it lost only 1.2 per cent of local children), of average size and, to her satisfaction, 'typical'. She compared it to a grammar school and a secondary modern school in the same area. There is a useful survey of other small-scale research in Griffiths (1971). Guy Neave (1975) studied the impact of comprehensive schools on working-class opportunity in higher education using a sample of 969 students from 163 comprehensives in 1968. Paul Bellaby (1977) studied three comprehensives in one town.

Several books on secondary reorganization were concerned with the politics of change, both national and local. Others were accounts of particular schools by local administrators or teachers. Still others, such as the Comprehensive Schools Committee reports, were from pro-comprehensive groups who were not, naturally enough, seeking evidence of failure of the comprehensive idea. Other pro-comprehensive academics described how they thought the schools should work. None of these publications, however, provided comparative analysis. As a result, those campaigners who argued about meritocratic results in comprehensives could only base their conclusions on statistical data about the results, and not also on some of the conditions which shaped them. In these circumstances, the examination statistics war has largely ignored the socio-economic and educational factors which would have provided the vital explanations of them. It would have enabled educators to make up their minds about the results. For instance, if results were slightly worse in comprehensive schools they might have accepted this as the price to pay for other benefits, such as better vocational education in comprehensive schools. If the results were as good these other benefits would be a bonus. If results were better and there were other types of triumph, in personal and social education, for instance, the comprehensive case would be unassailable.

Large-scale and longitudinal research might have unearthed strong socio-economic or even educational factors having a general effect on results over time. In other words, results might have declined (or improved) in any type of school during a certain period. As it is, the statistics of examination results always seem to imply that it is the type of school which affects results more than anything else, even though this is by no means proven.

No deep research was done, however, and it will never be known whether comprehensive schools are really better overall at the meritocratic game than the combined tripartite schools or whether their preoccupation with egalitarian ideals ruins their performance at this. Perhaps it was impossible to discover even in the mid-1970s, but this will never be known either.

The examination statistics war

The following account of the statistical war will demonstrate how such a mathematical maul is rendered virtually meaningless by the absence of factors explaining it. In any case, some of the conclusions of the protagonists seemed to be lacking in plain common sense. To discover, for instance, by adding up all the A level, O level and CSE Grade 1 passes achieved by school leavers between 1965 and 1973 that comprehensives improved their performance by 187 per cent and selective schools by 119 per cent is surely no more than a demonstration that comprehensive pupils did a lot of CSE examinations.

Yet R. W. Baldwin, for many years Chairman of Governors at Manchester Grammar School and a member of the city education committee, a leading figure in the numbers game, said that the result quoted above was a matter of taking advantage of the fact that comprehensive schools had hardly begun in 1965. Yet early comprehensive schools had good results. The point was that the entries to CSE in 1965 were low because the examination had only just begun. Baldwin (1979) paid attention to passes in 1 to 3 A levels between 1966 and 1977. The total of these had levelled off over the years, and since comprehensive school results had declined in comparison to grammar school results he concluded that secondary reorganization was to blame for the overall stagnation. In English, mathematics and French results had actually declined (as they had together with science in O levels and CSE Grade 1). Hilary Steedman (1982) also pointed out that the proportion of pupils passing O level English, Grades A to C, fell from 83.2 per cent to 78.8 per cent for boys and from 89.2 per cent to 84.9 per cent between 1975 and 1979 (this is a proportion of the candidates entering for the examination). Including A level passes at further education colleges, Baldwin (1980) found that the index of A levels per school-leaver (1970 equals 100) was 102.5 in maintained schools and 119.5 in independent schools by 1977. In another place (Baldwin 1981) he surveyed A level results between 1975 and 1979 and again associated a decline with the advent of comprehensive schools. He reminded us that the DES had forecast an era of improving results in 1971, but this was based on the contemporary performance of a system only half comprehensive. The promised land had not materialized because the next decade brought many more of the disastrous comprehensive schools. In 1971 the DES could gloat over the fact that the numbers qualifying for higher education had risen from 6 per cent of the age group in 1960 to 13 per cent in 1970. But, according to Baldwin, the comprehensives spoiled it all. If only he could have told us why, backed by good empirical research.

Poorer results in comprehensive schools can be explained by creaming, yet Baldwin was unable or unwilling to build in this factor and to give us any researched reason why bright pupils apparently failed in these schools, apart from a global 'dragging down' process. What dragged them down? And was it worth further reforming the system of schools to get rid of this effect or was there evidence that the whole idea of integration was wrong and had to go? As to DES forecasts of rosy futures these need be no more reliable than their prognostications about birth rates and how many teachers we will need. In any case, there is no evidence to disprove the theory that decline was caused by general socio-economic factors and that had it not been for the existence of large numbers of comprehensives this decline would have been even worse. For instance, there is a great deal of evidence for the poor performance of pupils of West Indian origin in comprehensive schools but their performance might have been even worse in tripartite schools. On the other hand, comprehensive schools could have made the decline even worse.

According to Philip Venning (1980b) Baldwin's conclusions were based on assessing A levels per school leaver, including those who left at 16. Venning reckoned that all this proved was that more 16 year olds were leaving school rather than staying on, especially in maintained schools. If the results of 17 and 18 year olds were isolated this showed an improvement for maintained schools from 1973. Moreover, if the results of 17 year olds only were considered (only those who left with one or more A levels) the trend in maintained schools in the 1970s was an improvement from 68,000 in 1967–8 to 78,230 in 1970–1 and to 92,500 in 1977–8. Venning's assessment of the situation was that apparent improvements or declines in results were mainly the effect of changes in the appropriate age groups. Any decline in the early 1970s was quickly arrested and comprehensives could not be specifically blamed for any decline except in some key subjects. It is difficult to know how he could make such assertions from the evidence of examination statistics, any more than Baldwin could.

Auriol Stevens (1980) concluded from her studies that the massive and dramatic disruption of reorganization had not raised levels at the top. On average it took their bright pupils longer to attain disciplined academic work, but comprehensive schools had helped pupils in the middle ability range. In 1967, 50 per cent of school leavers had no public examination passes but this figure was 16 per cent in 1977 (further evidence of the effect of the CSE). *Education Statistics for the United Kingdom* published by HMSO in 1982 gave the proportion as half in 1968 and a sixth in 1979. The same report indicated that the percentage of leavers gaining five O levels (Grades A to C or their equivalent) increased from only 24 to 26 per cent during the same period. The proportion of pupils passing at least one A level stayed steady at about one-sixth and the percentage of 19 and 20 year olds in post-compulsory education remained about the same at around one-third. What we really would like to know is why this was so.

Auriol Stevens (1980) at least tried to look inside comprehensives. It says something about the paucity of efforts of academic researchers in this field that journalists and the chairmen of education committees were left to fill the breach. Stevens tried to explain relatively poor results at the top with evidence of some poor teaching, low expectations and bad organization in comprehensive schools.

The National Children's Bureau's *Progress in Secondary Schools* (1980) was a detailed analysis of the data for their 1958 cohort from the aspect of progress between 11 and 16 related to the types of school attended (Steedman 1980). From this it appeared that comprehensive schools were doing well for bright pupils, especially in view of the finding that the social class composition of comprehensive schools was scarcely different from that of secondary modern schools in the survey. In mathematics and reading the top 20 per cent of the ability range (as shown in IQ tests at 11) did as well in comprehensive schools as in selective schools. Those below the top 20 per cent who managed to get into grammar schools did better than similar pupils in comprehensive schools. Results for comparable pupils in comprehensive schools and secondary moderns showed no significant differences.

These findings were based on tests given at 11 and 16. The author, Jane Steedman, was able to add findings from public examination results at 16 (for 1974) in a further report in 1983 (Steedman 1983). Taking into account ability and background at 11, going to a grammar school could be measured as an advantage of two-thirds of an O level. Going to a comprehensive school instead of a secondary modern (all other factors being as equal as a statistician could make them) provided a third of an O level more. Examination results of comprehensive schools compared to tripartite schools combined cannot be analysed as better or worse. Grammar schools were not better than comprehensive schools for bright working-class pupils.

This second report was very cautious and published its raw data because the first one had aroused a storm of protest from the Centre for Policy Studies and Black Paper contributors, largely the same people who serve the National Council for Educational Standards (NCES) (see Goldstein 1981).

Another well-known personality in the numbers game has been and is Fred Naylor, a prominent member of the NCES.

A typical example of his work (1975) was the appraisal of improved examination results at Woodlands Comprehensive in Coventry. He compared this progress with that at the City of Bath Technical School. At Woodlands results rose dramatically despite de-streaming in the late 1960s but Naylor said he could find non-grammar schools in the tripartite system which did even better. Even though Woodlands had many more entrants with IQs of over 100 than the Bath school (about twice as many), still taking into account the higher number of early school-leavers from Woodlands, the Bath school achieved about the same number of O level passes. But the head of Woodlands complained that comparing the two schools was a meaningless exercise. All pupils stayed on at the Bath school compared to a national average staying-on rate of 44 per cent (at that time). It was a well-established school with very high academic aims. Even though Woodlands had twice as many entrants with IQs over 100 only 2 pupils going to the Bath school had IQs under 100 whereas Woodlands had 96 of them in the year selected by Naylor for comparison. Woodlands thus had a wider set of problems to face.

Naylor was up to his tricks again in 1983 after Sir Keith Joseph had ruled against the closure of selective schools in Salisbury. He defended the decision on the grounds that the tripartite schools in the city did much better than comprehensive schools (Naylor 1983). A head of a Salisbury comprehensive school came quickly into the fray, pointing out the wider aims of comprehensive schools and highlighting manipulation of data by Naylor (Hood 1983). It was the same old story of superficial judgements based upon the complete absence of essential information.

The National Council for Education Standards (NCES) survey of results for 1981 (Marks *et al.* 1983) concluded that social disadvantage only accounted for a third of the difference between grammar school and comprehensive school results. This analysis was heavily criticized for research defects by statisticians. John Gray and Ben Jones (1983), with a similar survey, found that social disadvantage accounted for 70 per cent of the difference in results between grammar schools and comprehensive schools.

The NCES then embarked on a new survey, promising to

improve their previously 'crude and inadequate' allowances for the 'social class factor'. They looked at GCE results in 61 local education authorities (Marks and Pomian-Srzednicki 1985) and found that some comprehensive schools got four times as many O level passes per pupil as others in the same totally comprehensive local authorities and that the average number of O level passes per student was twice as high in some local education authorities compared to others even after allowing for 'social class'. However, it is fairly certain that statisticians (e.g. Gray *et al.* 1985) will not be satisfied with the way the NCES purported to allow for 'social class' (the Rutter Report (1979), finished in tatters after such an assault; see Tizard *et al.* (1980) and Exeter University (1980)).

Some of the protagonists in the examination statistics war contributed to an overview of the topic in the Oxford Review of Education. Yet the significant conclusion here from neutrals in the examination statistics war was that prevailing research provided no effective base for comparing the selective and the non-selective systems (Goldstein 1984, Lacey 1984, Clifford and Heath 1984).

One further problem about arguing on the basis of examination results, noted by Stevens (1980), was that grades in examinations might cloak rising or falling standards because they were unable to move with such changes, either from year to year or from one examination board to another.

Although educational projections into the future are notoriously suspect there is some justification for the view that the 1970s should have been an era of improving results. The teacher: pupil ratio in all secondary schools fell from 20.3:1 to 17.7:1 while the school population rose from 2 million to 3 million between 1955 and 1970. It fell from 18.4:1 to 16.9:1 between 1966 and 1978. Between 1955 and 1970 the staying-on rate beyond the age of compulsory attendance rose from 21.1 per cent of 15 to 17 year olds to 47.4 per cent, and this was massively increased by the raising of the school leaving age in 1972. Educational spending as a percentage of the GNP rose from 4.5 per cent in 1965–6 to 6.3 per cent in 1975–6. The proportion of graduate teachers rose from 1 in 5 in 1970 to 1 to 4 in 1976. All this makes the modest gains of the 1970s an intriguing mystery, to which some gurus apparently have the key.

In his study of 969 students in 1968 Neave (1975) discovered that a far higher percentage of them were coming from working-class homes, but he warned against any firm conclusions about the effect of secondary reorganization on university entrance. This could not be really calculated until about half of secondary pupils were in comprehensive schools. Unfortunately, he was not able to make further studies of such samples and his findings for 1968 were published at a time when such further study had become critical, that is when about half of secondary pupils were in comprehensive schools. In 1982, Neave noted that this country was the only one in Western Europe where the proportion of 18 year olds who qualified for higher education has remained static over the last decade (Neave 1982). In France, in 1980 25 per cent of this age group passed the Baccalaureat compared to 12 per cent in 1966. In England and Wales the figure for those passing two A levels had hovered around 14.8 per cent throughout the 1970s. Neave believed we had abandoned the notion of mass higher education. The same issue of the journal in which Neave's article appeared also showed the proportion of qualified school leavers going into higher education as declining from 93 per cent to 81 per cent between 1976 and 1979–80 in this country (although other European countries exhibited the same trends). Since 1980 cuts in higher education will have hastened this trend.

The Universities' Central Council of Admissions (UCCA) Report of 1978–9 showed that applicants for university places included 1.2 per cent from students born into the homes of unskilled workers. This figure was 1.4 per cent in 1977. Applicants whose parents were in occupations rated above the skilled non-manual level made up 60 per cent of the total applications in 1977 and 62 per cent in 1979. Ivan Reid (1981) reported that the number of entrants to universities rose by 100,000 between 1970 and 1977 but in the same period the percentage from Social Class 1 rose from 30 to 36 and from Social Class 4 it fell from 28 to 24. The proportion of working-class students may have fallen by a third between 1973 and 1983 (Venning 1983b).

None of any of this is likely to make a supporter of meritocratic comprehensives jump for joy (the bad news continues to pour in; for example, the Oracle research team found that one in three pupils regressed in English and mathematics in their first year after leaving primary school (Galton and Willcocks 1983). But nothing in the examination statistics war is convincing as to the reasons for possibly diminished performance. It was hoped that reports on secondary school standards from the DES Assessment of Performance Unit (APU) would provide a basis for tracing upward or downward trends over large samples of pupils but the Unit has been unable to mount the necessary statistical bases for this and it has made no attempt to compare tripartite schools and comprehensive schools.

Examination results now have to be published by all schools following the operation of the 1980 Education Act. They also have to produce brochures of information for parents. What could be hoped for here is that the schools attempt to explain their results. They are in a very good position to do this; only they know the difficulties they have to operate under. Perhaps their explanations should be taken with a pinch of salt, but at least they would be something to go on. Are schools in fact attempting to explain their results? I was able to study closely the brochures of 169 London comprehensive schools (about half the schools in the region) for 1982 and there were few general remarks about the contexts in which examination results could be placed. Two schools observed that examination results were not a true indication of a school's whole worth, and another two referred to the effect of environmental factors on school achievement. Only one school in the sample referred to creaming and yet all the schools in this region must be subject to this. If this is to be the extent of the 'information' in school brochures one despairs of them as providers of illumination about meritocratic performance. Only six brochures mentioned 'equality of educational opportunity' and 46 per cent made no mention of any sort about maximizing the development of individual potential, the very essence of the comprehensive movement (Weeks 1983).

7
Possible reasons for meritocratic success/failure

Introduction

The previous chapter demonstrated a dislocation of arguments about examination results and possible explanations for them, for which the necessary basis of completed research does not exist. This chapter, in the absence of this research evidence, attempts to sketch out the possible grounds for explanation of results (good or bad). The suggestions in the section titled 'Inside schools' are that the way in which comprehensive schools grouped their pupils, made special provision for 'gifted' pupils, organized vocational education, organized their sixth forms and created equal opportunities for girls, were major factors in shaping success or failure in meritocratic terms. Additionally, the incidence of disruption in comprehensive schools could be seen as accounting for poorer results and also poor quality teaching (see pp. 98–101). In isolating all these factors as being 'inside' schools this is not meant to indicate that they are not heavily influenced by pressures from outside schools, as indeed they are. The term 'inside' merely indicates that school policies in these areas can have some bearing on school meritocratic performance. In 'Outside schools' (p. 102) the factors discussed are plainly socio-political and schools can do relatively little to modify their effects. Creaming, the relatively small size of comprehensive schools, the limited reforms in public examinations, environmental disadvantage, the lack of public

finance and the inequality existing between different comprehensive schools are all cited as possible reasons for meritocratic
failure.

INSIDE SCHOOLS

Mixed-ability grouping and gifted pupils

A strong and persistent recommendation for the meritocratic
school is that it should make special provision for talented pupils
by separating them out from others, either by some form of
streaming or by *setting* (i.e. streaming in individual subjects).
This meritocratic objective has been modified by the practice of
mixed-ability grouping in the lower years of secondary schooling. The idea here is that since selection at 11-plus had been
abandoned it seemed a retrograde step to stream pupils at this
age in comprehensive schools. Removing selection at 11 was
intended to encourage later development in those who might
just have failed a selection test and immediate streaming in the
secondary school would have defeated this objective. However,
meritocrats would not support the delay of selection too long in
case talent was lost to a general mediocrity. At the same time,
pupils could still be encouraged to develop in preferred directions in a system of setting subject by subject.

Evidence of the grouping policies of comprehensive schools is
patchy. Early comprehensives were strongly committed to
streaming (Pedley 1963) and Crosland (1962), no less, warned
about sociology and egalitarianism 'running amok'. Streaming,
he maintained, was essential. If there were late developers they
could be promoted later – the 'achievement streaming' Bellaby
(1977) noted at a comprehensive school and the 'contest
mobility' referred to by some sociologists (as opposed to
'sponsored mobility' in the tripartite system). There is strong
evidence, however, of a lack of movement between streams once
they were established. This was noted by the music teacher at
Kidbrooke School in 1964 (and confirmed by her headteacher)
and at Nailsea School by Elizabeth Richardson (1975) in the
1970s. Here, transfers between streams were rare.

A move to mixed-ability grouping in the lower years was under way by the time Benn and Simon (1970) surveyed first year pupils in 389 comprehensive schools. Only in 19.5 per cent of classes was there pure streaming. More frequently, first years were divided into broad ability bands (banding), sometimes two of them (above average and below average) more often three (above average, average and below average). This was so in 31 per cent of cases. Setting was being introduced, used with streaming in 14.5 per cent of cases and on its own in 5.5 per cent. Mixed-ability grouping was used in 22 per cent of the classes, with up to two subjects setted in 6 per cent of these, remedial pupils separated in 12 per cent, leaving 4 per cent of classes completely integrated into mixed-ability grouping.

A follow-up of a representative sample of these schools in 1971 (Rubinstein and Simon 1973) showed that since 1968 the percentage of first year classes using streaming and/or setting had declined from about 40 to 13.5 per cent. Mixed-ability (with setting and separation of remedial pupils in some cases) had jumped from 22 to 34.5 per cent. Banding was used in 45 per cent of cases (31 per cent in 1968). Rigid streaming had fallen from an incidence of 19.5 per cent to 4.5 per cent.

The 1966 NFER sample, including practically all the comprehensive schools then existing (Monks 1968), showed a greater incidence of banding and mixed-ability grouping and a lesser incidence of streaming and setting than the Rubinstein and Simon results. Setting seemed to be declining because it was being replaced by mixed-ability grouping in these early years, but setting was maintaining its hold on the senior years, which later it was going to dominate.

The NFER study of 1100 comprehensive schools in 1974–5 found that 54 per cent of them had mixed-ability grouping for 'most subjects' in their first years, 37 per cent in first and second years and 24 per cent in the first three years. Ninety-one per cent of the schools had setting in some subjects. A survey for *Comprehensive Education* (Lydiat 1977) looked at eighty-six Yorkshire comprehensives and found that just over half of them had mixed-ability grouping in their first years and about a quarter for their first two years. Nine per cent had mixed-ability grouping throughout the whole five years of compulsory schooling.

During the HMI survey of 10 per cent of all secondary schools between 1975 and 1978 the inspectors found that mixed ability in 'most subjects' existed in 35 per cent of the first years of comprehensives, 23 per cent in years 1 and 2, 11 per cent in the first three years and 2 per cent in all five years (reported in DES 1978a).

Thus the schools studied by the NFER and in Yorkshire appeared to be more mixed-ability than the national average, and the same is true of the sample of 500 teachers who provided the material for the later NFER sample (Reid *et al.* 1981). The percentage of first year groups given as mixed ability in this report was 55, and this proportion remained unchanged in a survey of both 1975 and of 1980, indicating that the national trend to mixed-ability grouping had levelled off. In these two surveys the percentage of third year groups organized on mixed-ability lines fell from 25 to 18. The practice of setting, however, had increased from 9 to 23 per cent, which now appears to be the trend. This was certainly the case in my study of London comprehensive schools in 1982. Only 39 per cent of first years here (of a half sample of the schools in most of the region) were mixed-ability groups, but a further 32.5 per cent of them combined mixed-ability with setting. Only 12 per cent of second years were fully mixed ability but a further 50 per cent combined mixed ability and setting. In third years, only 7 per cent were mixed ability but a further 46 per cent combined the two systems (Weeks 1982).

A deeper analysis of the material (Weeks 1983) showed that setting is more prevalent than mixed-ability grouping in years 1 to 3, with banding infrequently used and streaming even less. In years 4 and 5, setting rules the roost being used in 70 per cent of cases, either on its own or in conjunction with other types of grouping. Banding (separate GCE and CSE classes) came a poor second, with the incidence of mixed-ability grouping and streaming very low. The most consistent pattern in these schools was a mixture of setting and mixed-ability grouping in years 1 to 3 followed by a move to setting on its own in years 4 and 5. About half the schools in the sample had this clear pattern.

In the particular batch of schools studied it seemed that the meritocratic system of delayed selection and setting by subjects had come into its own. However, there was also evidence that this pattern is not favoured by many teachers of particular subjects, and the incidence of mixed-ability grouping is severely restricted by the reluctance of these teachers of prestigious subjects to embrace it. At Nailsea School there was mixed-ability grouping for art, crafts, home economics, music, physical education and games but setting or banding for English, mathematics, French and science (as well as history, geography and religious education, although later these subjects went over to mixed-ability grouping). The recent NFER survey by Margaret Reid and others (1981) showed that 47 per cent of mathematics teachers and 56 per cent of modern languages teachers in their sample considered that their subjects were unsuitable for classes with wide ability ranges. In other studies science teachers have appeared equally reluctant. In the NFER study teachers of English, the humanities subjects and arts subjects in general had little objection to mixed-ability grouping in the early years of secondary schooling.

In my 1982 sample (Weeks 1983) there was often a predominantly mixed-ability organization in the lower years but with one or two subjects setted out. In 66 schools the subject was mathematics, in 51 schools it was modern languages, in 29 schools English and in 18 it was science.

Meritocrats were concerned that mixed-ability grouping in the early years should not adversely affect later public examination results. Research at the 2000 pupil Banbury School looked at one 16-form entry, 8 of them divided into mixed-ability groups and 8 streamed for their first year only (Newbold 1977) and found that high ability and low ability pupils did not suffer academically from their one year of mixed grouping, and in some cases low ability pupils were advantaged by it. A later study at Banbury by Postlethwaite and Denton (1978) reported that lower ability pupils who had been in mixed-ability groups in their first year did better at O level and CSE than pupils who had been streamed in their first year. Moreover, high ability pupils mixed in year 1 did better at O level. The National Children's Bureau study of its cohort at 16 years old confirmed that mixing ability in years 1 and 2 did not adversely affect examination results and positively helped pupils of lower ability (Fogelman 1976).

An Assistant Masters' Association (AMA) study of sixty-four schools with some mixed-ability grouping (1974) led to the conclusion that there was a tendency for clever and average pupils to become slack, bored or frustrated in mixed groups, while less able pupils seemed to benefit from them. The report concluded that poor results might have more to do with inefficient teaching than the notion itself of mixing ability.

The HMI's (DES 1977a) working paper *Curriculum 11 to 16*, written during its large-scale survey of secondary schools, picked out mixed-ability grouping as one of the reasons for poor achievement in modern languages, mathematics and science, especially among the more able. Here, again, however, criticism was directed at poor teaching rather than the type of grouping. The less able, on the other hand, once again seemed generally to gain from mixed grouping.

Conclusions such as these have led to the belief that it is the practice rather than the theory of mixed-ability teaching that causes poor results. A number of publications have offered advice on practice, warning, for instance, that the change-over in any school should be gradual and not foisted on the unwilling. The initiative for such change-overs tended to come more effectively from a group of teachers within a school rather than from the school's headteacher. The 1981 NFER report (Reid *et al.*) indicated little or no consultation by headteachers with their staff (or parents) in two-thirds of cases where mixed-ability grouping had been introduced. The advice given in the report generally refers to the extra expertise, effort and resources needed for mixed-ability teaching. Maintaining work for various levels of ability at the same time is exacting work. As a result, there are constant calls for more initial and in-service training to prepare teachers for it. The NFER report (Reid *et al.* 1981) indicated that the lack of consultation and preparation often meant that the far-reaching changes needed in teaching methods and class and staff-room relationships had not materialized. Teachers tended to base their work on the middle of the ability range and they had extreme difficulties in analysing what it was the very able and the less able needed.

One well-trodden way of managing different levels of work was the use of graded worksheets. Yet the standard of these have been roundly condemned by many critics, including HMI (see DES 1978a:37–54). Not only was presentation, content and structure poor but there were too many worksheets. HMI called for more of a balance between whole class teaching and the use of worksheets, either in the form of discussions or plenary sessions. In its opinion, too much individualized teaching prevented essential learning through verbal interaction. There was also a pressing need for more detailed and efficient recording and assessment because of the amount of individual work (see Shapland 1977).

There was evidence of less able pupils gaining through mixed-ability grouping but the evidence regarding more able pupils was conflicting. No one could be certain that the comprehensive school was suitable for them, or that comprehensive schools were potentially the right place for them but in practice were making a poor job of teaching them. The view of Auriol Stevens (1980) was that there were no automatic gains in comprehensive schools for the top 20 to 25 per cent of the ability range. In their early days these schools were fairly conscious of the need to help the least able, but it was now time for them to look positively at the more able student. In a 1977 pamphlet, HMI also expressed fears that the gifted child would either finish work quickly and be left with nothing to do, or would have to work on without direct teaching help (DES 1977b). This was mixed-ability grouping without the mixed-ability teaching that was needed to accompany it. The inspectors thought that mixed-ability teaching above the second year required very exceptional teachers, experienced, hard-working, ready to write a great deal of their own material and carry out numerous ancillary duties.

Educational commentators create a problem when they refer to 'clever' or 'gifted' children. What exactly does this mean? The top 20 per cent or so or the 3 or 4 per cent with very special talents? 'Giftedness' has been defined as IQ in excess of 120, but there are a few children who might not score as high as this and yet be gifted in one particular activity. If it is this 3 or 4 per cent then 'gifted' children cannot be said to represent any more of a problem for comprehensive schools than in grammar schools where they would equally be in need of special attention. Cyril Burt, however, claimed that the gifted working-class pupil was better off in a grammar school were there was likely to be advanced mathematics and science and special activities such as poetry or ballet (Burt 1975). He said that teachers in comprehensive schools modified their material to suit slower pupils. Often, some gifted pupils knew more than their teacher in certain areas of knowledge. Burt objected to teachers straightjacketing the curriculum to external examinations and called for lessons dealing with broader aspects of life, with more creative work, an interesting view of merit and one that contrasts with narrower definitions.

Elizabeth Hitchfield (1973) agreed that grammar schools had tended to give more attention to giftedness than comprehensive schools but she pointed out that it was not only determined by IQ but also by motivation, personality, drive and social background. She believed that comprehensive schools promoted these qualities more than grammar schools.

Special provision for the gifted child is, however, always likely to be a political question for those who believe that positive discrimination should be reserved for the child who performs poorly at school for some reason or another, especially for those who are disadvantaged. In 1979 Nottinghamshire set up a special unit in the George Spencer Comprehensive School at Stapleford, costing £300,000 a year, providing special help for gifted children in local schools. When the county went Labour in 1981 the new council closed the unit on the grounds that it was 'socially divisive'. The unit had been set in a predominantly middle-class area.

Caroline Benn (1982) regards 'giftedness' as an elite substitute for the 11-plus, a new excuse for selectivity, and as such it had the advantage of operating without the need for a separate school system. It did not appear to advantage any social class, race or sex, and did without mass and crude testing. Moreover, the number of 'gifted' was small so that creaming was avoided.

Benn claimed that the National Association of Gifted Children's newsletter had 'sent out subtle counter-comprehensive messages' under banners such as 'mediocrity' and 'dull uniformity'. The concept of 'giftedness' ensured that selection was retained in the inner workings of comprehensives. What had once been a rare quality or genius had been transformed into a commodity. After all, she pointed out, Edward Boyle had collected 167 definitions of the gifted child. It was thus a vague idea turned to the use of selectivity.

Possibly, such strictures make comprehensive schools reluctant to make special provision in fear of the label of elitism. From my survey (Weeks 1983) of London comprehensive schools in 1982 it is clear that either such provision is not available or schools are not going to write much about it in their brochures. Twelve schools out of 169 mentioned gifted pupils. In 5 cases practical schemes of enrichment were described, on the timetable in 2 cases and as an extra-curricular activity in the other 3. Two schools monitored the progress of exceptional children and 2 others simply commented that the gifted must be cared for. From the other 157 brochures there was silence.

Vocational education

Another mark of the meritocratic school is its arrangements for vocational preparation. Section 4 of the Joint Statement of comprehensive ideals by educationists in Appendix A of the NFER longitudinal research (Ross *et al*. 1972) was that pupils must be acquainted with the circumstances of work in modern industrial society. But a running complaint in English education is that secondary schools ignore the needs of industry. In 1965, there were numerous examples of this inadequacy (e.g. see the *TES*, 19 March 1965 and a statement by a teacher speaking at the Royal Institute, reported in the *TES*, 19 November 1965), although local authorities had begun to respond to demand by appointing industrial liaison officers (about half of them had done so by 1970). Work experience was suggested as a way of linking careers education in schools and industry but trade unions have consistently been wary of such schemes.

One of the reasons advanced for the lack of school–industry links is the academic nature of English education. 'Meritocracy' as a 'system' with academic examination results on one side and vocational education on the other contains internal conflicts. Martin Wiener's thesis (1981) is that the puritanism the Victorians applied to sexual morality has been transferred to an anti-industrial spirit in our century; industry is squalid and unworthy.

The DES (1978b) called for 'bridges' to the world of work. Work experience schemes had been very limited. The theme of school and work had been a central part of government concerns during the Great Debate on curriculum, generated by James Callaghan in 1976. That the Government and the DES continued to refer to the matter indicated dissatisfaction with the efforts of comprehensive schools in vocational education. Ford (1969) found no evidence in her comprehensive school that the occupational horizons of pupils were widened, one of the claims of comprehensive supporters. Neave (1975), studying comprehensive school leavers about the same time, however, found that it was more likely for comprehensive pupils to follow a science-based course or a mixture of arts and sciences.

It could be that comprehensive schools have maintained an anti-vocational mentality which results in their relegating vocational preparation to 'non-academic' groups. Benn and Simon (1970) noted that many schools left vocational preparation to early leavers' courses or remedial departments. The TES editorial of 11 September 1981, sixteen years after a similar complaint in the editorial of 19 March 1965, complained that there was still comparatively little response to the demand for more school–industry links. Since then, there have been some schemes, mainly based in comprehensive schools. The Schools Council Industry Project started in twenty-five schools in five local areas (Cleveland, Wandsworth, Mid-Glamorgan, Sandwell and Wiltshire) and spread to twenty-six local authorities by 1981. The Centre for the Study of Comprehensive Schools set up in York in 1980 had financial backing from industry. By the end of 1981 just under half of all local authorities, together with fourteen teacher training institutions, were involved in developing school–industry links. Eggleston (1982) and Watts (1983) have good accounts of case studies of these links.

Experience in some projects led many of those involved to demand greater resources and financial support for teachers to be seconded to industry (Venning 1981). Courses in Sheffield seemed then to be for low ability pupils only (which Benn and Simon complained about in 1970) and were preoccupied with specific jobs. The DES Further Education Unit recently warned of the old danger of the division of academic and vocational work, especially in sixth forms swelled by young people unable to find work. Vocational education could become the 'tertiary modern' sector of education.

There have been extensive national and local initiatives to put microprocessors into schools, partly as an aid to vocational preparation. The effect of this can be seen in the results of my survey of London comprehensives in 1982 where 124 out of 169 schools taught computer studies (Weeks 1983). In 1982, there was a 50 per cent increase in the numbers of candidates for public examinations in computer studies.

A new concept of vocational education now emerging in some quarters is the notion that there should be an integrated vocational package for the whole of the 14 to 19 age group. Coventry has advanced furthest along this line, proposing to house all its 16 to 19 education in extended 11 to 18 community schools. A recent suggestion is that some of the Government funds being channelled through the New Training Initiative, which replaced the Youth Opportunities Scheme in 1983, should go towards special vocational courses in schools starting in the fourth year. Quite a few commentators see this as a retrograde step, re-creating old divisions between the 'academic' and the 'leavers' with all its tripartite overtones. Despite this, by February 1984, 60 out of 104 local education authorities had Technical and Vocational Education Initiative (TVEI) pro- grammes funded by the Manpower Services Commission (MSC), which has since invited all local authorities to adopt such programmes.

The evidence in my study (Weeks 1983) is that the organization of vocational education is patchy. Only a handful of schools made a reference to the maximizing of career opportunities for all pupils. Careers education was timetabled in only 57 per cent of the schools. Perhaps schools without this timetable provision can still do an effective job through individual counselling. In this case, one would expect to find that a large number of them referred in their brochures to strong links between the academic and/or pastoral systems and careers work, or to careers information services, specialist rooms or careers centres in the school. However, the total number of brochures describing such links or services was 110 (out of 169) and this included the 97 with careers on the timetable. So 59 schools out of 169 gave no indication in their brochures how they tackled careers education, if at all. How important do they regard this if they forget to mention it? The DES regulations of 1981 for brochures specifically asked schools to detail their efforts in this direction.

Apart from timetabling careers education and/or providing other services schools can make direct links with local or national employers in a variety of ways but nearly half the schools in the sample did not attempt to do this in their brochures (82 schools). In the schools that did describe activities connected with employers 40 had guest speakers, 33 had visits to firms, 33 held careers' conventions or conferences, 52 had work experience schemes, 14 followed special school–industry schemes such as Trident and 14 had special liaison with local personnel managers (some had several of these activities in tow).

The Great Debate on curriculum generated by the Government after 1976 and official demands for better vocational education were closely connected. A central idea of the Great Debate was that schools would do better to have more compulsory items on the curriculum. If they had certain responsibilities to the economy this should be reflected in a compulsory core of studies. The subjects which the DES (and HMI) particularly wanted to see in the core were very closely connected with vocational education, namely, English, mathematics and science. The HMI (DES 1979) survey of 1975–8 discovered an 'anarchy of options' which resulted, for instance, in 17 per cent of girls and 9 per cent of boys in their senior years not doing any science at all. In my survey (Weeks 1983) 88 of 169 schools did not appear to have science in compulsory cores, although, of course, pupils in these schools studied the subject voluntarily. The argument of the inspectors (and others) was that more science would be done and results would improve, presumably in terms of quantity and quality, if science was part of a compulsory core. The implication was that this argument could be applied to all subjects considered important and that meritocratic failure was partly the result of the lack of compulsion in the curriculum. I found this argument hard to swallow, especially as neither arguments nor evidence was presented to substantiate it. As a matter of fact, I was able to test it out in 103 of my 1982 sample of schools and the general conclusion I reached was that entry to science examinations and subsequent results in them were far better in schools where the subject was not part of a compulsory core (Weeks 1983, 1983a).

Obviously, this small piece of research would have to be repeated elsewhere and in other years but it does suggest that compulsion and educational progress is a connection which has to be substantiated through argument and evidence. As to the extent of compulsory cores in my sample generally one school had a core of 8 subjects, 3 had a core of 7 subjects, 28 had a 6-subject core, 24 a 5-subject core, 41 a 4-subject core (22 of them in English, language and literature, mathematics and science) and 76 a 3-subject core (English language, English literature and mathematics) (reported in the *TES*, 21 May 1982 on the sample of 169 schools plus four others in 'The conservative curriculum').

Sixth forms

To make sixth forms as meritocratic as possible the trend in the mid-1960s was to have selective entry to them. This was attacked, however, on the grounds that the economy relied heavily on those with average ability and that further education for them (and new public examinations, see pp. 112–13) would be in the national interest. Therefore, new sixth forms should not be overzealous in restricting entry and should provide courses in CSE (and later CEE) and O levels and in vocational education as well as A levels. Pedley, as early as 1966, had seen the need for the new sixth form concept (Pedley 1978) and the Schools Council quickly became involved in this field, its Working Paper No. 16 (Schools Council 1967) suggesting a wider curriculum and more general studies – not exactly what meritocrats had in mind. The new sixth form became a necessity for many schools building up from an ex-secondary modern population in order to get sixth forms of economic size (Monks 1970). Naturally enough, official pressure for larger sixth forms also supported open entry and wider courses.

The NFER study of twelve comprehensive schools (Ross et al. 1972) showed only three of them with open entry policies. The DES reported in 1968 that 12.3 per cent of sixth formers in comprehensive schools were not doing A levels compared to 2.8 per cent in grammar schools. Benn and Simon (1970) found that two-thirds of the schools they looked at allowed entry to sixth forms with no O levels, with 14 to 18 schools being the most open and the 13 to 18 schools, many housed in ex-single sex grammar schools, the most restrictive. Neave's (1975) study showed that open entry resulted in more mixing of science and arts subjects. In a recent study of sixth form colleges, only three out of over a hundred had entry qualifications (Watkins 1983). But in the NFER study by Dean et al. (1979) many sixth formers were very critical of work in general studies and in vocational education. They suggested that students not going on to higher education were treated as second-class citizens, even more so in schools than in sixth form colleges. Various Schools Council plans for more general courses and watered-down A levels have met the solid objections of meritocrats (see pp. 112–13) and A levels remain as the solid rock of sixth form work, with the implication that it is entry to higher education with which sixth forms are really concerned. The CEE made very little impression and has now been cast adrift by the DES (although some CSE Boards are trying to keep it going) and there now exists the Certificate in Pre-Vocational Education (CPVE) for sixth formers who have not left school mainly because they cannot find work. Youth unemployment is now providing ample opportunities for a new tripartism in sixth forms.

In my sample (Weeks 1983), sixth forms offered a variety of courses into which the majority of sixth formers were banded. The brochures often did not make clear whether they could take sections out of different courses, more like setting than banding. The general pattern is that sixth formers stick to one course, only joining students on other courses for some type of general studies. In the sample, 131 schools had sixth forms and 68 of them, or 52 per cent, had sixth forms divided into three courses: a two-year A level course, a one-year course leading to more O levels or CSEs, and a one-year course in vocational preparation (other schools without this element promise it in the near future). A further substantial number of schools have two-course sixth forms, either split into two-year A level and one-year O level/CSE courses (32 schools) or two-year A level and one-year vocational courses (2 schools), making up about a quarter of the sample. In the remaining 25 schools, the indication was that students can take a mixture of all kinds of courses, and open entry to the sixth form was allowed (2 other schools also had open entry). Three schools required 3 to 5 O levels for entry and another a Grade C at O level in each of the subjects to be studied in the sixth form. From this sample, it seems that schools are anxious to fill up their sixth forms, especially in view of the competition coming from the New Training Initiative which gives young people a weekly income, and are looking to extend their courses to accommodate them. The only pity is that perhaps they could have done this years ago instead of waiting for mass youth unemployment to set them going, another case of expediency calling the tune rather than educational ideals.

Equal opportunities for girls

Deprivation in education is mentioned for large numbers of pupils suffering possible socio-economic disadvantage, working-class pupils, ethnic minority pupils and pupils with special needs, but perhaps the largest potential disadvantaged group is female pupils. If, generally speaking, girls are not offered equal opportunities to boys this must be one of the gravest causes of meritocratic failure. Girls are so poorly represented in some school subjects, especially vocational ones, that this must represent a massive waste of talent. In O levels in 1972, 96,000 boys took woodwork and metalwork compared to 300 girls; 285,000 boys took physics with chemistry as against 88,000 girls.

In 1976, Sue Sharpe interviewed working-class girls in Ealing schools (Sharpe 1976). They did not seem to have much ambition apart from getting married and perhaps doing some sort of clerical job, a vision thrust down their throats from all directions. The head of English at Thomas Tallis School, Margaret O'Connor, wrote (1977) about the sexism in academic counselling in schools, especially for working-class girls. The presence of a majority of male teachers in some subjects and female teachers in others was a clear indication of what was expected from girls even if they went on with their education.

The Sex Discrimination Act was passed in 1975 and an Equal Opportunities Commission has tried to make it work. Yet in 1979, four times as many boys as girls gained O level physics and 78 times as many boys studied design and technology.

Very few local authorities seem to be taking their own initiatives to achieve sex equality but one of the exceptions is the ILEA which is now questioning its secondary teachers on sexism in their schools. One should mention here pioneering work in equal opportunities in schools such as Clissold Park. The Research and Statistics Branch of the ILEA is monitoring the under-representation of girls in mathematics and science and promotes DASI (Developing Anti-Sexist Initiatives). This is very urgent work because my own survey (Weeks 1983) revealed that very scant attention was being paid to equal opportunities for girls in London; in 76 out of 105 mixed schools there was no mention of the topic. The other 29 schools made arrangements for boys and girls to do all craft subjects in their first two or three years. Only 3 directly referred to a general school policy of equal opportunities. This is not an encouraging profile for a philosophy of equality of opportunity for all.

Disruption in schools

Equating disruption in comprehensive schools with socio-economic disadvantage is very tempting. Disruption tends to be reported from the large cities where there is considerable disadvantage. David Hargreaves (1982) attributed disruption to the defence of dignity which pupils feared they stood to lose in school. Dignity and status could be recovered through a physical, anti-intellectual stance, calling trouble-making, toughness, smartness, excitement, fatefulness, freedom and independence its attributes. Merit was sought in these areas but it was an anti-school merit. Hargreaves claimed that the reasons for this could be found in the destruction of working-class communities, confirming for him a connection between disadvantage and disruption.

Less recently, Christopher Price (1973) suggested that disruption in comprehensive schools tended to receive special publicity because people were out to knock them. If these schools came in on a wave of ideology it suited their opponents to find juicy evidence of violence, disruption, theft and classroom disorder. Similar events in secondary modern schools had never attracted such publicity. A typical example of these attacks was Jean Rowan's book (1973) which is a bleak tale of disruption. Life in London comprehensive schools was generally chaotic and noisy (made worse by tannoy systems), teacher morale was low and teacher absenteeism and turnover was high. Nobody seemed to care and any innovation had a derisory reception from disjointed, dispirited and constantly changing staffs. There is a similar story in that now classic anonymous piece 'Comprehensive Casualty' in the *TES* of 4 January 1974. In the school depicted, beleaguered staff ran to a far-off staffroom and there sank down with a fag or a flask. The staffroom was a frenzied arena where desperate teachers tried to contact each other in the mob. They were absent with impunity; newcomers were faces without names. The place was filled with pupils in their thousands, swarming over it like ants.

In 1974, two articles in *The Guardian* by Janet Watts suggested that it was not dramatic disruption which was prevalent but a creeping contempt which acted like a water torture (Watts 1974a, b). Some pupils kept 'on and on' and it was an exhausting job trying to contain them. Penny Blackie, a teacher in Bristol, wrote that pupils did not regard teachers as real people (Blackie 1977). The job placed her in constant opposition to herself, making her tired and irritable. Later she left to have a baby. She was glad to be out of it. In school she felt there was a 'deadness', a lack of growth, and people seemed concerned only with their own interests (Blackie 1980).

Marsh *et al.* (1978) found, like Penny Blackie, that pupils tended to treat teachers as not 'serious'. They had structured rules for dealing with them. Crises in inner city comprehensives seemed to reach a peak in the mid-1970s (see Thornbury (1978, ch. 1) and Raynor and Harris (1977)). Thornbury (1978) reported that 21 per cent of boys and 16 per cent of girls in inner cities exhibited aggressive and abnormal behaviour. There was drug-taking, glue-sniffing, lunchtime drinking and mugging, suicides following instances of bullying, and pilfering. During 1973 to 1975 over half the 37 per cent increase in London burglaries were committed by 11 to 15 year olds and most juvenile crime took place between 12 noon and 3 pm. In 1973 there were 89 major school fires (18 in 1963), most of them in London, Merseyside, Manchester and Birmingham. School damage costs were esti-mated at £17 million in 1977. One London comprehensive in 1974 spent £50 a day repairing broken windows (*TES*, 4 January 1974). The physical appearance of schools deteriorated rapidly. Pupils were afraid to leave any of their belongings and trudged around all day loaded down with coats and bags.

Devices of suspending pupils or horse-trading them were only stop-gap solutions. Insurance for damage in some schools began to cost more than the damage. Teachers truanted (reports in *The Times*, 28 January 1974 and the *TES*, 2 May 1975) or fled to other schools. The teacher turnover in London in 1974 was 29.8 per cent, twice the national average (in the country as a whole there were 40,000 new teachers in this year). In some schools in the capital the average stay of teachers was seven months.

The years 1973 to 1977 witnessed a rapid expansion of special behavioural units attached to schools. Eighty-three per cent of the units surveyed by HMI (DES 1978c) were opened during this period. The majority of pupils in the units studied were aged between 14 and 16 and were not likely to return to the main school before leaving. This was obviously connected with the raising of the school leaving age in 1972. Rob Grunsell (1981) revealed a rapidly increasing rate of the practice of suspending pupils in one local authority between 1975 and 1978.

Truancy may also be increasing. In November 1982 the truancy rate for Inner London Education Authority (ILEA) schools was 16.4 per cent, the highest rate since the raising of the school leaving age. Six of the ten divisions had a truancy rate in excess of 25 per cent and 32 of ILEA's 169 secondary schools had a rate over 20 per cent. Some explanations for this state of affairs may be sought in Jean Davies's (1980) report for the ILEA or the article by Caroline St. John Brooks (1982). Perhaps schools did not want to face up to the possibility that pupil disaffection was an indictment of poor teaching. Instead of inviting the articulation of this condemnation they allowed pupils to 'leak out' of school.

One of the most publicized events of the 'blackboard jungle' era was the Faraday School affair. This was an Ealing comprehensive which was the subject of a BBC Panorama film (screened on 21 March 1977 as *The Best Days?*). The staff thought that the film showed too much of a rather disruptive class with inexperienced teachers but the producer defended herself in a letter to *The Times* (28 March 1977) in which she claimed that she had co-operated fully with the staff and given them every opportunity to see the finished film in advance. In 1982 a comprehensive school in Corby became the subject of another BBC documentary. The head there, Brian Tyler, said that television had to be interesting and therefore it had to pick on the extraordinary, the un-typical, the disasters and distresses. The real life of a school was missed, although the producer in the case of his school was described as a 'brilliant imposter' (*TES*, 31 December 1982).

A recent study of an East Midlands comprehensive (Turner 1983) categorized pupils there as 'swotters' and 'dossers'. The 'dossers' were intelligent enough not to work at school, but did so privately. Hargreaves commented that this was old hat and not confined to comprehensive schools. The real trouble for comprehensive schools was in the social anomie in which many pupils were left and they had to seek their own social grouping hostile to the school.

Richard B. Dierenfield, Professor of Education at Macalester College in St Paul, Minnesota, surveyed secondary headteachers and other teachers about classroom disruption and reported the results in the *TES* (Dierenfield 1982). From a sample of 875, 465 replied (69.1 per cent were classroom teachers, 15.7 per cent were heads, 13.5 per cent deputy heads). The Professor warned about inferring too much from the results, but about two-thirds of the respondents saw disruption as a problem but one with which schools could cope. Half thought the problem was not getting worse or better but two-fifths thought that it was becoming more severe. Seven point one per cent thought that the extent of inappropriate talking was serious, 4.9 per cent impertinence, 4.9 per cent other inattention, 21.9 per cent abusive talk to teachers, 23.6 per cent physical violence to teacher, 4.3 per cent making inappropriate noises, 13.1 per cent aggressive behaviour among pupils, 4.9 per cent hyperactivity. Analysis of the reasons given for serious misbehaviour was unsettled home environment (about half), peer pressure (35.6 per cent), lack of interest in a particular subject (30.7 per cent) and general lack of interest in school (30.5 per cent).

Teacher quality

It is the firm and persistent view of Sir Keith Joseph that comprehensive schools perform relatively poorly because they contain too many inefficient teachers. At present he is trying to persuade teacher associations to agree to the regular assessment of teachers in return for higher salaries. But teachers want 1985 salary negotiations dealt with before addressing the question of assessment. A further complication is local authority enthusiasm for agreement over conditions of service, especially with regard to lunchtime supervision of pupils (which is also connected with the incidence of pupil disruption). Again, teachers want more money for this.

There are daunting theoretical and practical difficulties in the assessment of teachers, not least the lack of hard research into how it could be done. Who is to say what 'good' teaching is? It might be possible to highlight features of good meritocratic teaching, which is probably Sir Keith's objective. However, a glance at Chapter 8 will indicate that there is much more to teaching than meritocratic results. These wider educational aspirations might be put at risk by any attempt to produce a narrow and mean concept and measure of 'teaching' (such as the 'payments by results' in the nineteenth century). This is the fundamental problem with the current preoccupation with educational accountability. Are teachers to be accountable merely on a narrow meritocratic basis or on a much wider one, embracing a more universally applicable set of education values?

OUTSIDE SCHOOLS

Intakes to schools

It was obvious that creaming would have a marked effect on the performance of comprehensive schools. For many, a crucial part of the comprehensive principle was a balanced intake, ideally made up of 25 per cent of pupils who might have expected to pass the 11-plus, 50 per cent of average ability and 25 per cent of below average ability. The demands for balance gradually became more strident, overcoming egalitarian preoccupations with the neighbourhood school concept (Marsden noticed this drift in DES policy after 1965 (Marsden 1971)) as creaming drained the new comprehensives. Some 'sink' schools became over-burdened with disadvantaged pupils of low ability. Even those such as Caroline Benn, who might have been expected to support the neighbourhood concept without qualification, made noises about balanced intakes. This meant that the pure neighbourhood ideal lost its place in the evolving comprehensive principle, now regretted by some, such as Hargreaves (1982).

There were practical problems in obtaining the right intake mix. How should the catchment area or zone for schools be constructed? If it was too large, trying to garner in a fair range of ability and varying socio-economic backgrounds might cause transport problems and complaints from parents about their children travelling to far-off schools when they preferred the one nearby. If the catchment area or zone was too small perhaps it would not get its proper mix. One way of overcoming this was to have a zone for a number of schools. The social and intellectual profile of the zone would be measured and each school would be entitled to an intake which was a smaller replica of the zone profile.

The patterns of intake construction in the early 1970s were described in the CCE survey of 1973 (Benn 1973). A third of the areas in the survey had catchment areas, although it was not specified how many of these had zoning. Fifteen per cent based intakes on catchment area and parental choice, 7 per cent on particular primary schools, 8 per cent on primary schools and parental choice, 19 per cent on parental choice with/without informal zoning to avoid over-subscription of particular schools, 8 per cent on selective entry and 10 per cent on 'guided' parental choice.

Zoning over whole districts or whole authorities was not common. At the time of the 1976 Education Act the ILEA, Bromley and Lincolnshire were the only whole authorities practising zoning but it was also operated in the districts of Blackpool, Exeter, Hull and Norwich. These were places where the distribution of population made it extremely difficult for particular schools to get a fair intake without zoning. The Act of 1976 allowed these areas to keep zoning but forbade any more areas to adopt it, trying to hold on to the neighbourhood principle. The ILEA desperately needed its zoning policy in order to persuade 40 voluntary grammar schools to go comprehensive. These schools would have resisted much more strongly if their intakes had to come solely from the neighbourhoods in which they happened to be situated. Now, however, parental choice of schools will surely mean a further decline of the neighbourhood concept (unless it is homogeneously middle class).

There is an abundance of evidence for the existence of a wild variety of intake profiles for comprehensive schools, due partly to creaming but also to inequitable distribution between competing comprehensive schools due to the nature of some catchment areas, parental choice, selective entry and the varying calibre of feeder primary schools. The inequality became crystal clear in the NFER surveys. The first one (Monks 1968) reported that 13 schools in the sample (of nearly all 1966 comprehensive schools) had less than 5 per cent above-average pupils in their locality, but 74 schools had less than 5 per cent of them in their actual intakes. Forty-two per cent of the schools were in direct competition with grammar schools for bright pupils (mostly in county boroughs and the ILEA) and 70 per cent of these schools received less than the 5 per cent plus of above-average pupils in the locality. One in five of these schools said they had more below-average pupils than in the locality profile and 34 per cent of them received more average pupils than expected from locality profiles. Children from the homes of semi-skilled or unskilled workers were heavily over-represented in these comprehensive schools. In the 1970 NFER sample (Monks 1970) the more able were under-represented and the schools contained 28 per cent of below-average pupils whereas 20 per cent were expected from the localities in which they were situated.

The DES report of 1978 showed that the intake of pupils with IQs in excess of 115 ranged from 6.1 per cent to 25 per cent in comprehensive schools and pupils with IQs of 85 or below ranged from 6.6 per cent to 31.3 per cent of intakes (DES 1978b). The HMI study of 384 secondary schools (a 10 per cent sample) between 1975 and 1978 indicated that one in five comprehensive schools in the sample had no pupils from the top 20 per cent of the ability range (DES 1979).

Particular examples confirm these general figures. At Risinghill School, Islington, an amalgam mainly from four ex-secondary modern schools in 1960 (closed in 1965) half the pupils were in the lowest band of the ability range (Berg 1968) and a similar creation in Hull, the David Lister School, had 53.7 per cent in the lowest ability range (Rowe 1971). Twenty-three of 204 London comprehensives could not recruit half the above-average pupils they were entitled to, despite ILEA banding or zoning (Rowan 1973). In 1966, the ILEA began their policy of balanced entry (ILEA 1966) in an attempt to provide each school with 20 per cent of pupils in each of five ability ranges, but by 1972 it was struggling to maintain this spread (which was very thin because of creaming) and announced that it would transfer some bright pupils to arrest the growth of sink schools. There was a violent parental protest reaching suffragette proportions and the ILEA hastily abandoned the idea. The zoning, however, was maintained but its lack of success can be gauged in the twelve inner London comprehensives studied by Michael Rutter and his team (Rutter *et al.* 1979). In this small sample in one area the percentage of children admitted with behavioural or reading difficulties ranged from 7 per cent in one school to 50 per cent in another.

The creamed comprehensive has always been in an unenviable place as far as possible pupil alienation is concerned. Rather desperate measures for meritocratic success can result in selection by co-operative attitude rather than by ability (perhaps Turner's 'swotters', p. 100; see also Young and Brandis (1971)). With high unemployment it may be even harder to motivate pupils.

One of the problems of systems based on parental choice and large zones is the number of feeder primary schools there is for each secondary school, making liaison and continuity especially difficult. Writing in the DES report (1978b) the Chief Education Officer for Manchester, Dudley Fiske, reported that with parental choice operating in the city schools, they had from 15 to 57 feeder primary schools.

Creaming by grammar schools and direct grant schools was a fact of life which the Labour Government of 1974 to 1979 was intent on removing. By 1975, the attack on the direct grants had begun and the 1976 Act sought to finish off what was left of the tripartite system. This, however, left the independent sector. Since the late 1960s the Labour Party Conference had sought to abolish this sector but the Labour Government of the late 1970s did not move far in this direction. At its fall in 1979 the comprehensive system was being creamed of something like 4 or 5 per cent of the total secondary school population, the vast majority of them pupils of above average ability. With the Conservatives in power the independent schools had a mandate to continue and to flourish, especially with the new Assisted Places Scheme.

The Labour Government of 1966 to 1970 set up a commission to inquire into the public schools. This commission was told by its research workers that the public schools would not and could not be integrated into the state system (Marsden 1971). *The Public School Commission First Report* (Donnison 1968) reported that in 1966 16 per cent of entrants to universities and 35 per cent of entrants to Oxford and Cambridge were from 273 schools in the Headmasters' Conference or the Governing Bodies Association or the Governing Bodies of Girls' Schools Association. The Commission ignored the advice of the research workers and recommended that the schools develop a socially mixed entry to counter their influence for social divisiveness. They were to aim at a much wider academic achievement and cater for maintained pupils who needed boarding education. This report did little more than gather dust. It not only ignored advice but also the fact that 90 per cent of state pupils in need of boarding school education had abnormal family backgrounds and half of them were classed as maladjusted (Griffiths 1971). The report was universally condemned and ignored.

The *Second Report* (Donnison 1970) was on 178 direct grant schools which had 3 per cent of the secondary population and 10 per cent of all sixth formers. At this time they took up 20 per cent of admissions and 23 per cent of awards to men's colleges at Cambridge. Sixty per cent of all their pupils and 80 per cent of all their costs were provided by the state. The evolving integration with comprehensive schools had not materialized except for a handful of experiments, such as those in Blackpool, Wakefield and Leeds (Benn 1968).

The Commission reported that the schools were on the whole rather too small to be used in the state system. Also, only two of them were mixed. They were told to relinquish their special status and integrate more with comprehensive schools, and to abolish fees or go independent. Ralph Allison and Robin Woods (1970), in a minority report, thought that direct grant schools should become 14 to 18 schools with selection continuing for a number of years and a graded system of fees. Allison and Woods thought that the report should have made more of the liaison with comprehensive schools that had developed in some places.

The Tory Government of 1970 ignored the report and, in fact, provided extra funds for direct grant schools. In 1975 came the Labour decision to phase them out, after which 119 out of 171 schools became independent. With the Tories back in the 1980s came the Assisted Places Scheme, of which most of the former direct grant schools took advantage. This new scheme was regarded as superior to the direct grant scheme because it awarded places on the criteria of merit *and* need rather than merit alone and it provided a better balance of places between the north and the south.

When the scheme was under way nearly all Labour-held authorities refused to allow transfer at 16-plus to independent schools but the Secretary of State removed this power of veto in 1983. Of 5302 places in England in 1981, 4243 were taken up and in 1982, 4417 of 4736 places (in this year only half the sixth form places were taken up). Phasing out direct grant schools undoubtedly reduced creaming, but not very much. Before the phasing out had finished the Assisted Places were under way.

For 1968, the NFER calculated that 42 per cent of 11 to 18 comprehensives were creamed by direct grant schools and creaming was reduced to a trickle only in 20 local authorities (Griffiths 1971). Rubinstein and Simon (1973) calculated that the real percentage of pupils in comprehensive schools was 12 per cent in 1970, and not the official 32 per cent, because of the incidence of creaming. They reached this figure by discounting as 'comprehensives' schools which were heavily creamed. Benn (1973) considered the figure to be 12 per cent in 1972 when the official figure was 43.4 per cent, and 15 per cent for 1973 instead of 50.7 per cent. The profiles of ability in comprehensive schools were thus hardly different from secondary modern schools, and this was confirmed in the National Children's Bureau's *Progress in Secondary Schools* written by Steedman in 1980. Until the late 1970s, 40 voluntary grammar schools in Inner London took 17 per cent of the area's secondary population.

Hill (1972) calculated that 71 local authorities had mixed economies of comprehensive and tripartite schools. A quarter of all authorities had comprehensives and tripartite schools in the same catchment areas. A further 11 per cent had separate catchment areas for the two systems of schools but allowed transfer to selective schools across districts. Fifty-two per cent of the mixed local areas had separate catchment areas with no transfers allowed. There was a general tendency in mixed authorities to test all pupils at 11-plus. Even though 32 local authorities had no selection test early in 1975, in 10 of them up to 10 per cent of pupils were creamed. The ILEA had no selection test yet 15 per cent of its pupils were in grammar schools (14 per cent in Durham and 13 per cent in Barnet). Little *et al.* (1972) considered that 10 per cent was a ceiling above which local comprehensives could not be genuinely comprehensive.

Caroline Benn continued her campaign against official estimates of the number of pupils in 'comprehensive' schools. She took the official figure of 83 per cent in 1980 and then subtracted pupils at direct grant and independent schools (Benn 1980). This reduced the 83 per cent to 72 per cent. A further 2 per cent could be knocked off by excluding 'bogus' comprehensives in Kent and Cumbria which selected pupils for grammar school at 13. Another 3 per cent went by excluding secondary modern schools with no sixth forms and comprehensive schools with unbanded intakes. The resulting 67 per cent was further robbed by creaming grammar schools, fee-paying schools and voluntary-aided schools. In fact, Caroline Benn considered that only about a third of our secondary pupils were really in comprehensive schools. I find it rather difficult to follow her accounting and am under the impression that she counts some pupils twice.

The size of comprehensive schools

One of the main advantages claimed for comprehensive schools was their potential for being larger than tripartite schools. A large school could command a larger capitation and thus a wider range of teaching expertise and resources (Monks 1970). The object here was not only to improve results but also to improve them over a wider range of subjects and pupils. It is quite clear, however, that these early hopes of large comprehensives were gravely disappointed. Circular 10/65 referred to schools of a thousand pupils or more, a 6- or 7-form entry, and Pedley (1963) to schools of 1500, which would provide sixth forms of 120 students. On average, schools have not reached a thousand pupils since 1965, the main reason being the general lack of buildings to house large schools. Existing schools were either too small or too far apart to be joined in the majority of cases and new buildings proved too expensive. The various end-on solutions outlined in Chapter 5 (tiers, middle schools and separated sixth forms) all resulted from the existence of comparatively small schools and the possible uneconomic division of teachers and resources. Perhaps comprehensive schools have not done as well as they could have because they are generally too small. Early comparisons of examination results (Benn and Simon 1970) showed that large schools had better results except in the case of the basically small 13 to 18 schools which had generally taken over from ex-single-sex grammar schools. The trend for better results in larger schools was still there ten years later according to the DES Statistical Bulletin of July, 1981 (based on a very large sample of 2200 comprehensive and grammar schools).

The concept of the big, economical, all-embracing school pervaded early comprehensive ideology and its show-places. Margaret Miles was proud of the large size of her comprehensive (Miles 1968) and wrote in support of the 2000-plus school. If selective schools had on average about 500 pupils for about 25 per cent of the school population then simple arithmetic told her that comprehensive schools could be about 2000 pupils strong. She regarded size as impressive and dignified. It provided a lively and varied social community which rose above petty strains and jealousies. Other heads have also defended their large schools, such as John Sayer at Banbury which was organized into fairly autonomous houses or halls. Mike Durham (1983) recently reported on the 2200-pupil Beacon School in the heart of rural Sussex at Crowborough. Like the split-site school, large schools, their proponents believe, have to try harder – a curious ideology. Crowborough, like Banbury, tries hard, and like it, too, accounts for success in effective house and tutorial systems. To compensate for the failure to construct many schools of more than a thousand pupils the DES hoped for an improved staying-on rate which would produce viable sixth forms. It was here that the worst diseconomies might occur.

Official policy recognized a losing battle over size. Sometimes the urgency surfaced and the DES would turn down a scheme because it thought the suggested schools were too small. Yet it accepted Hertfordshire's plan for 5-form entry schools in 1967 and continuously granted permission for 11 to 16 schools, 60 per cent of which in 1970 had below a 6-form entry (36 per cent had a 4-form entry or below). Circular 4/74 suggested that schools need not be all that large. But the DES report of 1978 bravely advocated schools of up to 1200 pupils and warned against ones of under 600. Rather cheekily it was suggested that schools of 3000 would work if the internal organization was right. Yet despite strictures about schools of less than 600 pupils the same document reported that 545 comprehensive schools were of this size in 1977, about 15 per cent (this figure includes middle schools deemed as secondary schools) (DES 1978b).

In 1966, 58 per cent of nearly all comprehensives had less than 1000 pupils (Monks 1968) and 13 per cent had more than 1600, with two schools having over 2000 pupils. Tiered schools had a majority of 400- to 600-pupil schools. The average for all the comprehensives surveyed was 865 pupils. In 1963 it was 1036, and this was the all-time peak (so far, anyway). Benn and Simon (1970) in a survey of 728 schools in 1968 found that 23 per cent of them had over 1200 pupils but 19 per cent had under 600 and 30 per cent were below Circular 10/65's suggested minimum of 1000. Benn (1973) reported the average size of comprehensives as 850 pupils (11 to 18 schools had an average of just under 1000). The official average in 1975 was 870. A complete break-down of sizes for 1977 is provided in the 1978 DES report. Fifteen schools had over 2000 pupils and over a third had over 1000 and for schools which took pupils up to 18, 1341 out of 2977 had over a 1000. The average was well below that figure. One hundred and thirty schools, including some 11 to 18 schools, had under 400 pupils.

Sixth form size has always been the most worrying aspect of pressure on scarce resources. This is now critical in an era of falling rolls, leading to a new wave of reorganization (see Chapter 5). It is doubtful whether many schools have fulfilled early visions of large institutions with wide-ranging sixth forms, and this obviously hinders meritocratic achievement. An improved staying-on rate has not solved the problem because an exceptionally good staying-on rate was needed to produce a large sixth form from a 6-form entry of about 200 pupils. The early NFER reports showed that average sixth form size was 70 in both 1966 and 1968 (Monks 1968, 1970). According to Benn and Simon (1970) many local authorities were content with 40 pupils in sixth forms. In their 1968 sample of 391 schools, the average size of sixth forms was 83. In the mushroom 11 to 18 schools the average was 150, but this was the take-up rate for whole areas. For upper-tier comprehensives the average was 115. Benn and Simon calculated that where comprehensive schools were competing for sixth formers with grammar schools their sixth forms averaged 75. Elsewhere, the figure was 92. Twenty-eight per cent of schools with sixth forms had fewer than 40 students in them. Alan Little *et al.* (1972) complained that it was impossible for comprehensive schools to get large enough sixth forms in a mixed economy with grammar schools. Comparison with direct grant schools throws into relief the small size of comprehensive sixth forms. Boys' direct grant schools had an average size of 616 but average sixth forms of 164. The corresponding figures for girls' direct grant schools were 518 and 112.

When Eric Briault studied the implications of falling rolls in the late 1970s he concluded that sixth forms under 150 were not viable, an admission that even without falling rolls sixth forms had been too small (Briault and Smith 1980). The DES thought that 100 was the right figure. Official statistics gave the average of all maintained sixth forms as 79 in 1977 (84 in the 1981 Macfarlane report for the DES). Forty per cent of sixth forms in 1977 had less than 50 students.

Not everyone was convinced that bigger schools were better at the meritocratic game. Elizabeth Halsall (1973) agreed that they could provide a wider range of studies but not much more. On purely educational grounds she believed that the ideal school would be between 400 and 1000 pupils and it was only cost and administrative factors which forced up these boundaries to 800 and 1200. Michael Armstrong (1970) suggested consortia of schools which could have fewer than 300 pupils each.

The final NFER report, a close study of twelve schools (Ross *et al.* 1972) concluded that the evidence against large schools was negligible (confirmed in another study of twelve schools, Rutter *et al.* 1979). Perhaps the big, bad comprehensive was a part of educational folk lore? Perhaps there had to be some bad comprehensives and the bigger the bad ones were, the worse they were? The correspondent who wrote 'Comprehensive Casualty' (*TES*, 4 January 1974) certainly thought so.

Whether these were only teething problems or the result of poor leadership and organization we shall never know. In fact, the large school has never had a chance to show its paces in our system except in isolated cases. In meritocratic terms, the economic use of scarce resources and a wide curriculum, its case stands. The most serious challenge to it has been on egalitarian grounds (see p. 128).

Limited examination reforms

One of the possible reasons for meritocratic failure could be inadequate adaptation of the examination system to cater for a wider range of ability and skills. The solid preservation of the GCE O level and A level, so far, can be viewed in terms of the maintenance of standards but the particular failure to develop alternative examinations at sixth form level as a follow-up to the CSE, perhaps a successful innovation at fifth form level, may have meant the loss of talent which could have been developed during post-compulsory education.

After 1970, the Schools Council tried to generate reform in the shape of N (Normal) and F (Further) levels to replace A levels by a two-stage examination but there was fierce opposition from the universities, head-teachers and sixth form teachers. Pilot schemes for the Certificate of Extended Education (CEE), a sort of one-year advanced CSE, did go ahead, and subject entries in the examination increased by 84 per cent between 1979 and 1981.

The present Conservative Government scrapped N and F levels and has given no backing to the CEE. The DES by 1984 had plans for an AS level, an examination based on half an A level syllabus. The current Certificate of Pre-Vocational Education (CPVE) is given official preference over the CEE and the CSE Boards may well have to switch their attention to the CPVE unless they want the Government to use other agencies to develop it – major initiatives have already been taken by bodies such as the City and Guilds Institute and the Business and Technician Education Council (BTEC). Thus the present situation is that no definite system has evolved for the non-A level sixth former, apart from re-sit and extra O levels and CSEs. DES support for the CPVE appears to be in response to youth unemployment rather than to ten years of thinking about a new examination at 17-plus.

Environmental disadvantage

A great deal of recent educational research has been directed to the theme that children from lower socio-economic groups lose out in education. Secondary reorganization was specifically designed to put this right, whether the view was from that of the interests of the national economy or from a wider humanitarian concern. It has been asserted that schools, being the tool and reflection of society, cannot create such socio-economic changes or individual attention. Thus, a good reason for meritocratic failure is socio-economic disadvantage. Even if educational progress shifted from a 'sponsored' mobility to a 'contest' one, the contest was potentially unfair because some pupils could not take advantage of what was on offer, whether it was in a tripartite school or a comprehensive.

There was a suggestion in Ford's research (1969) that comprehensive schools could, in fact, increase disadvantage and working-class hostility to schools. It was clear in her research that comprehensive schools would not necessarily make education a more powerful force in reducing social inequality, at least for those pupils who were streamed. More middle-class and working-class pupils were looking forward to leaving the comprehensive school than either the secondary modern school or the grammar school, in Ford's sample, indicating an increased waste of talent, not the reverse. There was evidence that comprehensive schools fossilized class attitudes, reduced occupational optimism and worsened attitudes towards work. Aspirations in the lower streams of comprehensives were much lower than in the secondary modern school. The streams in the comprehensive were as socially homogeneous as in the grammar school and class attitudes were much harder in the comprehensive, possibly because of the proximity of more middle-class pupils which may not have been the case in the secondary modern.

Ford's research has been criticized because it was centred on only one comprehensive, one grammar school and one secondary modern, but it was just the sort of hard research that was needed. Griffin reported work with a larger sample in Manchester which gave him different results (Griffiths 1971) but nothing was done on similar lines elsewhere. T. S. Robertson (1977) followed up 1844 pupils who were in the NFER surveys of 1966 to 1972 and found that they generally finished up with better jobs than their parents. Michael Rutter's team tried to find out if the internal organization and policies of twelve London comprehensive schools made any difference to their examination results, pupil behaviour, attendance and delinquency (Rutter *et al.* 1979). The main effect on these was from the type of intakes the schools had as far as their scores in verbal reasoning (VR) tests and their socio-economic backgrounds were concerned. But, according to the report, schools did make a difference, if only a slight one. Yet the acclaim (even hype) with which the report was greeted in some quarters hardly squares up with the flood of criticism about the statistical methods used and its lack of reference to social interaction in the school, the curriculum and social forces acting on the schools (see Tizard *et al.* 1980, Exeter University 1980 and Radical Statistics Education Group 1982).

The overwhelming evidence of working-class educational disadvantage is somewhat untroubled by superficialities in the Rutter report, look no further than Fogelman (1976), or the 1982 National Children's Bureau's surveys by Wedge and Essen (1982), which, for instance, discovered that 33 per cent of disadvantaged pupils in the top 20 per cent of the ability range in English were entered for O level English compared to 80 per cent of other pupils in this range. The figures for overall disadvantage are there and also those for its increased severity in the midlands and the north compared to the south. At the beginning of the period (1963) 8 per cent of school-leavers in the south passed two or more A levels compared to 5 per cent in the north. In 1977–8, capitation levels in ILEA were three times as high as the lowest spender, and in 1980–1 they were four times as high, in each case the lowest spender being a northern authority. Compare, for example, a teacher–pupil ratio in secondary schools of 12.9 : 1 in Brent to 17.6 : 1 in Dudley (1980–1).

Lack of public finance

It is quite clear from earlier chapters that secondary reorganization was achieved on the cheap. One official utterance after another urged the use of existing facilities, and this resulted in a retreat from the ideals of the 11 to 18 school and the single-site school. If success in meritocratic terms relied on the large all-through, single-site school it must be possible to attribute failure to the fact that such schools made up much less than half the system which evolved – a proportion which may decline even further.

The whole period is characterized by financial stringency. Had reorganization come in the preceding decade it might have been based more on its ideals. But the new Labour Government was plunged into an economic crisis in 1965 and in the next ten years the best that can be said of this time is that the sun peeped out at times. Then the country fell prey to world recession in the late 1970s. Nevertheless, educational spending as a percentage of the GNP rose from 4.5 per cent in 1965–6 to 6.3 per cent in 1975–6 (it fell to 5.4 per cent by 1978–9, see DES 1982d). But there were great demands on this increased spending from a whole host of directions. The school population rose from 8.43 million in 1965–6 to 10.69 million in 1977–8. Expansion in sixth forms, further education, higher education, nursery education and priority education all had to be met. When the DES-sponsored journal *Trends in Education* came out in January, 1966, its opening salvo was to cast doubt on the Government's ability to finance all the new developments.

What this has meant is that this country did not buy comprehensive education but allowed it to muddle its way into existence. The Labour Government, having satisfied its rank and file on ideology, was only too happy to let local authorities solve the practical problems of reorganization and take the responsibility for it. The raising of the school-leaving age planned for 1970 could have brought in much needed financial support but Labour postponed this until 1972, when the Conservative Government provided most of the extra teachers needed as well as a few million pounds – 'peanuts' (as Eric Midwinter once described Government funding in priority education).

Anthony Crosland spent 1965 and 1966 trying to get more teachers to meet the growing waves of pupils, even promising a salary rise above the going rate if the teacher unions would co-operate (but they drew the line at accepting 'ancillary' staff to help out in overcrowded classrooms). The shortfall of teachers was estimated to be 40,000 in January, 1967, and this number of extra teachers would only reduce the average primary class to 40 and the average secondary class to 30 (9000 of 26,000 classes in 1965 had more than 30 pupils). Campaigns were mounted to persuade married women back to the classroom, even on a part-time basis. The 1968 NFER survey (Monks 1968) showed that one in five women teachers were part-timers. The shortage was most serious in mathematics and science (where it still remains in an era of over-supply of teachers) with French and crafts not far behind. In 1965, 17,000 places in science and technology at the universities were not filled.

Crosland put pressure on the training colleges to jam in extra trainees, and even suggested that technical colleges could do some teacher training. Amazingly, the colleges met the 20 per cent increase demanded for September, 1965, perhaps in some desperation to avoid losing customers elsewhere, and perhaps embracing a reduced concern about selecting appropriate candidates for teacher training. That the supply of new teachers managed to keep anywhere near the demand was something of an achievement. But in the early 1970s the combination of financial stringency, reorganization, problems of getting used to larger schools and new internal organizations and policies, all coupled with the rush of new teachers, a promotion merry-go-round and a rapid turnover of staff, made meritocratic success difficult. Teacher turnover reached 25 per cent a year in some cities in 1973 when there were 40,000 new teachers, many of whom had not been subject to a rigorous selection procedure.

Financial stringency had to affect the teacher–pupil ratio, and thus the effectiveness of teaching. Of course, there is no clear evidence that smaller classes bring better results (in fact, there is some evidence to the contrary) but there must be something in the fact that independent schools consistently did better than state schools as far as results were concerned and they consistently had smaller classes. The ratio for the whole maintained secondary sector was 18:1 in 1965 compared to 11:1 in the independent sector. In comprehensive schools in the NFER survey (nearly all comprehensives in existence in 1966), the 11 to 18 schools had a ratio of 18:1 (Monks 1968) compared to 16.7:1 in direct grant schools and 16.6:1 in grammar schools. Thirteen and 14 to 18 schools had a ratio of 17:1 but 11 to 13, or 14, or 15, or 16 schools had an average of 20:1. The general secondary ratio for maintained schools had fallen to 17.8:1 in 1970, at which time the grammar school rate was 16.1:1. In 1978, the maintained secondary figure was 16.9:1, still worse than the grammar school rate of 1966 and very much worse than the picture in independent schools.

The National Union of Teachers (NUT) survey of 1962 (*The State of our Schools*) recommended the re-building of a sixth of secondary modern schools. The Newsom Report of 1964 found that only 21 per cent of secondary modern schools were 'up to present standards' and 41 per cent were 'seriously deficient'. Many of these inadequate buildings were used to kick off 'new' comprehensives. The NFER survey for 1966 (Monks 1968) reported that 48 per cent of comprehensive schools were on new buildings on one site (3 per cent were new on separate sites). Twenty-two per cent were on split sites, a half of them with buildings over a mile apart. It was calculated that at least half the schools, and probably considerably more, were not purpose-built comprehensives. This was at a time when the incidence of the 11 to 18 school was at its highest, as was that of the purpose-built school. The proportion of both in the evolving system declined with tiered schools, middle schools and separate or linked sixth forms. These were essentially based on existing buildings; in other words, they were cheap.

Many comprehensive schools were developed from rather small establishments into much larger campuses over the years, and the piecemeal and uncertain growth was often not conducive to good results. Brookfield School, Kirkby, grew from a school for 120 pupils to one for 2000 over eight years (Halsall 1970). B block was the original building and the sequence of additions was B plus $\frac{1}{2}$A, B plus A, B plus A plus Annexe, B plus A plus $\frac{1}{2}$C (plus swimming baths), B plus A plus C (plus Dolcorsllwyn Hall), and B plus A plus C plus Annexe. Such changes put a heavy workload on staff, and teachers needed great organizing ability and stamina. The head here wrote that if comprehensive schools relied on teachers who could work in counter-purpose buildings with a high workload they would fail. Benn and Simon (1970) made the point that a purpose-built building had the potential advantage of a purpose-recruited staff (see Chapter 5 for the pros and cons of split-site schools).

Benn and Simon gave the percentage of comprehensives which were purpose built as 28 (in 1970), rather less than the half the NFER mentioned for 1966. But even teachers in purpose-built schools had plenty of their own grumbles about planners and architects, the lack of facilities, flexibility and room, especially for sixth forms. Teachers were rarely consulted by planners and pupils never. The standard of fittings and materials varied enormously. At Countesthorpe College one of the early serious problems was the fragility of the fabric of the building which soon became delapidated. At Risinghill the new school was drab, graceless, stark and impractical (Berg 1968). The school had seven different playgrounds which shared four exits, none of them large enough for a vehicle to get through. There were no covered ways outside the school and no outside drinking fountains. The cloakrooms were inaccessible and insecure.

Add all this to many other problems and you get some idea of what the head, Michael Duane, was up against. The head of the expensive Gateacre complex in Liverpool complained that architects never returned to see if their buildings worked (Dawson 1981). Very few head teachers have the advantage that Geoffrey Cooksey had at Stantonbury Campus, Milton Keynes of being *in situ* three years before the school opened (Makins 1985b).

On the lay-out of buildings there was increasing support after 1970 for a series of smaller blocks rather than single large blocks in order to house horizontal or vertical organizations. This was the plan in the eight units at Wyndham School (Sharp 1973). Perhaps this is the reason for the comparative success of the split-site school which provided ready-made blocks of the right size. Even where new buildings were planned, with money and plans available, there was often considerable delay in starting work because of administrative problems and delay over freeing sites.

Education spending cuts in recent years (1 per cent in real terms in 1981–2) have brought new problems for would-be meritocratic schools, or any sort of school. Details of the cuts and their effects are given in the first section in Chapter 9.

New inequalities for schools

In the early days of comprehensive reorganization, Sir William Alexander said that these schools would be as differentiated if not more so than tripartite schools. Of course, it is possible to argue that excellent results at some comprehensives compensate for a mass of indifferent results, but this hardly squares up with the 'comprehensive principle'. It is more like a new form of elitism.

The potential for variance was there if ex-grammar schools made up the whole or part of the new schools or if ex-secondary modern schools did, apart from the potentiality of varying intakes in different areas. Many ex-secondary modern schools had a double disadvantage in not being associated with ex-grammar schools nor being situated in salubrious districts. Bellaby's (1977) study of three comprehensives in one town is the most illuminating example of this local variance. One was an ex-grammar school, with many of its teachers remaining in the new school, and with a high proportion of graduate teachers. Another school had inherited a technical bias and had many non-graduate teachers. The third school was a struggling ex-secondary modern with a high staff turnover and a younger staff than the other two schools, many of whom were non-graduates. Bellaby's detailed description of the three schools gives the strong impression of a new tripartism.

It comes as no surprise to learn that a Schools Council survey of parents in 1968 (described by Taylor (1978)) uncovered the fact that they were interested above all in good examination results and good jobs for their children. They strongly supported the meritocratic principle. An ideological vacuum created by the rise of a non-selective system could be filled by parents looking for the meritocratic best created by reorganization and intake policies. Parental support could further confirm the success of particular schools and the failure of others in meritocratic terms.

Perhaps the best example of a new inequality of schools partly created by parental choice is in Manchester. The Chief Education Officer there until recently, Dudley Fiske (1982), explained how parental choice after 1967 has created a hierarchy of schools which did not conform with any comprehensive principle (see also the DES report (1978b)). In 1967, parents were able to choose any three schools in order of preference from a list of twenty-eight. Priority was granted to choice, to proximity, for schools already attended by siblings and for medical reasons. First choice success rose from 77.4 per cent of cases in 1973 to 82.3 per cent in 1977, assisted by a surplus of places created by rapidly falling rolls. Meanwhile, six of the schools became heavily over-subscribed, in one case 270 places were sought by 546 applicants in 1975. The number of feeder primary schools for over-subscribed schools escalated (up to 57 in the case of one school). The percentage of intakes with IQ in excess of 115 ranged from 6.1 to 25 per cent and IQs below 85 from 6.6 to 31.3 per cent. When, in 1981, Manchester tried to reorganize its secondary system because of falling rolls the Secretary of State turned down the first plan because he could not justify the closure of 'good' sixth forms at Burnage, Parrs Wood and Whalley High Schools (schools whose parents had figured prominently in the campaigns to save 11 to 18 schools in the city). Sir Keith Joseph called them schools of 'proven worth'. Schisms created by historical accident were thus widened by parental action and confirmed by Sir Keith Joseph. Such a meritocratic tale could be billed as 'The Rise of Son of Tripartism'. Were the successes of the few compensation for the failure of the many in a 'comprehensive' system?

Sir Keith Joseph has pursued the theme of differentiation and parental choice remorselessly, so that some educators see an incipient process of privatization in the maintained system through an expanding Assisted Places Scheme. A parallel move to open enrolment and voucher systems now seems less likely because of only modest support for these ideas in the Conservative ranks. The open enrolment experiment in the Tunbridge Wells and Tonbridge area represented the only practical application of these schemes so far in this country and this is now really defunct because the present arrangements do not allow for the expansion of 'successful' schools. But the Assisted Places Scheme can expand in a number of ways and parental choice (and financial contributions) can create more elitist comprehensive schools as a substitute for those not able to get into independent schools on state grants.

In conclusion, schools in pursuit of 'egalitarian' objectives might have difficulties with the merit criteria of success. Thus one of the potential reasons for meritocratic failure is egalitarianism (and vice versa). It is feasible to imagine a school falling between these two stools, perhaps committed to equality but striving also to be meritocratic. Bellaby (1977) noted that one of the comprehensive schools he studied, an ex-secondary modern, had a rather superficial progressivism which merely restricted its chances of meritocratic success. Perhaps it was wiser to adopt the single-mindedness of Peter Dawson, Head at Eltham Green School for a number of years, and get out the red cards and the binoculars (Dawson 1981) and 'strike first' with 'dramatic action'. He had no doubt that parents wanted discipline, uniforms, homework – anything that would lead to meritocratic success.

In her school, Margaret Miles (1968) thought everything was possible. It was large, could offer a wide range of specialisms, it was meritocratic, but with a strong commitment to pastoral care and to healing social class divisions through links with the community. One wonders whether any single school could do all this, although all the well-known 'egalitarian' schools mentioned in Chapter 8 had reasonable, often good, examination results.

8
The egalitarian school

Introduction

It is obvious that all schools have to pursue meritocratic objectives. The extent to which comprehensive schools have been successful in these ventures, and the possible reasons for this, have been discussed in the two previous chapters, albeit suffering from information malnutrition.

The search for egalitarianism in comprehensive schools is a completely different matter. They can get away with pure meritocracy. But there will be few political traumas over schools neglecting a pure egalitarianism as depicted by Denis Marsden in his article 'Which comprehensive principle?' (1969). The best that can be done in this chapter is to scratch around for the few crumbs of comfort provided by a handful of exceptional schools and teachers. Most comprehensive schools provide examples of some egalitarian work but this is extremely patchy. The modest and piecemeal efforts of the bulk of schools is thrown into relief by intense and radical experiment in the exceptional schools.

Marsden's account of the egalitarian school sees its objectives as the creation of a more equal, just, and peaceful society. The inequalities of pupils would be minimized, especially those based on traditional theories of 'intelligence'. The school would seek to develop the child's qualities of citizenship. It would be co-operative, permissive, pluralistic, not looking to any one class or group for leadership. It would stand against the demands of the occupational structure. A few egalitarians would go for the neighbourhood school with no zoning or banding or sex segregation. The school need not be large. An all-through 11 to 18 was to be preferred. The school must have its own sixth form; sixth form colleges were only permissible if all-comers were allowed in. Some work could be done in further education colleges. The school must be non-streamed, co-operative, progressive in methods with flexible teaching, possibly in teams. Positive discrimination towards the less able was favoured. The curriculum must be common, although there could be some individualized work. The school would be open to the community and a community centre. Specialization would be delayed as long as possible. The aims of such a school would be concerned with good general education for all, the social maturity of pupils, good community links and high quality in art, music and drama.

The community school

In Marsden's Fabian pamphlet of 1971 he seemed to add a third ideal type of comprehensive, the community school (Marsden 1971). This was a corollary to the egalitarian school, an extension of some of its radical features. It covered a whole range of educational innovations, openness in curriculum and teaching methods, especially in relationships with the community. This would bring about a new school ethos and a new view of the educational world.

More recently, David Hargreaves (now Chief Inspector for the ILEA) has suggested that we need this type of school in order to revitalize the comprehensive principle (1982). This was being eroded by a culture of individual success in examinations and vocation, by pupil egoism and a social anomie caused by the destruction of working-class communities. The children of these lost communities had lost the value and dignity of belonging to a social group. In order to put right this state of affairs schools had to become 'approachable', and become total neighbourhood educational institutions regenerating community life.

A few early comprehensive schools had in mind closer links with communities (there is an example of one in Bristol described in *Trends in Education*, April 1967). The community work at Thomas Bennett School, Crawley was publicized in a book by its headmaster (Daunt 1975). The objective here was to 'know' the community, to pursue social and recreational activities for all, to encourage community concern for the school and its facilities and community service for pupils, and the co-ordination of local voluntary services.

However, for the majority of schools 'community education' has the status of an optional extra and not that of a central philosophy of the type Hargreaves envisages. It means perhaps having Parent–Teacher Associations and community education and/or community service on the curriculum, and consecutive use of premises and facilities for the school, with older people using the facilities at other times, rather than common and simultaneous use. In the 1968 NFER study (Monks 1970) of 59 comprehensive schools, 47 headteachers answered the question on community education. Twenty-nine said that they had PTAs, mainly engaged in fund raising. In 20 cases attendance at meetings was poor. Thirty-one had community studies but in 29 cases it was a voluntary subject. Since then projects and courses in community service have become fairly common in comprehensives. (See accounts of the work and case studies in DES 1974, Groves 1980 and Scrimshaw 1981.)

Some local authorities have latched on to the community education idea with some enthusiasm as part of a general programme of social reform, many of them springing out of the Community Development Projects sponsored by the Home Office from 1970. Coventry developed a complete system of 11 to 18 community schools, including the well-known Sidney Stringer College and Community School (see Jones 1980 and 1983 and McHugh 1976). Other well-publicized schools in the community education field are the Sutton-in-Ashfield Centre in Nottinghamshire (see Robbins and Williams 1977, Wilson 1981, Flecknoe 1983 and Fletcher 1983), and Abraham Moss Centre, Manchester (Thompson 1983), which is in fact an 11 to 16 school, and Madeley Court School, Telford (Toogood 1984). So grand are some of these communal palaces some critics suspect them to be show pieces in a sort of 'terminology race' to keep up with the Jones's of community theory. How far they attain the ideals listed for Peter Daunt's school above it is hard to say. Are any of them attempting Hargreaves's radical suggestions for community regeneration? Full-blown community schools are very limited in number, and not likely to increase much in the present financial climate, and there must be doubts about the extent to which the present schools can move beyond consecutive use of premises and a little community service for senior pupils.

The theory of 'community education' is no less clear than the practice of it. What is the 'community'? If this is simply a reference to the catchment area of a school, such a locality can be so geographically dispersed as to have little cohesive existence, especially now that parents can choose a school. Even if the catchment area is small it may have no 'community'. A 'community' can be a network of social relationships which have a vague and complex geographical arrangement. Maybe some areas have no 'communities' (which is the point Hargreaves is making).

In my study of London comprehensive schools (Weeks 1983) the search was for mention of localities, outside organizations, and so on, in the brochures. According to 150 out of 169 of these, neighbourhoods did not appear to exist. Yet 85 schools had community education or service on the curriculum. Community service on the curriculum of schools who cannot express a sense of fraternity with their locality does not ring true, added to which, twenty-two of the schemes were for sixth formers only.

Of the 19 brochures which did mention localities there was an interesting array of items (most of them in the schools of the outer boroughs and not in Inner London schools). Some saw the schools as the focus of community life; others expressed a respect and a desire to understand people in the neighbourhood. Two schools had school-based social workers and one school wanted to identify with the problems and plans for the future of the local population. This would make a stimulating school motto, but not in Latin, please.

This type of work is obviously reserved for a small minority of schools. Harry Ree was equally disappointed after a tour of the

Cambridgeshire colleges founded during and after Henry Morris's long term as Chief Education Officer for the county. Ree found that many of the colleges had stagnated in their ideas, and they failed to exemplify Morris's philosophy and his hopes for them (Ree 1980). Ree blamed outworn administration and a fear of the radical implications of community ideals. Evening work made little impact on or connection with work during the day or in the community at large. Many of the teachers hardly knew they were working in community schools. Secondary reorganization had brought in pupils (or, more exactly, parents) interested in straightforward academic success. The Federation of Village Colleges was defunct and county newsletters for youth work and adult education were produced separately.

Ree also reported how spending cuts were further reducing the prospects for community education. In Leicestershire they had hoped to move into phase three of the development of the community colleges, that is all staff contracts would contain obligation to do community work. Bernard Harvey, Principal Adviser for community education in the county, believed there was more than economy at work here. He thought the local authority was out gunning for the relatively autonomous community councils which administered the colleges (Harvey 1980).

Cyril Poster, Principal of Groby College, a well-known advocate of community education, described the effects of the cuts on his school (Poster 1981). He thought that the original concept of a community college had become a 'pipedream'. Like Hargreaves, he now believes that community service should be the co-ordinating zone of the curriculum (Poster 1982).

Evidence of the existence of egalitarian schools

If a powerful projection of the egalitarian ideal type exists in the genuine community school the sad news above seems to indicate that the average comprehensive school is light years away from the ideal. If they cannot hold out a hand to their localities are they transforming their inner lives and structures in readiness for the community millennium? Checking through Marsden's list for the egalitarian school we see that the preferred 11 to 18 school is in decline and the number of schools with their own sixth forms is in a similar contraction. There is no evidence that any school stands against the occupational structure. If any did there would be another Tyndale affair, except that it would be nastier, more brutish and shorter. The neighbourhood concept seems to have been compromised by the need for balanced intakes.

Meritocrats complain about small schools but perhaps comprehensive schools are too large for egalitarian ideals. Pedley (1978) mentioned that the large school could remove teachers from its centre of gravity, losing a sense of community. The ordinary and the average pupil could be lost in it. But a contemporary, Margaret Miles, believed that the large school was essential to an integrated community (1968). Halsall (1973) reported that research findings supported the view that smaller schools were easier to manage, provided a better educational climate, were more innovative and provided better pastoral care. Teachers in large schools had to make a much greater effort to succeed. Halsall thought that the range of 400 to 1000 pupils was right. The campus idea of linked small schools was a solution to the problem of restricted curriculum range. Yet the small school could widen its provision by using resource-based teaching. Taylor (1973) concluded that large schools fostered departmentalization, they needed very explicit arrangements for care and attention of individual pupils, they lengthened and complicated the channels of communication and created a very complex social structure.

Evidence for the rest of Marsden's list is sought in the remainder of this chapter in the sections: the caring school (p. 129); mixed-ability grouping, flexible teaching methods and a common curriculum (p. 145); positive discrimination for pupils with special educational needs (p. 150); multi-ethnic programmes (p. 152); and democracy in schools (p. 155). The remaining item on Marsden's list was the promotion of aesthetic subjects. Whatever progress schools have made here (e.g. Leicestershire's special promotion of these curriculum areas) the recent spending cuts have placed them in great jeopardy (see the *TES* series of articles on this surgery titled 'The Arts in Decline', 16 January to 6 February 1981). Affected were peripatetic instrument teachers, fees for music lessons, grants to youth orchestras, drama teachers and advisers, grants to youth theatres and theatre-in-education teams, specialist art teachers and artists working in schools, repair of kilns and their fuelling. Leicestershire had to launch an appeal for £300,000 to try to save its ambitious programme for music and drama.

The caring school

Marsden mentioned co-operation, permissiveness and cohesion rather than leadership and social maturity. The sphere of all this rests in what is called the pastoral organization of a school, although many who support this type of work have come to regret that it has been distinguished from 'academic' work (see p. 132). It has been observed that pastoralism in comprehensives has gone through three phases, represented by teachers as chief beaters, then counsellors and now curriculum developers. This is an evolution from simply dealing with miscreants to the idea of a separate and specialist staff dealing in pastoral care, and finally to the integration of pastoral and academic work involving all staff. This is not to say that many schools have left the second phase or even the first. In a school near London studied recently the pastoral organization was for the use of teachers rather than pupils (Best 1983). Pastorality here still meant authoritarian discipline, concerned with control and rule infraction. In the 169 school brochures I read (Weeks 1983) every single one of them detailed a pastoral organization in Years or Houses with their tutor teams. They looked for, sometimes demanded, the co-operation of pupils and parents. Far fewer of them mentioned mutual obligations on the part of teachers. Forty-three per cent of the brochures (72) had nothing about the co-operation of everyone concerned with a school. Eighty-nine per cent of them made no reference to education for democracy, a powerful aid to a co-operative atmosphere.

Comprehensive schools have basically moved away from House organizations to Year ones. In the NFER survey for 1966 (Monks 1968), 90 per cent of the schools had House systems but in 1968 (Monks 1970) in the smaller sample of 59 only 17 per cent of them had pure House systems although it was the main form of organization in 37 per cent of cases. A main reason for this was the large number of split-site schools for which House organization was inappropriate. The practice of separating sixth forms also defeated traditional schemes of vertical organization. Another reason for the change was the desire to create separate units for First Years and perhaps Second Years. In an era in which schools tended to become larger (although comprehensive schools became smaller) teachers worried that newcomers to secondary school would feel bewildered having arrived from a small primary school. They could be housed in small units with special teams of teachers, either on their own or in a lower school with Second Years (split sites could be used in this way).

In 1970, 40 per cent of schools in a large sample were using pure Year systems (Benn and Simon 1972) and 50 per cent used it in conjunction with other systems. It was particularly popular in schools with a limited age range. There was a strong move against 'artificial' or vertical units. At Mayfield School (Margaret Miles's school) tutors moved up with their groups year after year, maintaining a pastoral continuity. Horizontal organization concentrated potentially troublesome groups within single organizations (Miles 1968). Girls' schools had little time for Houses because of less enthusiasm for competitive games, one of the main functions of traditional Houses. The belief that leadership, if desired at all, should come from within a group rather than vertically added to the growing dislike of vertical systems.

Year units were often within the larger grouping of upper and lower schools, or upper, middle and lower (60 per cent of the large schools in the NFER sample were divided in one of these ways, Monks 1970). There are schools with quite separate Year units, such as the self-contained communities for First, Second and Third Years at Michael Marland's North Westminster School. Examples of special units for First Years were at Kenington House in Wyndham School (Sharp 1973) and in two London schools out of 169 (Weeks 1983 and 'The Conservative Curriculum' in the TES of 21 May 1982). The preponderance of Year systems does not mean that Houses were not important in some schools or areas. Coventry based its 11 to 18 community schools on Houses, often containing the teaching of some subjects within them, also true at Banbury School. Michael Marland discussed pros and cons for both vertical and horizontal organization in his book (Marland 1974).

Where a year was organized predominantly or partially on mixed-ability groups the teaching group often became the pastoral group, with the form teacher in a special pastoral role. Even if a minority of subjects were mixed-ability taught this group could become the tutor group. Ford (1969), in her small sample, found that it was the teaching group for most subjects that was the social group. But this was in a heavily streamed school and there were obviously more diffuse affiliations when the mixed-ability group was the tutor group with many lessons taught to differently composed groups. The decline of the streamed class as a base unit is indicated by the decline of the practice of giving class rank orders of achievement from 90 per cent to 50 per cent of classes between 1961 and 1968 (Benn and Simon 1970). This had been standard practice in grammar schools. In the NFER figures for 1966 (Monks 1968) 24 per cent of tutor groups were mixed ability, a much higher figure for the incidence of mixed-ability grouping in general at this time.

Comprehensive schools have rarely experimented with making up tutor groups from particular feeder primary schools or neighbourhoods. In fact, Marland (1974) warned of divisive dangers in doing so. He urged that the base unit should be as small as possible by employing all staff as tutors. In this way, the size of tutor groups could conform to the school's teacher–pupil ratio (perhaps 1 : 17 or lower). He presented arguments for and against mixed-ability tutor groups.

Marland supported a powerful tutor role in which the tutor was 'ascendant' (as opposed to 'neutral' or 'subordinate') in relation to senior staff. This placed a severe limit on the extent of referrals, and it supported a contained relationship between a tutor and her/his group. There are at least three reasons why this sort of semi-autonomy is not common: referral is convenient for overworked teachers; referral can be justified because senior or specialist staff are supposed to have superior pastoral knowledge and skills; referral can be explained as part of a chain of command or authority.

Marland could see justification for referral to specialists where the specialism was relevant in particular cases. There is obviously specialist knowledge in matters of discipline, attendance, welfare, counselling, general guidance, vocational guidance and record-keeping. The intermediate pastoral head could offer some of these advisory services to teams of tutors and, in certain circumstances, to any teacher when no one else could offer the expertise needed. Rather than using a referral system an intermediate head could lead her/his team, providing support and advice where necessary, linking the work of the members of the team. Should tutors move through the school with their group year after year? There are arguments for and against this in Marland (1974).

Senior management could link with intermediate pastoral heads but Marland deplored the split into sexes and into academic and pastoral management. Although senior teachers could have specialisms in pastoral care, which was very handy, Marland saw their main task as leading the intermediate heads. In this system there could be no pastoral/academic divide. But the common pattern of senior management in comprehensive schools is a sex division in which male and female senior teachers restrict their responsibilities to pupils of the same sex and in which they have a limited academic or pastoral role. Instead of a channelled system, 'pastorality' for Marland implies a total pyramidal system embracing the 'academic' and the 'pastoral'.

The 'management' of the headteacher over all this has led some educators to see headship in terms of management generally. This view is rejected by those who feel it is impossible for one person to oversee all the myriad activities of a school (see Barrow 1977) and by those who think educational management is very different from managing a business (Barker 1982). Taylor (1977) reported a poor correlation between training in management and management performance in schools. But a new centre for training senior staff has just opened in Bristol and there is still support for the idea that school headship is like the work of a chief executive in industry (Everard 1982).

Griffiths (1971) referred to a special breed of administrative heads pioneered by the London County Council (LCC) but one of their contemporaries was Michael Duane, appointed head of the ill-fated Risinghill School in Islington. It was said of Duane (Berg 1968) that he was a man in whom teachers and pupils could confide, who would talk to people for hours. Most headteachers of comprehensive schools have not been trained robots or gifted with pastoral talents like Duane, or John Watts of Countesthorpe or even Brian Tyler, who hit the headlines in the television series about Kingswood School in Corby in 1982. How it is men and women more human than robots or less gifted than Duane have been chosen as headteachers of comprehensive schools is not something anyone can be too sure about.

The NUT complained that headmasters were being selected in Wales because they could sing or play rugby. Bryan Allen (1968) has a fascinating list of questions actually asked at interviews, including, 'Why have you got a black eye?' Presumably, if this was in Wales the candidate could gratefully reply that it was sustained while playing rugby. 'What did you read on the way to the interview?' The answer to this was quite possibly, 'The Herts Committee text books', which was one of the reasons given to Allen for success at an interview. A third list in this book was a composite stereotype of qualities and circumstances which appeared to secure appointments. This revealed a man (not a woman) on the right side of 40 to 45 years of age with different kinds of experience not always to do with teaching, an ordinary, well-dressed, ambitious member of the teaching profession. It pointed to a man able to converse freely and easily if not deeply on a wide variety of topics, self-confident with a tendency to pomposity, a graduate (class of degree not important). In the north it should be a local man. The ideal seemed to be a man who desired to get into a school somewhere in the country between London and Oxford in fine new buildings backed by a liberal-minded local authority and 'easy' housing. All this makes interesting reading, especially if joined by Frank Musgrove's portrait of the aloof and hated head whom staff accept only because he has suffered like they have and he protects them from untold enemies (Musgrove 1971). He has to innovate ceaselessly so the staff never know where they are. Unless a head has a lot of power he could never do the almost impossible job he has been given. A friendly head puts a strain on everybody. If Musgrove's tongue is not in his cheek or even if there is an element of truth in what he says, what price the caring school?

John Watts can hardly be thought of in terms of the typical headteacher. Countesthorpe opened on a manifesto of collaboration, and decision-making was in the hands of the school moot, on which all the constituencies of the school were represented, including the caretakers. Watts maintained there was still a role for the head in such a school. He felt responsible for continuity and forward planning. He had to be on most committees to see what was going on and this was an important co-ordinating job. Since he had no control over promotions perhaps teachers had less to fear if they wanted to disagree with him. Watts remained as the essential contact with agencies outside the school. In this way he considered that he earned his salary. His authority came through being himself. But he warned against any school going over to participatory government; they had the initial corporate agreement for it at Countesthorpe. The model of government there was conflict, compromise, then consensus, and finally commitment to the consensus. The price of an effective consensus was living with temporary ambiguity and delayed decisions, but the result must be something towards the caring school.

The third phase of pastoral work to which a comprehensive school could aspire, in terms of present theory, is the 'pastoral curriculum', an integral part of the total curriculum. The formal separation of 'pastoral' staff seemed to deny that all teachers had this sort of responsibility. Could it be said that some teachers care and others do not? The unfortunate sequel to this separation in many schools (e.g. the one studied by Burgess 1984) was that the 'pastoral' teacher was a second-class citizen, subordinated to 'real' teachers of subjects and not connected with any intellectual rigour (whereas Charles Stuart-Jervis (1974) claimed such rigour for care and not a 'phony sentimentality').

It is not easy for one teacher to be instructor, disciplinarian and carer, but Marland believed that relief for the individual teacher could come from the specialists in the different pastoral spheres (although the tutor would retain the management of the care of individual pupils). Marland is very critical of present comprehensive schools where there is a tenuous link between care and the curriculum and teachers take a daily battering because of lack of planning, poor role definition and poor leadership.

A practical solution to a divided academic and pastoral work was the mini-school idea tried at Countesthorpe (Evans 1983). After the school had been running for a couple of years teachers there became convinced that there had to be a closer connection between subject lessons and personal relationships of teachers and pupils. In the mini-school, a small team of teachers took up half the timetable of half a year. The rest of the week was spent in option work outside the team's expertise, although some pupils were allowed to stay with the team all the time and other specialists decided to work within the team organization (Watts 1977 and Evans 1983). It was all towards blurring the academic/pastoral distinction. Madeley Court School in Telford has also had success with the mini-school arrangement. It was interesting to read that the headmaster at this school recently resigned partly in protest at the delay in making Madeley Court a community school (Toogood 1984).

But Countesthorpe was special. In its regard for individual pupils it stands with other distinctive schools, such as Marland's (he was earlier head of Woodberry Down School), Daunt's and Rowe's David Lister School in Hull, as a beacon of care. Excellent practice of this calibre could spread through in-service training (Marland is extremely active in this field) but few local authorities provide advisers in pastoral care. In the HMI survey, *The New Teacher in School* (DES 1982c), 54 per cent of the new teachers thought that the worst omission in their training was in pastoral care. A 1980 survey of 633 Inner London teachers showed that only 6 per cent of them had been on an in-service course on pastoral care, and only 3 per cent of senior teachers in the sample and 8 per cent of deputy heads (Jayne 1980).

If staff are to work in teams this makes staff fraternity in caring schools absolutely vital. Albert Rowe saw fraternity emerging from an organized solidarity in which tutors had multiple roles

(Rowe 1971). It should be remembered, however, that Bernstein has argued that organic solidarity is no passport to a new world because it builds in a new authoritarianism. We cannot rely solely on a new type of organization. It is the attitudes of the individuals involved which is essential to the defeat of fossilization and the sustenance of care.

At Countesthorpe the pursuit of equality progressed to the construction of special programmes for each pupil. The contact of staff and pupils which this made possible was continued in the informal atmosphere of the general social area (Watts 1977). There was no staff-room. At other schools differentiated treatment of pupils caused rancour and alienation among pupils. One of the schools studied by Bellaby (1977) introduced a system of positive points for good behaviour, with a trophy for the best class. But the teachers' committee introduced negative points for bad behaviour and the higher streams won the prize continuously. Possibilities of unequal treatment led egalitarians to condemn the Newsom Report of 1964 on the average- and below-average ability pupils. The prototype 'Newsom' child was the source of many complaints (e.g. from the headteacher of Deanery High School, Wigan in the DES report of 1978). Peter Daunt (1975) tried to remove competition as the motivator in his school and replaced it with emphasis on individual pupils' excellence within their own spheres. He liked the mini-school concept. Elizabeth Halsall (1970) wrote of the desirable social activities, the self-confidence and the self-esteem which resulted from attention to the capabilities of each pupil. Even Peter Dawson (1981), no egalitarian, wanted to make remedial provision a prestigious activity. Peter Daunt recalled one teacher saying to another, 'You realize that X can't read, and you respect him for it.'

Albert Rowe (1971), head of David Lister School, Hull, was concerned with the quality of living within his school, based on healthy personal relationships. Peter Daunt and David Hargreaves believed that the dominating characteristic of 13- to 15-year-old pupils was alienation. One of the crucial ways out of this *impasse* was to give equal value to all pupils in the pursuit of personal autonomy. Marland (1974) saw the starting point for this as the consideration of the intense social pressures on adolescents. Schools could not go in for 'massification' of young people whose outside lives provided them with a vast range of options, much change and much movement. We had to face up to the facts that adolescence had been democratized, and deference and hypocrisy had faded.

In the DES report of 1978 a number of snapshots of various schools was given. Easingwold School in Yorkshire regarded the development of individuals as its supreme objective. This school saw itself as caring; it had banding, school uniform, prefects (elected by peers) and prize days. In view of Daunt's strictures about the divisiveness and the alienating effects of rituals of deference and 'petty pomposities of rank' (Daunt 1975) one wonders if Easingwold could have been successful in its rather diverse endeavours, and the same could be asked about many comprehensive schools with a hazy mix of the egalitarian and the meritocratic.

In 1982 there was 'the fly on the wall' series of television documentaries about Kingswood School in Corby. A lot of comment was reserved for the relaxed informality of Brian Tyler, the head. Neutral observers praised him for good personal relationships but criticized him for confusing pupils by failing to produce disciplinary rulings. This was obviously a caring school but questions were asked about the lack of intellectual demands in lessons screened. Is this falling between two stools?

Seventy-two of 169 brochures in my study (Weeks 1983) or 43 per cent had nothing about the co-operation of everyone concerned with a school (1982) or about a good ethos or atmosphere in schools. The other 97 brochures compensated for this to a certain extent with an encouraging series of claims about the quality of life in their schools. Twenty-five simply referred to their schools as 'happy'. It is easy to take a very favourable view of a school which regards itself in this way. One would be equally annoyed if the description was unjustified, although schools are taking a bit of a chance using this adjective in a brochure if people connected with the school have a different view of it.

Thirty-four brochures (20 per cent) referred to their schools as caring communities, a heart-warming result. Some schools wrote about the desirability of a fraternal attitude by all concerned in education, and they clearly meant teachers as well as pupils and parents. Phrases such as 'concern for others' or 'concern for human relationships' or 'good personal relationships between staff and pupils' or 'service of one's neighbours' or 'the teacher as a friend' or 'pupils and teachers working together' or the word 'compassion' appeared in 26 brochures (15 per cent).

Were the 169 schools interested in their pupils as individuals and what special help were they ready to give them? Two schools wished to treat all their pupils as special. This was more than a pious wish because these were highly practical schemes where all subjects provided whole class or group or individual activities. In this way any pupil could receive special help within any subject in the remedial sense, in the sense of acceleration or for any other special reason. It seems like a good way to educate 'children with special needs' because it implies that everyone has special needs at some time or another. One of the schools had a 'personal development' theme linking all subject departments, a sort of 'people across the curriculum' idea.

Thirty schools out of 169 made a reference to 'the whole child' or 'personal development'. There were a number of other significant phrases, sometimes several within the same brochure. Six schools wrote of the 'importance of the individual' or the 'needs of the individual'. The sentiment 'everyone matters' was expressed by five schools. One school declared that it would accept the pupils 'as they are' and work from there. There was an interesting batch of comments about pupils making the best of themselves as if the schools concerned were worried that low self-esteem caused alienation and poor performance. Six schools wrote about the self-respect or self-esteem of pupils. Another school was concerned about the 'anxious' and the 'timid' and yet another saw the importance of personal development towards personal autonomy. Twenty schools were interested in education for leisure, obviously regarding this as an important personal need, closely linked to a young person's future happiness. One of the schools stated that education for leisure was aiming at 'happiness and success in living'.

A growing number of schools appointed specialist counsellors after 1965. In my 1982 sample of 169 there were 15. Even if a later ideology concentrated on the pastoral skills of all teachers there is still room for specialist help. Another argument in favour of the counsellor is that there should be on the staff a person who can be somewhat independent of the authority structure of the school, and this would encourage pupils to confide in her/him. However, this seems to imply that other teachers are unworthy of receiving confidences, throwing doubt on their pastoral role. The counsellor could get squeezed out in an integrated academic/pastoral system. C. James Gill (1974) wrote that counsellors could still operate in this system exterior to the hierarchy. But counsellors should not be denied the opportunity to work with groups of pupils as well as individuals.

The progress of the 'pastoral curriculum' must be dependent on the welcome it gets from the traditional curriculum. Only exceptional schools are moving towards this integration. One way to set this particular ball rolling is to give some priority in the 'academic curriculum' to courses in personal and social development. Some examples of this were given in the DES report of 1978. An 11 to 18 girls' school had as part of its common core curriculum a programme of 'personal development' which embraced consideration of the emotional, vocational and academic 'self', the development of self-awareness, social values and social interaction. Also involved were skills in decision-making, assessment of life styles and community studies. Another 11 to 18 mixed school had a second and third year course in community studies with modules in personal development, health education, careers education, leisure and community. This school's fourth and fifth year course included half days out on community service and two full weeks of work experience.

These personal and social programmes are fairly common in comprehensive schools but my experience as moderator in Social Studies for a CSE Board is that these were often offered only to small groups of senior pupils, very often those who were not going to get a battery of O levels.

A number of moral education courses were generated by central curriculum agencies in the 1970s. Perhaps the best-known was the Humanities Curriculum Project (HCP) of the Schools Council, although this was a programme in controversial issues and not specifically in moral education. However, the titles in the series, e.g. 'War', 'Relations of the Sexes', 'The Family', obviously pointed to moral issues. The distinctive feature of the HCP was the neutral 'chairman' role suggested for the teacher. Backed by considerable packs of relevant material and a teacher maintaining rational argument and moral neutrality it was hoped that pupils would develop their own powers of thinking and get used to making up their own minds on issues.

The Schools Council Moral Education 13 to 16 Project ('Lifeline') ran from 1967 to 1971. This was designed to lead pupils from simple situations involving ethical dilemmas to more complex and less easily recognizable problems. It also included consideration of democracy in the school. John Wilson's Farmington Project (later called the Warborough Trust) in moral skills was less popular than the HCP or Lifeline, although none of these schemes was used by more than a small minority of comprehensive schools. The idea here was that teachers could train pupils in moral skills rather like the development of skills in any curriculum area. Young people might want to act morally but might lack the knowledge to achieve this.

Religious Education has traditionally been thought of as helping towards personal and social development. However, if the subject is unpopular with pupils it might be counter-productive. It is quite apparent that many schools have given up trying with RE. Recent HMI figures suggest that 22 per cent of comprehensive schools provided no RE (the Religious Education Council think 25 per cent). Many teachers doing the subject were not qualified or trained in it and yet the Secondary Schools Staffing Survey in 1977 showed that there were 4000 qualified RE teachers not teaching the subject, and this did not include headteachers or heads of other subject departments. A survey in Hampshire (Souper and Kay 1982) revealed that only 17 per cent of county secondary pupils attended assembly at least three times a week. Only about half the county comprehensives regularly hold Christian assemblies of some kind. Four out of ten secondary heads took fewer than one assembly a week. In any case, religious leaders are not keen that the subject should be colonized by social issues. The Hampshire survey showed that 52 out of 72 non-church schools described the main purpose of their assemblies as social and educational. In March, 1982 the Archbishop of Canterbury, speaking to the National Society for Promoting Religious Studies, said that RE was in danger of being 'integrated out of existence by assimilation to moral and social studies'.

The 169 comprehensive schools surveyed in the London region (Weeks 1983) mentioned moral education (or something like it) in 69 per cent of cases (116 schools). Moral education was specified in 10 brochures and in 15 others as part of an RE syllabus. Sixteen schools had special general courses of the type described in the DES report of 1978 (see p. 139). But it was not clear how 31 per cent of this sample of schools provided for this vital area of the curriculum, at least from what they wrote in their brochures.

Daunt (1975) referred to alienation caused by school rules which encouraged a 'them' and 'us' mentality and which were not respectful of individuals. He thought rules should be about little more than safety regulations. It took him several years to get rid of corporal punishment and official detentions in his school. It was Daunt's belief that punishment wasted valuable time and impeded co-operation. Since punishments must be based on the truth, and it takes time in busy comprehensives to find out what the truth is, the result of punishment is very often injustice and the increased alienation this brings. Daunt had a poor opinion of rituals of deference such as prize days, school uniform, and so on. Malcolm Gooch, head of Stanbridge Hall at Banbury School, believed that rules were very irksome, especially those connected with the exclusion of pupils from the school building at certain times (and in most weathers) and those about dress (Gooch 1982). Peter Woods (1979) reported how much pupils dislike all forms of 'domestication', such as school uniform.

A major shift took place in English education in 1983 and 1984. These years saw the first government initiative to restrict corporal punishment in schools. It was not so much an initiative, rather an obligation following judgements from the European Court of Human Rights which placed Britain in contravention of the Convention of Human Rights. By January 1983 there were thirty-two complaints before the court from British parents.

The Government proposed to allow parents to refuse to allow their children to be beaten but the Lords defeated this proposal by voting in an amendment for complete abolition in July 1985.

Progress towards a national ban has already been achieved by local abolitions. Individual schools have always been free to ban corporal punishment and by the end of 1984 more than half of the local education authorities in England and Wales had a ban (16 authorities) or were considering one.

Peter Newell argued that the true basis of learning was a good personal relationship between teacher and taught and this could not possibly survive a beating (Newell 1972). Colin Bagnall (1977) reported on a mixed 14 to 18 London comprehensive which had last caned a pupil on 30 May 1966. School discipline there was now based on tutorial groups reinforced by a referral system. Caning had not been banned by an edict; it simply stopped happening. The school had had no serious case of vandalism for three years and violence towards teachers had stopped. In *Alternatives to Corporal Punishment* (1978) the Society of Teachers opposed to Physical Punishment (STOPP) listed counselling, referral, withdrawal of privileges, detention, placing on report, transfer to another school, suspension and the use of specialized guidance services. Another device which has evolved (and much of this costs money, now in short supply) is the special unit for disruptive pupils. The term used for some of them is 'sanctuary unit', denoting a connection with care. The idea is to separate these pupils into small units staffed by teachers taking a special and individual interest in their welfare. But the idea also has its source in schools being unable to cope with a small minority of disruptive pupils. The DES report of 1978 referred to candidates for these units as inadequate or withdrawn or shy as well as others who are extrovert, noisy and violent.

Teachers in the units take exception to being regarded as supervisors of 'sin bins' or dumping grounds for unwanted pupils (see, for instance Redpath and Ackroyd (1980) and their work in the centre for Willesden High School). But others have criticized the units in general for their narrow curriculum. Why should some pupils have whole areas of the curriculum removed from their programmes? Eric Bolton, an HMI, thought that the units absolved schools from the responsibility of examining why certain pupils were being disruptive. Geoff Whitty regarded the units as a punishment measure rather than therapy. They were tightly controlled, uncomfortable and uninviting.

In a study of ten Sheffield Schools, David Galloway *et al.* (1982) concluded that pupils getting in to the special units had their image as important members of an anti-authoritarian sub-group confirmed. The 'final accolade' was suspension. Headteachers in Augustine Basini's (1981) study of ILEA units seemed to regard the units as bureaucratic facilities for easing disruption. They frequently infringed ILEA guidelines on the units. It has been generally noted that pupils aged between 13 and 16 make up the vast majority of pupils in the units, and that most of them do not return to the main school, perhaps a new offence against the 'comprehensive principle', which is partly about a common schooling for all pupils. In these circumstances the epithet 'sin bin' may be deserved. Ron Dawson's investigations for the Schools Council suggested that there was little to choose between units and the best practice in schools which retained their malcontents in the main building (Dawson 1980).

An effective method of improving staff–pupil relationships is through extra-curricular activities providing the opportunity for prolonged contact with pupils in an informal social setting. Thus, some comprehensive schools have developed their field study centres (see an example of one in the DES 1978 report). The 20 schools in the 1982 London sample (Weeks 1983) interested in education for leisure may be examples of schools using extra-curricular activities to pastoral advantage. At Brook School in Sheffield one whole school day is devoted to extra-curricular pursuits, the academic timetable being squeezed into the other four days (see Wood 1983).

Home–school links create an important base for a caring school, with teachers supporting parental support for their children and parents supporting teacher support for pupils. These links also underpin a community awareness on behalf of the school. In 42 out of 169 London schools in 1982 there was a clear desire for strong home–school links (Weeks 1983). Implied was a two-way responsibility, in which teachers and parents had reciprocal obligations. Phrases such as 'friendly co-operation', 'partnership of home and school', 'mutual respect', 'close and harmonious dialogue' and 'liaison between home and school' were used in these brochures, just over a quarter of the sample. In a few of these schools parents helped out in a voluntary capacity, which must have enhanced home–school links. In three schools, parents helped with remedial reading, in four in the library, in another in the stationery shop. In other schools parents gave careers talks, invigilated examinations or supervised work experience at their places of work.

Schools are now obliged to provide information for parents under the terms of the 1980 Education Act. This must help parents to play a more productive role in their children's education, although my study of a large number of brochures suggests that many schools have a long way to go before they can claim to be fully informing parents and aspiring to frankness. At exceptional schools they not only made parents welcome and kept them informed but they also made a point of visiting them in their own homes (e.g. at Wyndham School in Egremont, see Sharp 1973). The 169 schools in my sample welcomed parents within their walls although quite a number of them reminded parents to make appointments. Just one of them had a home-visiting scheme. The desire to visit the homes of parents, if welcome, must be a great mark of fraternity and care. But the one school in my sample stood in splendid isolation.

This section has outlined some of the hallmarks of a caring school. It is not easy for an outsider to know whether any particular school deserves this description. At Risinghill visitors to the school spoke glowingly of the warmth, friendliness, and hospitality of the pupils who were in the fifth year in 1965 (Berg 1968). The school only lasted five years so these fifth year boys and girls were there from its birth to its death. The school's humanity could have received no higher accolade than this view of its graduates. It seems to me that care must be the crucial sign of the egalitarian school.

Mixed-ability grouping, flexible teaching methods and a common curriculum

In Chapter 7 the extent to which comprehensive schools had gone over to mixed-ability grouping was assessed in order to see how much they delayed selection for meritocratic reasons. Over-delay of selection could hold up talented pupils. To avoid this, setting in subjects now appears to be a prominant pattern (at least in London) in the senior years. The presiding principle here is equality of educational opportunity, but mixing ability on the fraternal principle is entirely another matter. The fraternal concern is to develop individual potential and to mix potentially alienated social groups. The potential attack on individuals and their self-esteem by placing them in low streams or sets (they could be in many low sets) is seen as acting against the development of potential and the large number of pupils from poor socio-economic backgrounds who find themselves in low streams or sets is seen as detrimental to social harmony. If mixed-ability is based on fraternity it could not be eased out in senior years. That is an opportunity device.

There were early examples of schools which completely abandoned streaming throughout the school, such as Vauxhall Manor, Woodlands at Coventry, David Lister in Hull and Bedminster Down in Bristol. At Woodlands the process took seven years, during which time examination results improved (Halsall 1970). Both Daunt's school and Countesthorpe were unstreamed, with emphasis on small group work and individual work, making GCE/CSE divisions unnecessary. At David Lister School anyone could opt for GCE and CSE in any subject (Rowe 1971).

The preponderance of pupils from working-class backgrounds in lower streams was confirmed in a number of researches before and after 1970. From the view of social harmony this was regarded as a condemnation of streaming. However, members of mixed-ability groups can also receive differentiated teaching.

Give them all the same material and achievement in it can vary: give some different material and unequal treatment is then manifest. Indeed, differential treatment may be more apparent in general in mixed-ability groups. One way round this dilemma is individualized work, which is discussed below, but we wait upon extensive research which clearly demonstrates increased pupil fraternity in mixed-ability classes. In the NFER study at Banbury School (Newbold 1977) it was discovered that a year of mixed-ability grouping in this enormous comprehensive resulted in pupils generally making friends from a wider socio-economic range than pupils who had a year in streamed classes. In the HMI *Matters for Discussion* called *Ten Good Schools* (DES 1977c) the schools were selected for all-round qualities, but with a central place for good relationships. None of them had narrowly streamed classes. In the numerous case studies of schools or subjects going over to mixed-ability grouping (see references pp. 172 and 173 of the NFER study, Reid *et al.* (1981) and the bibliography in Sands and Kerry (1982), neither of them exhaustive but a good start) the change very often improved the atmosphere in the schools, including the reduction of truancy and vandalism. However, on the possible social benefits of mixed-ability grouping, the NFER report of 1981 asked for caution in drawing conclusions because there was no clear evidence of such benefits.

The provision of individual attention can be done through the medium of graded worksheets, but the extensive use of these, even if they are well-constructed and well-produced, can undermine the essential group interaction and oral discussion (usefully discussed in DES 1978a and Shapland 1977). A mixture of large and small group work and individual work, as at Countesthorpe, may provide a better balance. But such a pattern demands flexibility in teaching and resource provision. This can be met by teachers working in teams and by dispensing with a few walls. Fluctuating demands by small groups or individuals is accommodated by varying expertise of different teachers in a large resource area covering perhaps larger knowledge blocks than traditional school subjects. Increased fraternity can arise from a more sensitive response to pupil needs and through increased co-operation by teachers (Rubinstein and Simon 1973; Daunt 1975; Rowe 1971). At Countesthorpe the building was purpose-built around resource areas and not teaching areas. Related subjects were located next to each other. There were some class-rooms but also many non-demarcated areas (Watts 1977). When team teaching came in here two years later the school lay-out was ideal for it. Team-teaching demands a high level of staff commit-ment, but at Countesthorpe it helped to produce an ethos of respect and warmth.

On the integration of school subjects there has been support from curriculum theorists, who either believed that the old subject barriers separated areas of knowledge which needed to be joined (e.g. Jerome Bruner 1972) or supported a topic approach which assisted the understanding of 'forms of know-ledge' (e.g. Paul Hirst, in Hirst and Peters 1970).

A number of comprehensive schools have tried integration of some subjects. There were early examples of this at the large Hartcliffe School in Bristol (Benn and Simon 1970) and Nailsea School in Somerset (Richardson 1975). At Nailsea, four arts departments joined for first year work and continued this in the second year. Elizabeth Richardson (1975) observed that many teachers were reluctant to join the team out of fear of losing their identity within a particular subject, in which most teachers seek their status and promotion. Indeed, evidence of subject inte-gration is patchy, and what was especially uncertain about it was the motives behind it in particular schools. Were they listening to the theorists? Did they understand Hirst's theory of 'fields of knowledge' and, more importantly, did they know how to make it work? Or was integration simply fashionable (it was very prominent in early Schools Council work)?

In any case, there has not been much of it and what there has been was largely restricted to the lower years, where it would not interfere with anything important. Very few schools were keen to follow in the footsteps of Hedley Walter School at Brentwood and integrate across the curriculum in the senior years (this school used a battery of GCE and CSE Mode 3 examinations to accommodate this reconstruction of the curriculum). The present incidence of integration, which is now not fashionable (along with the deceased Schools Council), may be reflected in the results of the 1982 survey of 169 London schools (Weeks 1983). In these schools integration was exclusively in the humanities and creative arts and exclusively in the lower school. In 32 schools, humanities was taught as a package in all or part of the lower school. In 10 cases this simply meant combined history and geography, but in 22 other cases one or more of English, RE, moral education, social studies, sociology or biology was added. Creative arts was taught together in 11 schools. Only 14 of the schools had a faculty organization (3 to 6 faculties; 8 in one school).

I also searched in these brochures for evidence of collaborative or participatory teaching methods suggesting a flexibility of approach based on individual learning and resource-based teaching. Ten schools clearly followed individualized pro-grammes, 2 had very active Resource Centres and 14 directly taught study and bibliographical skills, suggesting training in the use of resources and individual work. Two schools were very active in collective curriculum evaluation and development, requiring a committed teamwork. But these results represent very small percentages of the total sample (169). Indeed, self-evaluation and self-development in schools is in only a pioneer-ing stage despite a proliferation of handbooks telling schools how to do it and providing case studies to emulate (e.g. Eggleston 1980).

Two schools in my sample wished to treat all their pupils as 'special'. These were the two schools with special 'people across the curriculum' curricula in which all subjects united to provide large and small group and individual work. Schemes like this take a tremendous amount of planning and hard work but they must generate the same amount of goodwill.

Any school which is trying to give all its pupils a fair chance through mixed-ability teaching and flexible arrangements might see its efforts dissipated by a differentiated curriculum. For instance, some pupils might get extra science or a second foreign language whilst others do not. Or some get vocational education whilst others are too busy with O levels for this (or for courses in personal and social development). The common curriculum unites strange bedfellows. It is possible to support it on purely meritocratic grounds to guard against the early dropping of 'essential' subjects (see Chapter 7, p. 93). Arguing that varied provision is unfair on individuals, on the other hand, is an egalitarian view. If an educational philosophy can work out what the essential areas or forms of knowledge are into which all children have the right at least to be initiated then the corollary is that there must be a common curriculum. A number of educators, philosophers, curriculum theorists and sociologists have worked out plans like this. Some of them are very different, for instance Paul Hirst's and David Hargreaves's (1982) and also the Inner London Education Authority's (ILEA) plan of 1984 engineered by a committee chaired by Hargreaves himself (ILEA 1984). What they have in common is that they are saying there is a common experience which all pupils should have. Accounts of common programmes in particular schools can be read in Cornall 1983, Makins 1983b and Makins 1984.

The evidence from schools (e.g. Weeks 1982), an earlier account of my study of the brochures of London comprehensive schools) is that there is a common 11-subject curriculum in Years 1 to 3 followed by a wide range of options in Years 4 and 5 in nearly all schools. Only one school had a common core of 8 subjects. Seventy-six (out of 173) had a 3-subject core; 41 had a 4-subject core.

But in these schools there appears another of those yawning gaps between theory and practice. Generally, there was no Hirst (or Lawton, or Holt, or White, or Barrow). In fact, according to the brochures, most schools were happy to give no reasons for a core curriculum, or for one with loads of options. It just seemed to be something they did. One school actually mentioned 'forms of knowledge'. Another referred to the promotion of experience in all subject areas combined with the pursuit of individual interests of pupils. Twelve schools wrote of 'balance' in the curriculum without specifying what this meant. Two schools listed some areas of knowledge which they considered essential and then left some of them out of the compulsory core. For six schools 'balance' meant simply that there should not be over-specialization. No justification for this point of view was provided. No justification was given in any of these brochures. Perhaps schools thought that parents needed no reasons? Perhaps they reserve the reasons for a more informed audience? It would be nice to know whom this is.

The problem with the common curriculum idea for egalitarians is the question of individual difference and choice. Is it fair or fraternal to force individuals to do a subject in their senior years? To argue that the thinkers and/or committees (rational people, it is hoped) know what is best for young people cannot please all egalitarians. I found that London schools which forced their pupils to do science had fewer examination entries in the subject and worse results (Weeks 1983a).

Curriculum theorists have faced up to the dilemma. For instance, Denis Lawton suggested a common core individualized programme in which pupils followed common modules but then branched out to different projects. At Countesthorpe, the mini-school concept was meant to solve the dilemma (see Armstrong and King 1977). Here, the tutor, negotiating each pupil's programme individually, could hopefully weigh individual interests with the need for a wide and balanced curriculum.

Positive discrimination for pupils with special educational needs

Earlier terminology referred to 'remedial education' and to 'handicapped' pupils but the phrase now used to embrace these categories (and others, such as the 'gifted') is 'special educational need'. A Government commission of inquiry on educational provision for children and young people handicapped by disabilities of body and mind was set up by the Tories in 1973, under the chairmanship of Mary Warnock. Its report (Warnock 1978) was about the education of children with special needs, which meant that they had in mind the 16–20 per cent of children who had some type of special need, mild or severe, a percentage far in excess of that for the older category of 'handicapped'. Part of the comprehensive principle is that all children should be educated in a common institution, and the idea of integrating children who were in special schools because of severe mental or physical handicaps gained support in the 1970s as part of the comprehensive movement. The official policy of separating the education of severely handicapped pupils in the 1944 Act was reversed in the 1976 Education Act. But this Act was repealed by the Tories in 1979 and, although the separatist principle has not re-emerged, the Special Education Act of 1981 has a rather qualified support for integration. The Warnock Report went along with integration but warned of the severe practical problems involved and of the dangers of integration on the cheap (reminiscent of warnings about comprehensive education on the cheap). The 1981 Act obliges local authorities and schools to adopt a policy towards those with special needs. Up until now most secondary schools have restricted their attention in special needs to some form of remedial education for slow learners. Only exceptional schools have concerned themselves with children who had severe special need, although they are being forced into a position where they must consider those with emotional needs who are disruptive of school life. This is why so many special units have been set up. But as we saw earlier in this chapter this is regarded as a new form of separation rather than a chance to solve special need in the ordinary life of a school.

In the London sample of 1982 (Weeks 1983), 127 out of 169 brochures had accounts of remedial work but only 7 mentioned severe special need or handicap. Two of them had a partially-hearing pupil unit on the school site, each with a special teacher seeking to promote links with pupils in ordinary classes. Two other schools made special arrangements for partially-hearing pupils elsewhere. One school had special careers help for the handicapped and two schools arranged for the integration of physically handicapped pupils into normal classes with the help of specially qualified teachers.

There is an evolving literature on the practice of integration in comprehensive schools (see Hegarty and Pocklington 1982, Hodgson *et al*. 1984, Barton and Tomlinson 1982, and Booth and Statham 1982).

Multi-ethnic programmes

The egalitarian school would support a multi-ethnic approach from a philosophy of equal consideration of races or cultures. If one culture or race dominated certain items of school curricula this could not be equality. Another issue in this sphere is racism in schools. If this exists in any school, and if any teachers in it are racist, this must make the work of an egalitarianism almost impossible. For some egalitarians neutrality about racism is hardly better than racism itself. They believe in a policy of combating racism in schools. Are comprehensive schools developing multi-ethnic programmes and combating racism inside and outside their walls?

An early example of school work embracing the cultures of different races was at Michael Duane's Risinghill, mainly due to his own efforts (Berg 1968). The London County Council got rid of him in 1965 and eight years later its successor, the ILEA, issued its plan for multi-ethnic education and its blueprint for action twelve years later.

After the Fire (September, 1980), a report by the Bristol NUT on the race riots in the city, believed that one of the main reasons for racial tension there was the lack of multi-ethnic ethos and activities in the schools. In the same vein David Moore (1979) commented that the Indian Mutiny was still taught as if it were an atrocity committed against a civilizing force. The sole purpose of slavery, apparently, was to allow Britain to abolish it. Moore believed that a multi-ethnic curriculum was even more vital in the suburbs of the cities than in the inner areas because it was in these 'white highlands' that people were prone to stereotyping ethnic minorities.

There is an expanding canvas of material for multi-ethnic programmes. This is not so much the problem as the difficulty of knowing how to integrate such work into traditional curricula, especially in view of the demands of external examinations. Until the examination boards can be persuaded to shift the emphasis from something strictly Anglo-Saxon to something rather more multi-ethnic schools can do little to change their curricula. Apart from opposition to such a shift in the presiding councils of the

Examination Boards, which includes opposition from teacher members, there are external pressures on them to be conservative. These come not least from the present Secretary of State, who has scrapped the Schools Council and replaced it by separate Examinations and Curriculum Councils, with the former appearing to have more power. In these circumstances a move to multi-ethnicity seems unlikely.

These are the political realities. But even if schools felt free to be more multi-ethnic (and even then many would not want to be) there are daunting theoretical and practical obstacles to overcome. How can a teacher teach all the cultures represented in some schools? (At the last count about 130 languages were spoken by parents of children at ILEA schools.) How does a teacher reconcile the teaching of different cultures with the need for social harmony? A solution based on the common core individualized curriculum, in which the common modules are multi-ethnic and the subsequent options divide into the various cultures, would take very sophisticated planning and knowledge and place a heavy burden on teacher expertise and collaboration. And yet the egalitarian school demands teachers like this.

The problems of multi-ethnic teaching are well illustrated by the example of mother tongue teaching. For instance, Asian pressure groups may say that they want children of Asian origin to be immersed in the cultures of their forbears but when it come down to it many ordinary Asian parents simply want their sons to do well in English (and England). In other words, these parents are as meritocratic as any other parents. Some of the practical difficulties were revealed in the EEC funded project to teach Punjabi and Italian in Bedford. The Italian teachers tried to teach in standard Italian but this was almost like a foreign tongue to the Italians of Bedford. And it is costly; in Bedford only 2 per cent of ethnic minority children and 2 out of 70 languages were catered for. It seems hardly fair that some minorities should get lessons in their language and cultures and others not. In Bedford, probably with the highest percentage of ethnic minority children in its schools outside London, it would cost a fortune to provide for them all, and in London the cost would be prohibitive. Tit-bits for some, such as Black Studies for a few black children in some schools, might do more harm than good.

Evidence of racism by teachers has been a bone of contention for some years. The Schools Council's project on multi-racial education was abandoned after its project team produced an initial report full of examples of teacher racism. The teacher-dominated Council rejected this evidence. There is a lack of hard research into the topic, mainly because of its sensitive nature. There are plenty of anecdotes about teacher racism, such as that presented in Thomas Cottle's powerful documentary *Black Testimony* (1978). Peter Green of Durham University found a big enough sample of 'highly intolerant' teachers to construct some significant statistics about them. The origin of the Teachers Against Racism movement was in the seminars by the Centre for Applied Research in Education at the University of East Anglia in 1973. At one of these, a number of teachers walked out because they objected to even discussing the possibility that there was a psychological basis for race prejudice. To them, racism was firmly rooted in social institutions such as schools. In response to this anger the researchers in Norwich, with the aid of teachers, devised Strategy 'B' for the teaching of race relations, positive action against racism (Strategy 'A' was neutral teaching). But in 1982 only 4 out of 169 London comprehensives had a Strategy 'B' programme (Weeks 1983).

There might be some justification for expecting London schools to be in the vanguard of multi-ethnic education since it is one of the most multi-ethnic regions in the world. The last official estimates (1972) showed that the city had about half the 'immigrant' population of the nation. In 1975, 41 per cent of births in the ILEA area were to ethnic minority parents (64 per cent in Brent). The proportion of births for New Commonwealth and Pakistani parents was 26 per cent or more in Hackney, Islington, Lambeth, Tower Hamlets and Wandsworth (1975).

The ILEA initiative (long after Michael Duane's) was the 1977 'Multi-ethnic Education' programme promising policies for extra nursery education and more special help in schools. Resource centres such as the Afro-Caribbean Educational Resource Project have been promoted and an army of multi-ethnic inspectors, advisers and project leaders (now numbering about 150). Thus, I looked forward to reading the brochures of schools in the ILEA and outer London boroughs in 1982, expecting to find a great deal about multi-ethnic education (Weeks 1983). But such references existed in only 18 brochures, an amazing result. In the other 151 brochures, 48 had a brief mention of extra English for those whose first tongue was not English or of the teaching of a new local authority agreed RE syllabus which included Comparative Religion.

The 18 brochures with multi-ethnic references presented 46 comments on this topic. The term 'multi-cultural' appeared in 14 brochures and 'multi-ethnic' or 'multi-racial' in 8 (some had all of these terms). The desire to tolerate and understand different races and/or cultures is there in 16 brochures. One school had a multi-ethnic co-ordinator on the staff and another had set up multi-cultural liaison groups with local community groups.

If this is the response from the schools of this region (a half sample) with its vast range of races, its army of advisers, its enormous capitation and its fine official policies what are we to make of the 'progress' of multi-ethnic education? The result of my search for something multi-ethnic on the curriculum served only to emphasize the pessimism we can feel about such 'progress'. Only 4 of 169 brochures mentioned general multi-cultural emphases in their programmes. There was a special World History course in one, an emphasis on mother tongue teaching in another, and multi-cultural elements in a compulsory Development Studies Unit made up of English, mathematics and science in a third. These were all ILEA schools. One school in the outer boroughs mentioned ethnically-variated exercises in home economics.

Democracy in schools

Professor Peters has analysed the pursuit of democracy in schools as being concerned with curriculum items about democracy, democratic teaching methods and democratic government of the school (Peters 1970). In my London sample (Weeks 1983), 38 brochures out of 169 had something on collaborative or participatory teaching methods. These 38 schools had an interesting range of techniques. Seven wanted to develop inquiring minds, 2 used inquiry methods in science and RE. In 9 pupils were taught to be either critical or questioning or rational or coherent or taught to express opinions. In 6 others individual observation was encouraged along with clear and autonomous thinking and discrimination.

The HMI discussion papers *Curriculum 11 to 16* (DES 1977a) included one on political education. This recommended the teaching about the machinery of central and local government, industrial relations, the education system, pressure groups and an understanding of controversial political objectives, values, methods and procedures. The inspectors judged that existing courses were too tied to mere descriptions of machinery and ideologies. They should deal more with the processes of decision-making. The report extolled toleration of diversity of beliefs and compromise as preferable to war, imprisonment and censorship. Open-minded commitment was to be sought, and with it the denunciation of racism and the exploitation of the defenceless.

Since then, HMI has become rather silent on the topic of political education, in common with other plans which the DES considered expensive. Such delicacies are also rather indigestible for the present Secretary of State. Local authorities have scarcely been more active. The first local political education adviser was in Sheffield in 1977, and few others have appointed separate advisers in the field. The rather left-wing ILEA is at present trying to find out whether its schools are doing their bit in political education. My 1982 survey showed no reference to political education in 103 of 169 brochures (Weeks 1983). In the 66 brochures which had something on the subject this was basically the optional study of, e.g. the British Constitution, for public examinations (48 cases), with only a few senior pupils involved. In the other schools (18), 7 had a compulsory political element as part of a general course in social, personal and political education. Other schools had community service and referred to its importance in political understanding. Only one school referred to peace education, which is perhaps the sort of course George Nicholson and the ILEA want.

Three of the schools were trying to develop decision-making skills in their pupils. Some commentators think that pupils must be involved in some form of local political life, such as community politics, in order to get any understanding of politics, a view well expressed by Frederick Ridley (1980). To give lessons about a far-off Government or local council is like giving lessons about Martians to pupils caught up in a disadvantaged environment. One is reminded of that marvellous analogy in Douglas Adams's *The Hitch-hiker's Guide to the Galaxy* when the commander of the Vogon spaceship commented, after destroying Earth, that notices of impending destruction had been posted up well in advance in the nearest solar system only four light years away. A nationwide survey in the USA (Stradling 1979) showed that formal political education had little impact on pupils' knowledge, attitudes or behaviour, or their interest in political participation.

Many schools have tried to involve pupils in their political life through the medium of a School Council, a forum for discussion with delegates from classes or years. Elizabeth Richardson (1975) had a close look at the one in Nailsea School. She concluded that this School Council was not able to convey a democratic dialogue. She described staff and pupil apathy and the extreme dependence of the council on the established authority in the school, which virtually extinguished it. Such councils bear little resemblance to the comparatively successful moot at Countesthorpe, on which staff, pupil and ancillary staff delegates were the decision-making body for the school (Watts 1976, 1977).

Only 19 of 169 brochures of London schools appeared to refer to pupil participation in school government in 1982 (Weeks 1983). Twelve wrote of good or responsible or intelligent or sensible or mature citizens. What did they mean? Was it law-abiding citizens or people who could understand what was going on and play some part in it? Four schools mentioned developing pupils as members of a school community or simply of 'a community'. Three schools alone used the word 'democracy', two of which supported 'preparation for democracy' and the other understanding democracy and other systems of government.

As we saw from the Nailsea and Countesthorpe examples school councils vary greatly in their status and influence. It is obvious that the Countesthorpe moot is very exceptional. The brochures of the London schools in 1982 did not always make clear what the role of a school council was. Twenty-nine schools appeared to have one (17 per cent of the total). Four of these indicated that there was a hierarchy of year councils sending up representatives to the main council. In one school, the chairman of each year council was the year head from the teaching staff. One school had year councils but no school council. They debated 'topics of interest'. One school had form periods in which the school rules were 'discussed'. Twelve councils discussed school policy and activities and put up resolutions to the school governors. Four other schools had councils which helped with school activities and discussed ideas or problems brought forward by pupils. Not described anywhere was how far the members of any of these councils were delegates reporting back to their class or year. There was nothing on elections. One school had a public gallery where interested pupils could listen to the debates.

Only two schools had a pupil representative to the governing body. He or she was elected by all pupils from the second year upwards. Whether the pupil governor was able to vote or be present for all matters was not revealed in the brochures. The latest Advisory Centre for Education survey showed that only 15 out of 104 local authorities had provision for pupil governors, in many cases without voting powers or voting powers when the vote was close and in other cases not able to participate in matters about teaching staff.

Closely connected with democracy in schools is the question of their accountability, although this has been raised more in connection with their accountability to exterior agencies than with their interior democracy. A more sophisticated (and theoretical) accountability is through self-account and self-development in schools. This sort of activity is rare in schools (some of it is usefully traced in Professor Eggleston's 1980 study) although there is a developing industry of books on the topic. Despite the fact that the ILEA pioneered periodic self-accounts only eight schools in my sample had Staff Councils or Committees for curriculum development (Weeks 1983). Most current school reports are those which local authorities demand from their schools rather than self reports. In these circumstances the rendered account is often more to do with narrow accountability to resource providers rather than a mature self-appraisal.

A longer-standing method of curriculum development by schools has been through the use of the Mode 3 examination by which a school arranges its own syllabus and examination, moderated by an examination board. Hedley Walter School at Brentwood is the best-known example of this. But whether the Mode 3 is distinctively a comprehensive school development it is difficult to determine. It evolved (along with the CSE) in a period which coincided with the evolution of comprehensive schools. In the mature CSE system of 1974, 21 per cent of CSE courses were Mode 3 (Smith 1976) but the chances are that the Mode 3 (and the CSE generally) would have developed in the way it did even with a tripartite system. Indeed, secondary modern schools might have done more with the CSE and the Mode 3 in the sense that they might have made it more distinctive from the GCE. Because the comprehensive school has been geared up to offer both (in many cases to the same pupils) there has been pressure to make the two examination systems similar. This is another possible effect of expensive and disruptive reorganization worth pondering over.

Fletcher *et al.* (1985) suggest that it was basically because some of the exceptional schools attempted to promote democracy in education and in society that they had to endure public trials. The authors of this study of four schools – Risinghill, Summerhill Academy (Aberdeen), Countesthorpe College and Sutton Centre – rightly ask whether this country really supports democracy in schools (on the triple basis analysed by Professor Peters) when it can treat schools which attempt something in this direction in such a way (see also Fletcher (1985) and Toogood (1984)). Now that mecca of comprehensive school democracy, the Countesthorpe moot, has voted in a 'liaison committee' with executive powers which must curtail its own authority (Makins 1985a).

9
A bleak future?
cuts, falling rolls
and alienation

Financial contraction

Chapter 8, which was very much about a handful of exceptional schools practising the egalitarian ideals set out in Marsden's list (without failing in narrower meritocratic objectives), hopefully struck a note of optimism, although the recent book by Fletcher *et al*. (1985) suggests that such schools suffer persecution. But we now live amidst educational and general pessimism because of resource contraction or, at least, nil growth. A bleak future may await comprehensive schools. It was, after all, the financial cuts which started the erosion of democracy at Countesthorpe (Makins 1985a).

In the financial year 1981/2 there was a real cut in educational spending by 1 per cent and rather less than 1 per cent in 1982/3. The projection for 1983/4 (issued in February, 1983) still promised some contraction, its extent depending on how much the Government could restrain 'overspending' local authorities, on the rate of inflation and on the teachers' pay award. But whatever happens there is little likelihood of overall growth although there may be small improvements in some aspects of the educational service, notably in 'overspending' areas.

In the Autumn Term of 1980 HMI collected evidence of the effects of the cuts. This special information was added to returns from local inspectors to make up the report *The Effects on the*

Education Service of Local Authority Expenditure Policies, Financial Year 1980 (DES 1981b). I could not help noticing how by this title HMI appeared to be blaming local authorities for the lack of money. The inspectors reported that it was difficult to extricate the effects of cuts from those of inflation and falling rolls. Whatever the cause, the real value of capitation grants had fallen in four out of five local authorities. Fifteen per cent of authorities 'gave cause for concern'.

The report went on to detail some of the adverse effects on schools. Staff had fewer free periods and there had been reductions in the range of specialisms available. Probationers were put under more pressure. There was less help for slow learners and the gifted. In-service training was also adversely affected: courses held in teachers' own time were preferred by local authorities and headteachers more than ever. Induction work for probationers remained at a low level. Both advisory and ancillary services had been cut. Orders for books and equipment were well down. Half of all local authorities had cut their programmes of maintenance, repairs and redecoration. In a survey of 980 schools (Venning 1980c) premises were found to be in a poor state in 300 of them. An even worse story of delapidation was reported in the *TES* for 30 September 1983 (Venning 1983a).

Cash support from parents was accepted in nearly all schools visited. In some cases this exceeded the annual per capita allowance. This increased the inequality of school provision, between large and small schools and between schools in advantaged and disadvantaged areas. A *TES* survey in Suffolk (Venning 1980d) showed that parental contributions went towards basic needs and not just optional extras. The same was true of Gloucestershire schools in 1983 (Garner 1983).

HMI issued another survey report in 1982 (*Effects of Local Authority Expenditure on the Education Service in England – 1981*, DES, 1982b) showing worsening staffing establishments and special difficulties in providing remedial education, music, physical education, and avoiding more mixed-age teaching groups. There were more complaints about declining provision in in-service training, local authority advisory services, capitation allowances and the maintenance of buildings.

Disparities in provision were getting worse. Only five authorities had a 'satisfactory' or 'better' provision under every major resource heading compared to the previous year. More than two-thirds had reduced their levels of provision, 'slight' in 55 cases, 'moderate' to 'considerable' in 16. Four gave special cause for concern (not named in the report but later revealed as Gateshead, Wiltshire, Somerset and Norfolk).

A special survey of Dudley (fourth from bottom in the secondary school spending league for 1980–1) by HMI in October, 1982 led to the inspectors claiming that meagre resources were partly to blame for poor standards of school maintenance, inferior library and book provision, and restricted staffing and curriculum breadth. Examination results were steady, but school staffs were achieving them by making the best of a bad job (not an unusual tale of muddling through).

There is accumulating evidence that the cuts hit the already disadvantaged the hardest, noticed especially in Dudley. Louise Burghes's (1980) survey of 65 families for the Child Poverty Action Group found that children in nearly half of them had stayed away from school during the previous term because they lacked essential clothing. Six families kept children at home because of transport costs. Grants for clothing had been abolished in many authorities. The conference 'Pupils at Risk', organized by the NAHT (September, 1981), heard a paper claiming that cuts and the high unemployment rate were causing more and more pupils to stay away from school to see to problems at home.

A host of recent sources also indicate the declining economic position of many children. Indices of poverty and poor educational performance are so closely linked that this new depression must afflict their chances at school even further. In 1982, 1.3 million school pupils lived in families with the breadwinner out of work, 5.8 per cent of children under 16 lived in very low income families (in fact, a quarter of the total population lived on incomes at or below 140 per cent of the supplementary benefit rate), 10 per cent lived in bad housing and 8.5 per cent in one-parent families. In the same year only 33 per cent of disadvantaged pupils who had an attainment in English in the top fifth of all pupils entered O level in this subject compared to 80 per cent of non-disadvantaged pupils with similar attainment. Meanwhile, there is an overwhelming concentration of educational resources in the south-east so that the average incidence of poverty and poor performance in schools must be even worse in the other regions.

Falling rolls

Financial contraction must automatically make things worse on the whole but falling rolls do not necessarily mean bad news for schools. That is not to forget that in some cases they have spelt disaster. Good schools have gone and others submerged in amalgamations. Schools with a death sentence hanging over them can hardly be places of sweetness and light.

It was estimated in a DES Press Notice of 21 March 1981 that the school population would drop nearly 30 per cent by 1991. The last Labour Government had set up an inquiry into the effects and implications of falling rolls. Eric Briault and Frances Smith (1980) studied twenty comprehensives of various sizes in different parts of the country over a period of two years. They concluded that a policy of keeping open as many schools as possible would endanger curriculum provision in them, especially in their sixth forms. Subjects such as Latin, drama, music, physics, history, biology and a second language would be at risk. They recommended that authorities keep the smallest possible number of the largest schools they could, but by means of mergers rather than closures. Parental opinions of schools should be taken into account and authorities should be encouraged to build on strengths already existing. Briault and Smith called for generous re-deployment and early retirement schemes for teachers.

In February, 1981 the DES suggested cash incentives to speed up school closures. The Secretary of State asked for details of proposed surplus places which would exist in 1986. Such projections were 'urgent'. Local authorities were warned of possible 'penalties' if they did not speed up closures. The DES had earlier estimated a surplus of 3.1 million places by 1985 (1.1 million in secondary schools). The closure of places in what is regarded as temporary or sub-standard accommodation would reduce this potential surplus to 600,000. The Government wanted to take 1.3 million places out of use, mainly by getting rid of unsatisfactory accommodation, with 700,000 places going by 1984 and one-third of all surplus places by 1986. Local authorities told the Government this was all impossible. Mark Carlisle told them 100,000 places cost £10 millions a year. He offered more cash incentives but local authorities offered only to take out about 250,000 places by 1984. The Secretary of State further told them that the cost of heating surplus places in 1982 would cost more than all the purchases of books for that year. The NUT rated the DES Circular as misleading and very dangerous. It disputed the official figures and regretted the threat of 'penalties'. Later, the DES reduced its 1984 target from 700,000 places to 470,000.

Some case histories of falling rolls and school mergers or threatened closures afford interesting glimpses of the English education 'system' at work. In September, 1979, Labour-controlled ILEA threatened to close the prestigious Highbury Grove School, a school which its former headteacher, Dr Rhodes Boyson, described as 'over-subscribed' (1974). The *Daily Telegraph* followed the fortunes of a beleaguered Highbury Grove with interest (Izbicki 1979a and 1979b), reporting that the nearby Islington Green comprehensive, with a roll of 800 boys and girls, had only 22 O level and 2 A level passes in 1979, while Highbury Grove, with a roll of 1300 boys, had 220 O level and 40 A level passes.

Meanwhile, equally prestigious Highbury Hill school for girls was also under threat of closure. The *Daily Telegraph* reported that 600 parents and pupils from the two threatened schools descended on County Hall (22 November 1979) to hand in a petition with 40,000 signatures. The *Daily Telegraph* did not bother to give its readers details of the intakes of Highbury Grove and Islington Green (nor even how many pupils they had) but Peter Wilby of the *Sunday Times* provided the missing facts. His view of things was that Islington Green had been struggling with a very poor intake and was doing as well, if not better, than Highbury Grove.

The *Daily Telegraph* further reported that the head of Islington Green, Margaret Maden, believed in progressive teaching methods and was a well-known member of the Communist Party. It was alleged that she had 'enormous influence' at County Hall and she was definitely instrumental in preventing the North London Teachers' Association from supporting the strike of the teachers at William Tyndale Primary School. The current headteacher of Highbury Grove, Lawrence Norcross, complicated matters by revealing that he had also been a Communist, in his 'mis-spent' youth, as he put it. The Islington CASE supported the ILEA plans, which were to amalgamate Highbury Grove with Sir Philip Magnus School (470 boys) on the Highbury site, and Highbury Hill with Shelbourne Girls' School on the Highbury Hill site. The end of the story (or was it?) came when Highbury Grove was 'saved' and Sir Philip Magnus went to the wall. The Highbury Hill merger went ahead. In the language of accountability Sir Philip Magnus had been 'accounted for'.

But supporters of Islington Green could not easily forget the Press campaign against the school. Maurice Kogan (a Governor and parent and Professor of Social Administration at Brunel University) thereafter attacked the Press coverage of the affair (Kogan 1981) but was rebuffed in stiff replies from *New Standard* and *Daily Telegraph* journalists (Doran 1981). Anthony Doran of the *Daily Telegraph* reminded readers of an earlier attack on Islington Green which had been castigated in the *New Statesman*. But the editor of this, Doran informed us, was the husband of the Chairman of Governors at the school. The row was further pursued by Mr Norcross and Mr Wilby, who could not agree on the interpretation of examination statistics (Norcross 1981 and Wilby 1981).

It transpired that Islington Green came third out of three hundred schools in a national writing competition and ILEA inspectors had a high regard for the school. It was also revealed that some pupils from it were allowed to give vocal backing to the rock group Pink Floyd's 'We don't need no education'. To compound the complexity of it all the *New Standard* ran a feature on Islington Green's fund-raising bike ride across the United States.

With Rhodes Boyson as a former head and Lawrence Norcross, a prominent member of the NAS/UWT, as present incumbent Highbury Grove would find it difficult to keep out of the news. HMI inspected the school in 1982. On the basis of their report (reports were still confidential in 1982) a governor wrote to the *Times* attacking the school and its staff. The NAS/UWT branch at the school called for his removal. But there had been a previous letter which represented a fierce attack on the school's Labour Governors. And so it went on.

Perhaps for most schools the effects of falling rolls are not dramatic, more like a dripping water torture which can slowly reduce the effectiveness of the school. Schools in this situation have to struggle to maintain standards and curriculum coverage. But, as noted so many times in this book, adversity can bring out the best in teachers. Moreover, falling rolls do not necessarily spell only disadvantage. The process may get rid of sub-standard accommodation. And some schools are reporting some slack, i.e. rolls are falling faster than staff establishments, confirmed by the Government's inability to close school places as quickly as they would like. I was told that some schools (all in the rich and prestigious south-east) are trying to think of ways of using spare staff, including in-service training to administer to pupils with special needs in the ordinary schools. But schools should not be losing sleep trying to figure out how to use the slack; a look through the suggestions in Chapter 10 might help them.

Case histories of threatened amalgamations and closures show special groups of parents and community activists fighting for the lives of their schools, and sometimes winning. This concerted action could continue after the fight was won, bolstering the school in life as well as impending death, perhaps in ways suggested in Chapter 10.

Amalgamations could also mean life from death. If staffs are going to be reconstituted this could be an excellent opportunity for a reappraisal of school government, organization and curriculum, setting off a continuous process of self-evaluation and development, again outlined in the next chapter. This is a chance for a new headteacher to inspire the new establishment to better things. On the other hand, anyone with any experience

of amalgamations during the days of rapid secondary reorganization knows there is always some bitterness and recrimination in
these situations. Amalgamations are extremely difficult to
organize without upsetting someone. Such antipathy does not
bode well for a new school.

Contraction may bring a shrinking curriculum but this may
make schools plan their programmes more carefully. Smaller
schools *could* mean better teamwork and greater motivation for
evaluation and development.

Alienation

Hargreaves (1982) traced the source of alienation in pupils to the
destruction of working-class communities and a subsequent loss
of dignity. The attempts to re-establish personal status resulted
in anti-school attitudes and activities. The 1974 *Guardian* articles
by Janet Watts (Watts 1974a and 1974b) indicated a creeping
contempt and Penny Blackie in Bristol saw only a 'deadness' in
schools (p. 99). Hargreaves concluded that, outside the minority
of pupils committed to school objectives, there is a majority not
committed to them, reacting with indifference to what is offered.
Others are not committed but play the school game for what they
can get out of it. A few 'oppositionals' make a positive search for
a new solidarity based on physical superiority, toughness,
smartness and trouble-seeking. The situation has not changed in
the period under review because Leila Berg in 1968 wrote that the
pupils at Risinghill came from an environment hostile to
ordinary human growth; it 'spat at them' (Berg 1968).

The simmering hostility and dead apathy was also detected by
Bellaby (1977). The pupils were hostile to staff in two of the three
schools he studied yet this seldom surfaced in class except for
isolated outbursts by a few pupils, who expressed the inner
hostility of many of their fellows. He noted a division into
'leavers' and the 'ambitious', the latter learning to play the
academic game. The 'leavers', mostly from a working-class background, saw no point in acting in ways for which there seemed
no justification or pay-off. Unemployment worsens this situation
because there are fewer pay-offs for being 'ambitious'.

Ford (1969) noted increasing social class tension in a comprehensive school, not less. She thought that the role of the education system in legitimizing social stratification would be consolidated in comprehensive schools, rather than the opposite.

Alienation in comprehensive schools goes deep and solutions will not be found easily. However, there are a number of surface reflections of deeper troubles which could receive urgent oil. For instance, irksome and unnecessary rules (see p. 141) could be removed. Perhaps one of the most critical enemies of a fraternal atmosphere is the presence of corporal punishment, something of a model for successful violence. Yet, in the National Opinion Polls (NOP) surveys for the *TES* in 1979, 75 per cent of secondary teachers supported the use of the cane. Moreover, the official line of the NAS/UWT is that caning is part of the necessary *loco parentis* role of teachers. There has been stiff opposition from teachers in some areas where the local authority has announced a ban. Even though the European Court of Human Rights has made it quite clear that it regards the use of corporal punishment without parental consent as contrary to the European Charter the Government and local authorities are moving at a funereal pace to operate this judgement, taking cover under the practical problems involved.

When we get a unified 16+ examination (GCSE) its likely grading system will ensure the perpetuation of sheep and goatery. This would not matter so much if examinations did not have such a grip on schools. It was there as comprehensive schools were born and is now stronger than ever. Speaking at the Annual Conference of the Assistant Masters' Association (AMA) in December, 1964, Sir John Lockwood, Master of Birkbeck College, saw examinations as a great affliction in education, creating a mystique and a stranglehold, canalizing classroom work. An examination system should be a servant not a master, he said. The stultifying effect of examinations on the curriculum was also referred to in the Bullock Report in 1975 (*A Language for Life*). They had the most serious detrimental effects on higher reading skills. HMI continually condemn classroom work narrowly based on examination courses, e.g. DES (1979a) and in many reports on individual schools, made public since January, 1983 (see Makins 1983a). With the Schools Council gone and Sir Keith Joseph's new Examination Council calling the tune over a new Curriculum Council, the situation is not likely to change.

Hargreaves (1982) associated our examination system with a cult of individualism which did nothing to reconstruct lost communities. This reminded me of Harry Ree's report of his recent tour of the Cambridgeshire Village Colleges (1980). The decline of community ideals here was connected with a preponderance of parents and their children being interested only in meritocratic success.

Preoccupation with meritocracy has removed energy from egalitarianism and meritocrats also directly attack what they call 'sentimental egalitarianism,' most notoriously in the so-called 'Black Papers'. The first one (Cox and Dyson 1969) pointed out that its supporters were not enemies of all comprehensive schools (presumably they liked the ones which were like grammar schools). In fact, they thought that the 11-plus was an inefficient selection procedure. But they were completely hostile to progressive teaching methods, any non-directive teaching and to the integration of traditional school subjects. They loved streaming and formal examinations. The National Council for Educational Standards was set up in 1972. 'Black Paper Basics' were listed at the beginning of the Black Paper of 1975 (Cox and Rhodes Boyson 1975). They included support for competition and a competitive society and schooling instead of social engineering. Deprived pupils needed literacy and numeracy above all (rather like Maureen Stone's thesis about black pupils, Stone 1981) and bright working-class pupils needed examination success. Boyson (1975) attacked discursive teaching, mixed-ability grouping and the 'visual and electronic cult' and defended examinations and conservatism in education. The Black Paper tradition lives on with the NCES, the Centre for Policy Studies and the Social Affairs Unit, whose director, Dr Digby Anderson (1982), recently produced *Detecting Bad Schools. A Guide for Normal Parents.* In this he advised parents to ignore educators who talk about 'caring' for pupils, especially if they emphasize the first syllable of the word. Perhaps certain individuals are guilty of directly inflaming alienation. If they stay at the Social Affairs Unit they may do no harm but if they teach in schools they may do a lot.

But alienation goes much deeper than silly rules or beatings or examinations or reactionaries. David Hargreaves (1982) followed two pupils through one of their daily doses of school. For them it was like seven deadly dull TV serials which they could not switch off. They had fleeting moments of interest in the proceedings, but only for vicarious reasons not intended by the teachers. Now and again the volume of the 'TV set' rose and distracted them from their conversation. But they had lost track of the serials long ago (some of them were repeats, anyway). The lessons were no more than background noises which sometimes interrupted their gossip: good training for the world of work, if they ever got into it.

No school of any sort can thrive under these conditions. They were summed up pungently in Frank Musgrove's penetrating study *Patterns of Power and Authority in English Education* (1971). If a school follows slavishly what a meritocratic society wants of it this gives it no independent power. Training is pre-destined to subservience, as Musgrove put it. Yet if the school wants to be autonomous its 'irrelevance' to a meritocratic society makes it equally powerless ('the problem of the autonomous is still to be needed') and the wrath of the meritocracy might fall on its head. What can a school do in these circumstances? Perhaps very little on its own.

10
A brighter future? reconciliation in comprehensive schools

Opportunity, potential and culture

'Equality' in education can refer to 'equality of educational opportunity' or to the equality of 'culture'. In all cases the 'equality' rests with the basic human right of all young people to go as far as they can, in a socio-economic sense or in a sense of personal achievement or in the fulfilment of their cultural origins. In the real world the 'equality' must be diluted both through scarce resources and the accidents of life (a very broad canvas). But as long as we can be satisfied that as much as possible is being done for individuals we may rest content.

But there are inherent conflicts between 'opportunity', 'potential' and 'culture'. The fact is they often sit very unhappily together. 'Opportunity' might be gained at the expense of 'potential' or 'culture'. Personal interests or community activities are not necessarily gainful ones in a socio-economic sense. Yet success in money and status can frustrate personal interests and abilities and very often removes a young person from her or his cultural origins. If a 'culture' lacks socio-economic status and power the pursuit of its elements in a school curriculum may reduce the opportunities of the pupils. But sheer concentration on opportunities will remove the guts from a multi-cultural education.

It may be urged that schools do not exist solely to help individuals but also to support the economy. Without a strong economy schools will not have the resources to do anything. What I cannot understand in this argument is why supporting potential and culture as well as opportunity will harm the economy in the long run. Pursuing only opportunity has been producing large numbers of disaffected people, and continuing in this vein, now that we have high unemployment, seems doubly ridiculous. And a computerized future (if we get it) which is not labour intensive will only serve to intensify the disaffection of people who are not only unemployed but also frustrated personally and in their communities, which could themselves fall apart because of corporate personal unhappiness. Whichever way you look at it schools must go forward on a broad front. There may be something in a tough and single-minded political system but add a similar education system to this and you may be asking for trouble of one sort or another.

At the moment, even opportunity is heavily restricted. This puts an even severer premium on attention to personal and communal interests and abilities in the present meritocratic system. Priority for opportunity seems now to be stronger with scarcer resources and there is even more support for dispensing with what are, in meritocratic minds, fringe extras. There is no doubt that some of these 'fringe extras' can be very expensive if you think in terms of, for example, advisers, resource centres, in-service training, the sort of industry which grows up around specialist efforts, the best example being those initiated by the doomed ILEA.

But money is not everything. Perhaps these specialist industries have a nasty habit of ballooning all too quickly. I point again to the example of schools which have managed to do so much on Marsden's list (1969) and yet are not laggards in the meritocratic race, the schools mentioned in Chapter 8. These schools have not received outstanding resources, at least not in the ILEA league. The good example, especially the one based on good inter-personal relationships, can spread. Goodwill is not expensive if it spreads to a willingness to tell other professionals what you are doing, with a minimum of the expensive in-service training.

I do not believe that opportunity, potential and multi-culturalism are as mutually exclusive as different 'equality' theories suggest. In any case, the theoretical challenge is always to find a compromise between strongly-held ideas, with the result often standing as a new theory in itself. Indeed, a theory of 'equality' will only ignore resources and economic trends at its peril but cannot stand, at all, unless it refers to individuals and their cultures. But 'opportunity' so often embraces personal interests and aptitudes, and the socio-economic success it can bring potentially allows later cultivation of these interests. On the other hand, 'opportunity' standing alone is so harsh and inhuman. It desperately needs the softer edges of humanity and humility, caring for others (pronounced in any way). Is it asking too much for these programmes in opportunity to take with them some personal and social education? If 'opportunity' means grabbing what you can, all it teaches in a personal and social sense is competition and how dog eats dog. It's moral poverty. To say that a 'sloppy sentimentality' reduces academic success is nonsense. There is nothing sloppy or sentimental about humanity and humility: they are great strengths, and the suggestion is that they could be infused into the personalities of tomorrow's industrialists, trade union leaders and politicians. Even though 'wets' have a very bad political name at present, in schools, 'potential' and 'culture' must embrace 'opportunity' via emphasis on personal and cultural development within a spirit of goodwill and co-operation. No teacher can deny any young person 'opportunity' but it is possible to give it a shroud of humanity.

Good teachers know they can do an effective job with a public examination course and at the same time do much more. I am talking not only about teachers of the human subjects but teachers of all subjects. An unfortunate division ('two cultures') into physical science and human science is perpetuated strongly in our comprehensive schools, leading teachers in the former to believe that their subjects have no personal or social overtones, are somehow bodies of knowledge which owe nothing to society and have no effect on it. This is readily apparent in the work of mathematics teachers who believe their subject is not discursive nor susceptible to the environment or personalities of the pupils they teach. Such a view is rather arrogant nonsense (castigated in a number of official reports, such as Cockcroft 1982). These attitudes present enormous stumbling blocks to the pursuit of personal and social education.

A great deal depends on the attitudes of teachers now coming out of the colleges of education, and the people who teach them. The messages can be simple. We have to think of pupils as persons coming from particular environments. Whatever we teach them has to be related to these environments, whatever our subject is and whatever the public examinations syllabus is. Syllabuses are sometimes so frighteningly narrow-minded that reasonably imaginative teachers can provide lots of space for approaches based on the experience of the people being taught and their backgrounds, with many more discussion and project lessons (see pp. 195–9). Both GCE and CSE provide the flexibility of a Mode 3, ideal for embracing personal and cultural deflections, and the new 16-plus examination (the General Certificate of Secondary Education or GCSE) has school-based assessment built into it. In this way the meanness of an official syllabus can be removed, although the Moderators have to be satisfied. True, Mode 3 work and school assessment can be expensive, but they are there for teachers to use.

The education system is always short of money: this is nothing new. Looking back to 1965 (and beyond) there has been a fairly continuous financial crisis for education. The clouds may have lifted slightly around 1970 but not much. Grand schemes such as the White Paper *A Framework for Expansion* (DES 1972), heralding great progress in nursery education, in-service training, etc., fell on stony ground. As the proportion of the GNP dedicated to education rose steadily (4.5 per cent in 1965–6 to 6.3 per cent in 1975–6) so did the cost of everything connected with it. The 'fringe extras' (and the unfortunate industries which sprung up around them) were a real luxury. Then the GNP slice for education started dropping (from 6.3 per cent in 1975–6 to 5.4 per cent in 1977–9) and 'accountability' for spending raised its head (never far under the surface, led by Treasury monsters). The 'wild spending' had to stop. In fact, it never amounted to more than 'peanuts', which is how Eric Midwinter described the funding of EPA projects. The ILEA, for example, receives a lot of bad publicity because it spends highly in a sphere which is notoriously penny-pinching.

For educationists at all levels being short of cash is nothing new, and never will be. We have always planned our work on the assumption that we will be lucky to get funds so it is difficult to see how the present depression makes planning any more awkward than it has always been. This is no call for complacency. We want every penny we can lay our hands on. The point is we have always been short of money, and the other point is that money is only part of what we need in comprehensive schools. Indeed, adversity (cuts and falling rolls) can make people more determined to succeed.

But a narrow 'accountability' attitude can threaten and stifle the initiative of schools. Not only is money rather tighter than it was but those dishing it out are more suspicious than they were. They are looking for more control over how it is spent and this process always seems to favour opportunity rather than wider educational objectives. Heavily involved in this trend are the attempts by successive governments to intensify their supervision of the education service, marked significantly in the last decade by James Callaghan's Ruskin speech about the rights of constituencies outside the system to know about and participate in what is happening inside it. At present this sort of pressure is exactly in step with meritocratic pressure. Thus, Sir Keith Joseph preserves schools of 'proven worth', i.e. with meritocratic sixth forms, and sends state pupils, whose parents cannot afford fees, to independent schools on 'assisted places'. The present official support for these schools only increases the emphasis on opportunity. One only hopes that the independent schools, as some of them try to do and as all of them have been asked to do many times, can think more of wider educational objectives, especially in proving to the world that they are not socially divisive. If they are really guilty of this perhaps they should go.

Some Tories would like to do even more towards the privatization of the education system, including open enrolment or even educational vouchers, possibly involving independent schools. At the moment this all looks highly unlikely because the Tonbridge and Tunbridge Wells scheme of open enrolment is having its problems. Now the Kent Education Committee is limiting the expansion of successful schools. This means that some parents will be disappointed, defeating the principle of open enrolment. Sir Keith has recently admitted that open enrolment, not to mention vouchers, have too many practical problems to make them a viable proposition, but even more recently (August, 1985) the Prime Minister hinted that she was not averse to new experiments with open enrolment.

Narrow meritocratic attitudes take the lifeblood from schools which want to do more towards wider objectives. Comprehensive schools, for good or ill, have inherited the responsibility for educating the great proportion of our young people. If so much is expected of them give them a chance to make their own destiny. The evidence in this book is that we have comprehensive schools because most people want them. The re-establishment of grammar schools has succeeded in only one case, and, at present, the local Tories and parents in Solihull and Redbridge are split over reversion, which is now postponed, and a recent poll in Kingston-on-Thames, the last fully selective authority, showed a large majority of parents opposed to selection (Passmore and Durham 1984). Perhaps comprehensives were voted in because they were expected to provide meritocratic results for a wider spectrum of pupils. In this case, they should be encouraged to do their own work. Who is going to complain if they produce the meritocratic goods at the end of the day plus some personal and social benefits both for their pupils and for society in general? Who is going to object to self-reliant and thoughtful people?

But schools will have their work cut out for them, not only because of shortage of resources but also through hotch-potch planning which makes the future of some schools most uncertain. Indeed, economic stringency caused the hotch-potch in the first place because of the demands for reorganization on the cheap, which produced a bewildering variety of types of school. Thus middle schools flowered in the economic desert in an oasis of an 'ideology', constructed around them to give artificial irrigation. Now it is the turn of the 11 to 16 school, created by area sixth-form colleges or 16 to 19 institutions. Educationists will strive to create an 'ideology' for them as well, whereas, in fact, they are schools simply deprived of their older pupils, relieved of their successes, truncated. If they have the morale to do something special the notorious difficulties of liaising with other schools awaits them. The creation of 11 to 16 schools is probably the worst effect of falling rolls.

The case for the 11/12 to 18 (or 19) school is as strong as it ever was. The case rests on the facility for maximum flexibility to pursue wide educational objectives (opportunity, potential and culture) and executive power to carry through plans. Truncated and divided schools must put a premium on flexibility of government, organization and curriculum. Collaboration between schools even in theory is no substitute for the whole school. In practice collaboration has never worked. The 11 to 16 school is the strongest reason we could have for feeling pessimistic about the comprehensive system. What can they do? If they are purely meritocratic lack of specialist teachers and resources makes it difficult to achieve much. If they are more than meritocratic their personal and social educational objectives may be ignored by the schools they feed. There is a lot to be said for hanging on to 11 to 18 schools (and 13/14 to 18/19 schools embracing the 14 to 19 concept of vocational education) and trying to eke out scarce resources by pooling certain activities, the 'consortium' idea tried in Birmingham and the 'cluster' idea in Leicestershire (Kerrison 1985). This is very difficult to administer (as Briault and Smith 1980 found) but it must be better in the long run than 11 to 16 schools. I think schools could try harder with the consortia idea: it must be worth doing to preserve the basic all-age school. The trouble is that many of the arguments used to promote the 16 to 18/19 institutions are meritocratic ones. Concentrate the specialists and the specialist resources, it is argued, and you get better meritocratic results. As soon as wider objectives are considered, personal and social education, the more the division at 16-plus becomes a yawning and disastrous gap in the development of an all-round programme of opportunity, potential and culture. As the obverse of the grammar school was the deprived secondary modern school so the obverse of the 16 to 18/19 institution is the deprived 11 to 16 school. Some 11 to 16 schools may look fit on the surface (people make the best of a bad job) but suffer from organic illness. They can never be true comprehensive schools.

Schools may suffer, too, as the embarrassing success of some of the schools in the Kent open enrolment scheme demonstrated, from intakes largely made up from pupils who have done badly at primary school or who live in areas with severe socio-economic problems which make educational success elusive. Evidence in this book showed how unequal intakes have been throughout the comprehensive era (the best example being in the Rutter (1979) research). This situation is now potentially intensified by parental choice of schools and by Government support for schools of 'proven worth', with the Manchester 'league' as the most notorious example of both (Fiske 1982).

If poor intakes are born out of socio-economic disadvantage then evidence of the worsening disadvantage (see Chapter 9) heralds even poorer intakes for some schools. Schools of 'proven worth' will move rapidly in the opposite direction. What price 'equality' in this situation, and how is it any different from tripartism? What can 'sink schools' do about meritocracy let alone personal interests and culture, not to mention humanity? Short on gifted and specialist teachers, short on resources (many such schools have falling rolls) they are also short on morale and prospects, especially if they have no sixth form. It is difficult to tell the difference between such schools and the former secondary modern schools. Indeed, I think the secondary modern was able to hold on to a little more dignity than an impoverished 11 to 16 school, labelled 'comprehensive' and expected to do everything with nothing.

If there are schools of 'proven worth', and other sorts, parents will make their 'choice'. There is also a league of parents in which some are able to find out more easily what a school is like and more able to do something about it. We can hardly blame parents for being preoccupied with the meritocratic message because this is the dominant message schools transmit. It was the message present-day parents received when they were pupils and they still get it, undiluted – 'academic' subjects, examination results, further and higher education, well-paid job.

Of course, there is nothing wrong with the message, just as long as it could be wrapped in a little more humanity. The chances of this are reduced if the government of the day bangs out the meritocratic message to the exclusion of all else. Weaning parents away from a purely economic message is hard going for schools which have something more embracing to offer. But one of the jobs schools have is to educate parents (albeit if they believe fervently themselves in wider objectives).

If parents do not constitute an independent force in education because of their submission to a dominant theme, 'communities' hardly fare any better. 'Communities' could very much promote the stature of a more social message from schools, especially one about cultural fulfilment. The very fact that 'communities' traditionally have been kept at arm's length from schools has supported the predominance of a purely economic message. Of course, such a message is absolutely vital to localities in the present circumstances of unemployment and the launching of a national youth training programme (YTS), but not to the exclusion of other values in education.

'Communities' remain cut off from schools, blocked off by local government and its political representatives on governing bodies. Since local councils increasingly preoccupy themselves with party politics rather than local needs (economic and social) they seem more and more unfit to lead schools to wider objectives. But they are not likely to loosen their grip on schools, centres of political interests themselves. Local politicians say 'community' representatives are not 'accountable' because they have not been voted in on a ballot paper. But as many politicians become more and more remote from the localities they are supposed to serve other institutions may have to take over.

'Communities' have to remain in inverted commas, not because they do not exist, but because it is difficult to define what they are in any locality. They most certainly consist of complexes of local interests and organization, sometimes in conflict with one another. But I defy anyone to go to a locality and not find them. They are part of the fabric of our society and it is about time that educators realized that schools belong to them as much as they do to governments, parents, employers, educators.

Youth unemployment must constitute one of the worst prospects for comprehensive schools, even worse than financial stringency. It must be demoralizing to educate for unemployment or even to educate for YTS. To be cut off from work is to be cut off from a vital part of life. Even the motivating effects of the pure economic message of schools decline, making the social and personal message even more remote. Teachers in the early days of comprehensive schools had the security of an employment market to fall back on. So my old head could get up on the platform on Monday morning and warn pupils about punctuality because of the confidential reports that went out to prospective employers. Such traditional ploys to motivate pupils must be fading.

But we can prosper in this sort of adversity by taking the chance to take a square look at our provision for vocational education. The most exciting challenge comes now from the 14 to 19 concept, pioneered by local authorities such as Bradford. In this idea a wide range of personal, social and vocational needs are considered in an integrated programme for all 14 to 19 year olds with diverging patterns of work towards the top end of the age range. This is a true 'comprehensive' plan, in the sense that it is going for a wide range of objectives backed by the right flexibility and planning for all pupils. This is what puts the 11 to 16 school in such a poor light, and the 16 to 18/19 schools have the task of constructing an integrated package without being able to administer the formative 14 to 16 years.

The purely meritocratic sixth form stands as a barrier to the 14 to 19 idea. It is not that sixth forms are not taking in a wide variety of pupils. The evidence from London comprehensives in 1982 (Weeks 1983) is that schools are rapidly converting to two-or three-course sixth forms. But the evidence here is that the courses represent clear divisions between pupils going for A levels, those doing extra O levels or CSEs and those following a mainly vocational course. All the courses seem to be lacking in personal and social education, and the possible desire of the Manpower Services Commission (MSC) to remove this sort of education out of vocational training will only confirm the sharp edges of a meritocratic hierarchy in which 'academic' work is top of the league and 'vocational' is menial and not about people or communities.

Yet integrated sixth-form work would not interfere with A levels, which can remain as the specialist hurdle to higher education, but a broader base of work is necessary (and has been necessary ever since comprehensive schools were born). It seems to me that if employment is now delayed until 17 or 18 for most young people there is no reason why higher education cannot be postponed until 19. This would help to ease pressure on higher education places (the Government seems to be forcing in more entrants on declining per capita grants). The new entry age could be phased in gradually.

There is one very sizeable part of the school population which could do with more opportunity, and that is the female segment of it. If merit and opportunity are the names of the game then it is a male game we are playing. Governments and educationists go on about opportunity and 'proven worth' and yet we wonder if they mean girls, as well. The lack of opportunity for them is the most anachronistic feature of our education system. And you never know, perhaps there is something in the claim that with more women in prestigious positions there will be increasing fraternity in society generally, a social as well as an economic message.

School government and organization

The implications for school government and organization which emerge from the section above are that schools must maintain high academic standards within a shroud of greater humanity and humility, with individuals and cultures in mind, in an era of stagnant budgets and economic depression.

The theme of using threatening circumstances to advantage can be used to turn 'accountability' inside out. The prevailing 'accountability' demands an account to resource providers on a narrow meritocratic front. The only answer to this is a professional and exhaustive self-account given on a much wider, or 'holistic', front. A continuous self-evaluation subsumes mean prying and turns teachers into better professionals. The rights of teachers to more autonomy, and to their esoteric professionalism, must rest in their readiness and ability to look into their own efforts. In the future no one will come along with their periodic and mean claims for 'account' if schools habitually review and reform their own work as a natural part of their lives. If one of the fundamental problems for schools is to establish themselves more as independent entities in our society they will only do this via their own professional standing, which includes offering up periodic, mature and exhaustive self-accounts without any nagging from outside constituencies. So, self-evaluation and self-development have to be a vital part of school government and organization. Thus, it has to be outward-looking. It is not enough to leave it to the head teacher. An integral part of a school's government must enable it to present an account to constituents and so part of this process is to educate those constituents, i.e. the nature and structure of the account should in itself seek to widen the views of those receiving it, particularly those who may be in great need of this extra understanding, such as parents. This, and the special problems which comprehensive schools now face, means that the schools have a particular need to communicate with the outside. As we have seen, these problems especially trouble the truncated 11 to 16 schools and lower tier schools. Educational coherence in a hotch-potch of separated institutions is most elusive. Only about half the system is made up of all-through schools and the history of co-operation among feeder and receiver schools is not encouraging. Other problems are poor intakes and unemployment. The point is that schools need all the outside help they can get in these circumstances. Schools standing alone may suffer even more. If school government and organization is to be outward-looking then it must actually contain elements from outside schools which may support it.

This must mean the 'community' in all its vagueness and complexity. But these interests and institutions are there, for every school, and they can be allies in the struggles to come. If governments and local government are hostile to wider educational objectives and to the self-initiative of schools, communities appear as the major accomplices independent-minded schools can have. Moreover, if parents listen only to economic messages communities might help to broaden their views.

Government of schools must also take cognisance of the new vocational training needs, the exigencies of unemployment and the integrated 14 to 19 concept, a real fusing of economic, social and individualistic messages. The risks in separate 16 to 18/19 schools or colleges are of dominance by meritocratic objectives. Only the right form of school government and organization can avoid this. Curriculum reform is not enough. It is all so much easier in the all-through school, as Coventry realized in its plans for 11 to 19 schools, to be built out of the existing 11 to 18 community colleges. It is a visionary fusing of secondary and further education. The case for the large school has never been refuted. The only real evidence set against it has been from big bad schools, easily more disastrous than small bad ones. The secret is not to have bad schools. The benefits of a large school not only rest in the availability of wider expertise and resources but also in the opportunity to construct large-scale government and organization structures to accommodate maximum flexibility. Flexibility here means embracing wide meritocratic, personal and cultural objectives, with a basically integrated course for all increasingly modified by the needs of various groups and individuals, culminating in a sixth form which caters for all needs while maintaining common courses in personal and social education to the age of 19.

A better account of large schools emerges from the more successful ones, such as Banbury. This school based its development on efficient government and organization. It has consistently educated more than 2000 pupils yet has the flexibility and organization to build in activities such as the longitudinal NFER research comparing the effects of streaming and mixed-ability grouping (Newbold 1977, Postlethwaite and Denton 1978) and, more recently, the integration of pupils with special needs (Booth and Pym 1982). School government and organization must also build in opportunities for girls. Again, this cannot be left to curriculum reform alone.

How exactly can school government meet all the needs set out above? First of all, governing bodies might be able to influence events far more than they have up until now. As far as some independence for schools is concerned these bodies have been a dismal failure, confirming only local political influences and the dominating influence of head teachers within their own schools. Governors can only have an influential future through blessing and encouraging school self-awareness and self-development. Only in this way can schools constitute an independent (but accountable) force in society and the only real role for governors is to support them all the way. Governors are in an advantaged position to tell the outside world, proudly, what their schools are doing.

Governors, too, can be a substantial link to the 'communities' which might support schools in their more independent roles, and to local industry. The implication here for governing bodies is that they must use to the extreme the present statutory right to include community and parent governors. The sort of wide-ranging membership recommended in the Taylor Report of 1977 was unfortunately watered down in the 1980 Education Act but, at least, the Act lays down minimum numbers of community and parent governors (although before September 1984 the DES was forcing only new or reorganized schools to conform to this statute). There can be more. This could balance out party political representation, such a deadening weight on the initiative of governing bodies. Fortunately, at present, Government thinking is in the direction of more parent governors. Indeed the Green Paper of 1984 (*Parental Influence at School*, DES 1984) suggested parental majorities on governing bodies and the DES consultative document of 1985 (*Better Schools*) recommended equal represent-ation of parents and local education authorities on governing bodies. As lackeys of local parties governing bodies are useless, at least in supporting self-evaluation and wide educational objec-tives. In the few places where some form of community council has been created for schools, for instance in the Leicestershire Community Colleges, they constantly feel the strain of opposition from local politicians who claim that such bodies are not 'account-able' and that they 'atomise' local government. But such councils can win their 'votes' by standing up for the rights of schools and the needs of communities. If politicians deny and block such rights it is they who are undemocratic. 'Votes', as mere crosses on a ballot paper, have their democratic limits.

To sum up, the governing bodies of the future should represent the interests of independent and truly accountable schools, which are self-aware, pursuing wide educational objectives and opportunities for girls and telling the community, parents and local industry what is going on and enlisting their aid for the school. This may sound fine but the major problem is to reconstitute governing bodies so there is less dead wood in them. Political representatives sit tight under the instructions of their political masters because they fear that other political elements will take over the government of schools, madmen, fanatics and the like. What a good excuse for keeping out genuine community representatives, who have to prove to the world they are solid citizens who believe in an education not tied only to the purse strings of the nation. The only way to change governing bodies in the right direction is for more responsible and open-minded activists to come forward and tip the balance.

At least politicized and anaesthetized governors do not normally have the *de facto* power to stifle initiating schools. The vital appointment here is the head teacher. No school is going to be self-evaluating and self-developing, broadening the personal and social base of education, looking to its neighbourhood, negotiating with other schools and non-sexist unless the head wants it to be all these things.

All this demands a democratic school government, simply because one man or woman cannot do all these things, but the head teacher still has to be a leader, as John Watts showed at Countesthorpe. We are thinking here of people who believe very strongly in wide educational objectives and will not let the governors nor the school rest until they are achieved, getting people thinking and working together, cajoling and encouraging them. We are looking for very special people, and very special people to select them. A more alert and supportive governing body would certainly help here. The selection of the next head teacher must be seen as the crucial event in the life of the school. It amazes me how the whole process is over in a day; a momentous decision made in a few hours. I have seen it done so many times. And suddenly here is this person, with the school until he or she evaporates, for better or worse.

Self-aware staff must involve themselves in interviewing the candidates at length. Teacher governors must be in the final selection (or teacher representatives). These are the people who are going to work with the head teacher, so let them have a say in the appointment. We are not asking for a sea change. The CEO is still going to be there and so is the Chairman of Governors. It may be more expensive than the present system but poor head teachers are even more expensive.

How are we going to make progress without good leaders? We are probably not, given the present influence and power of heads. If the right people are in short supply we might consider reducing their powers. Staff keen on self-evaluation and self-development could fight for their rights. Poor heads are sometimes reluctant to do very much at all, and their redundancy or semi-retirement might leave the field clear for energetic staffs. In any case, so much is down to individuals in the system, from probationers to deputy heads. If they let heads get away with inaction they are just as much to blame.

The present arrangement of deputies, senior teachers, house teachers, heads of department, provides a workable pyramid of government. The deputies along with the head must represent executive power in the school. Absence of authority to act without constant referral to the wider staff is not democracy but anarchy. The deputies need bits of the head's power to act, perhaps a little more than they have at present, to provide more elbow room for action, especially in large schools.

This small executive team can make countless day-to-day decisions, as individuals or as a body. The democratic backcloth to this is direct answerability to the whole staff council. This sort of body is there in nearly all schools but often lacks teeth because members are loath to question senior staff, although the presence of teacher association officers can make a difference (even if the influence here can be narrow-minded). This situation could be eased by giving the staff council a place on the executive council during its official meetings. This place could be taken by a staff delegate reporting back to the full council.

Given the tasks facing school government in models presented in this chapter the most urgent need is for a staff development council, responsible for self-evaluation and development, constant appraisal and planning. The head teacher must lead this work, establishing a public role of encouraging staff to participate in this work. The development council could be empowered to set up its own working parties, consider their reports and order executive action. The work here must be the heart of the school's decision-making process. Here the crucial plans must be approved and ordered, plans affecting the whole life of the school. And here the account based on all the work must be prepared and issued to the outside. Its objectives must not only be meritocratic, but must also be for individuals, for society, for communities. The council must contain the head teacher and at least one other representative of the executive council, and representatives of the governing body, parents and the community (how else can these constituencies play their proper part in school life without being present at its heart?). But the majority of seats must be reserved for the whole staff council, the ultimate stroke for democracy and shop-floor evaluation and development. These representatives should be elected by the whole staff. Only such a widely representative body could accommodate the tensions and traumas of self-evaluation and development.

It must contain experts, experts in traditional curriculum ranges but also experts in personal and social education, to maintain the wide-ranging objectives necessary to a humane education. Someone must also speak for vocational education and opportunities for girls and for special educational needs. The development council must have a special responsibility in assisting the head teacher to link with constituencies outside the school, made easier by having direct representation from some of them.

The concern for personal and social education must permeate the whole government and organization of the school and this is best achieved by a thorough integration of the 'pastoral' and the 'academic' energies of schools and the roles of individuals within them. These distinctions, in fact, have to go – from the head to the newest probationer. It is the only way to overturn the narrow academic tradition and the poor status given to personal and social education. Most head teachers are obliged, in any case, to adopt on integrated role, although some of them still seem to distance themselves from the 'pastoral', cushioned by deputies whom they turn loose in this arena. The leader in the enterprise must show the way and be in the thick of all types of school activity. Deputies must be equally diverse. Obviously, they will have their expertises, of which the school may take full advantage, but their main role must be a general one supporting the whole life of the school, and not restricted to the 'pastoral' and the 'academic', or girls or boys, because this simply perpetuates disregard for personal and social education and promotes sexism.

The essential backing to this integrated government is a curriculum integrated in the same way, with equal status for personal and social education. The inferior place of these activities in many present schools is marked by a distinctive organization of separate intermediate heads, some for 'pastoral', non-curricular responsibilities, and some for 'academic', curricular tasks. In an integrated system intermediate heads, like their seniors, must be integrated animals themselves. Thus the traditional role of head of department needs careful scrutiny. If the great divide is to go then the head of department is an anachronism. If we are going to call on all teachers to assume responsibilities for personal and social education, which is what this sea change is all about, we cannot have teachers in special positions of responsibility destroying it by allowing them to ignore the 'pastoral'.

The role of experts in particular curriculum areas, however, remains crucial to schools, especially to the work of the development council. But it is equally crucial to the evolution of a more humane education to ask any teacher who has gained promotion to pay special attention to personal and social education. We cannot afford to promote people out of this role. There is too much promotion into specialisms in education. It would help if all intermediate heads had a general title, perhaps 'senior teacher', embracing existing roles of house or year tutors and heads of department. The addition 'with special responsibility for x' would indicate their expertise, which would be of general use to the school. But the title would indicate, above all, their position in a hierarchy dedicated to wide educational objectives. If some teachers, promoted or not, feel unable to play a part in this enterprise one wonders why they are teachers at all. What matters at the end of the day are the young people in the school and their communities and not the predilections of teachers.

At the base of the integrated organization must be a tutor system. Marland's idea of using every single member of staff as a tutor meant that tutor groups were small, as small as the tutor–pupil ratio for the school. The small consultancy group is the firm basis for personal and social education (see Button 1980). This also means that the full staff council is in fact the council of tutors, emphasising the crucial nature of this part of school life. Such a council can create a 'pastoral curriculum', an integral part of the whole curriculum (Marland 1980). Supporting the structure of development council, executive council, tutor council and the head teacher would be experts of all types, the more the merrier. They can be called in by individuals or by one of the councils.

If experts are freed in this way the notion of 'ascendant' roles for group tutors is feasible. Present schools seem prone to using experts in rather tight working parties or in rather exclusive gatherings, shielding them from approaches made informally by any member of staff. Experts, who are going to be tutors in any case, should be consulted independently by any tutor when the need arises. An 'ascendant' tutor role means that the tutor has executive power within his or her own consultancy group, with far less referral to intermediate heads. If the basis for inter-personal action between tutors and pupils is squarely within the life of the group, and not constantly transferred to third parties, then such relationships may take on a more realistically personal nature. The tutor can act within guidelines promulgated by the development council and on the advice of experts but he or she does the talking with the pupils.

A further responsibility of 'ascendant' tutors would be work connected with the locality, which is not to be left solely to teachers of community studies or careers teachers. Community resources, industry, local services can be used by all tutors regardless of their specialisms and they should let such material drift into their general teaching, especially in subjects which seem to disallow socially relevant material. A broader and more aware government of a school can only work through the genuine efforts of individual teachers in personal and social education, and it is no use leaving it to others. Every teacher is responsible for this.

I have used the term 'personal education' many times and it should be made clear that I am referring generally to 'individual potential' here, including not only consultancy in personal relationships but also group work in moral, social and vocational issues, and consultancy in the pursuit of personal interests through the school curriculum. Whereas the tutor will cover much of this work all teachers are responsible for moral, social and vocational issues, and consultancy in the pursuit of personal interests through the school curriculum.

Far too often at present 'pastoral' work is left to specialists appointed for it or to senior staff. Personal education, as defined above, and social and vocational education including work in the community, must be everybody's mission in a school. In this way everyone can share in or support the tasks of the development council. It involves a determination to participate in all processes of a school's life, which is the only way a school can really be a self-evaluating and self-developing institution. It is also the only way a school can be truly 'accountable'. At the moment far too many staffs point to their senior colleagues and say it is they who are accountable – a sort of protection racket.

Before leaving this account of a type of school government and moving into more details of organization it should also be made clear that in describing a fraternal system, one based on good interpersonal relationships, internal conflict is not ruled out. Any body of people, evaluating its own efforts (which involves the application of different and possibly conflicting values) is very likely to suffer internal disagreement over what is happening and what should happen in the future, forcing a debate. John Watts claimed that the Countesthorpe model was institutional democracy, conflict, compromise and the solid support of the compromise via institutional democracy. The final decision had the authority vested in it from the participation of all constituencies in the school. Intermediate heads, or senior teachers as we might call them, provide a potential link between senior executives and the tutors, as they do now in most schools. They also need to consolidate this platform by being leaders of teams of tutors which, again, is not all that unusual. The normal pattern is for these teams to centre around identifiable batches of pupils, usually now year groups. But some year groups will involve twelve or more tutors, especially if the groups are commensurate with the teacher–pupil ratio. At Countesthorpe the teams were often made up from tutors spanning half years, or 'mini schools', and having teams of about six tutors seems to make sense. Six people could conduct their collaboration in countless informal ways whereas a team of twelve would find itself involved in formal meetings and communication problems and inability to act swiftly. The teams, and their leaders, can provide special support for probationers and students on teaching practice, again, something far too often left to senior teachers or specialists.

The 'mini school' idea was created expressly as an instrument acting against pastoral/academic divides. In it the tutors would try to do a lot of the teaching for their own groups and other tutor groups in the team, providing an organizational link between subject teaching and consultancy work and maintaining the composition of the tutor group in many activities. At Countesthorpe the tutor teams took up about half the timetable. Obviously, this sort of proportion may have to decrease in the senior years as specialisms abound, but the base must not disappear, even in the sixth form. This is the trouble with separate 16 to 18/19 schools or colleges. The consultancy group solidarity and permanence is lost, and if it is replaced by a plain meritocracy and disparate courses all the work in personal and social education may be undone.

How should tutor groups be formed? In many schools whole subject departments or individual teachers demand the separation of 'bright' from 'dull' pupils. They may mean this in a general intellectual sense or only in relation to their own subjects. Other teachers may demand mixed-ability groups.

Both systems demand that tutor groups be formed on the basis of measured or suggested ability. There is a strong preference in schools at the moment for mixed-ability tutor groups and objections to this are rare. In fact, setting has replaced streaming as the basic teaching group organization in secondary schools (there is overwhelming evidence of this in my study of London comprehensive schools in 1982 (Weeks 1983)) and this means that all subject teachers are worried about, if they want sets, is that mixed-ability tutor groups are timetabled together for their subjects so that they can be reshuffled into sets. There is a lot to be said for mixed-ability groups, especially if they work together much of the time, because of the dangers of divisive intellectual elitism and rejection and because of the connection of measured ability with scales of socio-economic disadvantage.

Unfortunately, the creation of mixed-ability groups still involves precise and public measurements of ability. Through this process pupils are made quite aware of their standing, likely to be confirmed in setting arrangements. Possibly, by the time they get to secondary school pupils are well aware, anyway, of how teachers assess their abilities. But it might help if there were less public signs of these assessments (although, again, teachers easily give themselves away). It is possible to make up groups by the alphabetical order of surnames, or ERNIE might do it for you. But, it does not really matter if a system of whole group, small group and individual teaching is adopted by teachers. In this system the tutor group may be taught altogether or split into several small groups and/or individuals. It is difficult for one teacher to supervise some of this and so one or two more teachers could join him or her. However, no school can normally afford luxuries like this and so two or three tutor groups have to be involved in this work to make it viable. It is possible for a large group of pupils to be listening to one teacher whilst the others administer to small groups and individuals. Additional economy can be provided by occasional talks for all two or three groups together. The advantages of teacher collaboration or teamwork rest in the application of a wider expertise, better planning, more small group and individual attention and more variety of material and teaching methods.

Not all teachers could be expected to work in this way and even those who would at times perhaps need to apply their specialisms more in senior years. But there is no reason why some teachers could not work in this flexible way and maintain it to some extent even in sixth forms, especially for work in personal and social education. A serious barrier to the creation of flexible teaching groups is unsuitable accommodation. The resource areas at Countesthorpe have facilities for large group, small group and individual work. But it depends to a large extent how keen schools are on flexible teaching; in other words, it is a matter for the development council. This shows how important the details of government are. Individual teachers cannot knock down walls and invade corridors but development councils can.

Educational theorists like to use the words 'discipline' and 'punishment' in connection with schools but I would like to see these words fade away like old soldiers. It is not that I am opposed to some of the activities these words indicate but what is dangerous is the separation of these activities from other aspects of a school's life. In fact, too many schools have these divisions into 'academic pursuits', 'discipline' and 'punishment', 'pastoral' work, 'extra-curricular activities', and 'vocational education' as if there were six schools in the building, not one. Some of these parts seem to have nothing to do with the others. For the 'academic school' those nasty, brutish 'punishments' in the basement have nothing to do with it. Some pupils go off to Wales but that is nothing to do with the 'real' work of the school. There is some work experience, but that is only for some, as if the others will never go to work, or will never need to know about dreadful 'industry'.

School 'discipline' and 'punishment' are very much like this. So often it is a system only called into life when pupils fail to do what they are told or make a nuisance of themselves. Instead of emanating from the evaluating and developing centres of schools the system seems designed merely to safeguard teachers from irritations and a troubled life. If they want this they should work in a monastery.

As in their own educational debates and disputes teachers should welcome conflict in the classroom. Conflict is at the very heart of self-evaluation and development in a school. If teachers have participated in or approved the deliberations in a development council and they know that they and their colleagues have done all that they can to make their schools an effective educational force, they are in a much better position to assess the behaviour of pupils. This is because any decent evaluation and development plan will contain the details of personal and social education in the school. They know the accepted guidelines to tutors, who the experts are and what they can do and they know what the development council expects of 'ascendant' tutors. Tutors have had a hand in or have approved the total curriculum package.

Viewed from this solid ethical and intellectual position the behaviour of pupils can be assessed. Teachers must always be ready to accept that non co-operation may suggest that they and the development council ought to think again about their plans because we are asking that these plans take cognisance of pupils' environmental and personal needs. Perhaps the plans are not good enough in these respects. Rather than being a case for 'discipline' or 'punishment' it is a case for more evaluation.

The plan may be good but some pupils are in need of special help to take advantage of it. In other words, the plan must include ways of persuading pupils of its worth. This is simply another dimension of special need, rather like physical disability or cultural difference is a special need. Being very gifted at a particular activity is a special need.

But if special and/or individual work fails there is some logic in going beyond persuasion and trying to force pupils to co-operate through threat of sanctions and then, if necessary, the actual use of them, perhaps opening up with negative sanctions, such as the withdrawal of privileges.

But schools have to accept there are always going to be pupils who are not going to respond to the efforts of the school to educate them. No matter how good the plan some individuals cannot respond to it. Sanctions are irrelevant: they turn off the pupil even more. The school cannot give up trying but the major consideration here is whether the work of others is being disrupted. There is a case for removing the disrupters to special classes or units. But the continuous hope must be that they can return to normal classes because they retain their rights to education like anybody else. It is very dangerous to keep pupils in permanent isolation (it certainly defeats any sort of 'comprehensive' principle).

Schools must be in a position to justify their programmes (through self-evaluation) and thus justify the removal of pupils from its mainstream. Special units used to prop up schools which are not in the habit of evaluating their own work are very dubious. Many pupils do not return from these sort of units.

A proper process has no need of words like 'discipline' and 'punishment', bringing with them a tradition of non-evaluation, narrow-mindedness and injustice. The proper process reads: evaluation, development, special need, temporary removal if necessary. Certainly, one or more of the school's experts can administer these temporary devices.

If all members of staff are tutors there is no room for experts who are not tutors. Some schools have employed 'counsellors' for special work in personal education but this role must dilute the 'ascendant' role of tutors and perpetuate the separated 'pastoral' idea and the idea that teachers are either 'pastoral' or 'academic' creatures.

Curriculum

How can curriculum support the structures of government and organization already outlined and the needs of opportunity, potential and culture? It calls for wide curriculum objectives covering personal and social education (including political education and democracy and community work), vocational education, the pursuit of personal interests and special opportunities for girls. The total package is enormously eased by the presence of tutors who feel responsible for all parts of it even if their expertises emphasize various parts of it.

However teachers carry out their work there is a lot to be said for collaboration between them wherever possible. This is a straight 'education through example' in personal and social education and it makes far better use of resources and expertises.

The staff becomes a community in itself. This does not gainsay that they are specialists or that they need 'private space' in which to operate. The 'ascendant' tutor may provide some of this. But basic teamwork aids the concept of a development council.

There is a problem about compulsion in the curriculum. If a school is democratic and based on good interpersonal relationships is not compulsion against the grain? It depends on whether you are compelling particular material or types of activity. From all that has been written in this chapter it is clear that no curriculum should be without personal and social education. Moreover, because of the need to work with communities some form of community education must form part of the social education, and this includes political education (because communities are political entities) and vocational education because work is a crucial part of personal and social education and because localities have work places. In the range of personal education the potential of individuals must be considered and their economic opportunities, possibly through further or higher education. Personal and social education should also include questions of health and physical well-being and moral issues. All these activities require communication skills and most of them require numerical skills.

Compulsion simply asks here that all these matters should be attended to. How a school does it or what material they use is really up to them, the experts. But in addition we could ask for the stimulation of interest among pupils, material relevant to their own experience but also material which engages crucial issues, many of them controversial. Teachers cannot go blithely teaching on without response from pupils. If they do so they are not teaching. No education will take place unless something happens in the minds of the pupils. There is no point in them being present if this does not happen. We are not only referring here to direct work in personal and social education but to all ranges of the curriculum; indeed, this makes all ranges of the curriculum personal and social. Since personal and social approaches must involve the pupils perhaps we are looking here for more verbal interaction with pupils, more discussions, more pupil research, in short, more pupil thinking and language development. School subjects which have these activities in very short supply will have to consider whether they deserve the label 'narrowly meritocratic'.

In this compulsory package – of types of activity, not material – it is interesting to note that the flexible arrangement of whole group, small group and individual teaching works very well. In personal education consultancy can take place on an individual basis but can also involve group work on interpersonal relationships and some whole group work on information related to this and wider moral issues. In political education there can be individual projects connected with issues in the locality, group discussion on these and some fact-giving sessions to whole groups on wider political issues. Physical education is traditionally conveyed in flexible grouping and individual work. For community education there can again be projects, discussions and talks, and the same is true of vocational education. Obviously, many of these activities are closely related and can take place simultaneously within the same lessons. Work in traditional subjects or integrated topics for opportunity or for personal interest can be treated with similar flexibility.

Such flexibility is a friend of education for special need, especially embraced by small group or individual work. This will accommodate cultural exemplification, special intellectual and physical needs and emotional needs (including disruptives). Even if some teachers cannot modify traditionally monolithic approaches to allow in other teachers and their expertise, new resources and flexibility of teaching methods this does not mean they also have to cut out other cultures and responses to special needs.

What should be the priorities in framing curriculum items? The first priority must rest with the development of language and numeracy, underwriting all curriculum areas. Language needs may largely be served by the school subject called 'English', special lessons in the English language and its literature, but not to the exclusion of concern for 'language across the curriculum', the Bullock Report slogan (Bullock 1975). This report noted the neglect of oral skills, still neglected according to the HMI follow-up of Bullock (DES 1982a). There is clear evidence (e.g. in the

HMI secondary survey (DES 1979), in DES (1982a) and in Weeks (1983)) that few comprehensive schools have responded to a policy of 'language across the curriculum'.

Similar criticisms also refer to the teaching of mathematics. In far too many schools this is not related to the everyday, practical world nor to science and technology (DES 1979, Cockcroft 1982). The Assessment of Performance Unit (APU) of the DES found that 15 year olds were much better at mathematics when they thought that it was useful, i.e. related to practical and scientific matters (DES (APU) 1981). Cockcroft (1982) concluded that there were far too few discussion, practical and problem-solving lessons in mathematics (see also Burkhardt 1982).

Priority two must be scientific and technological awareness. Whether we like it or not science and technology hold out the promise of health and prosperity, leisure and happiness and the threat of destruction. Schools should also adopt a slogan of 'science and technology across the curriculum'. Teachers of all subjects should show awareness of it in their material and methods.

If priority three is personal, social and vocational education, for which I have argued strongly in this chapter, equally persuasive arguments now refer to awareness of people and concerns beyond our national boundaries, an international, world-wide awareness (priority four).

The problem in having a mounting list of essential curriculum items is lack of time for all of them. But a certain economy may be achieved in two main ways: one, by using the mantle of multi-cultural education, two, by using the device of options for individual pupils. The economy of multi-cultural education, in terms of the priorities outlined above, rests in combining studies of the lives of people in the neighbourhoods of schools whose origins were in other parts of the world with studies of those other parts, including their languages.

Individual choice can be made available in the upper school curriculum, essentially the present system in schools. It is essential to maintain here a compulsory module in personal, social and vocational education but, beyond this, there is room for specialization, possibly a selection from social studies, political studies or economic studies. Choice in multi-cultural education can be between language, literature, drama, history, religion, art or craft, with one element related to the locality of the school and a second element to another region of the world.

The pastoral curriculum must continue into the sixth form, a compulsory personal, social and vocational unit for all students, embracing the 14 to 19 concept. To give multi-cultural education the status it needs one of its elements, either local or foreign, should persist in the curriculum. Elitists may complain about the edging out of specialisms directed towards further or higher education, especially where three A levels are expected, possibly in the physical sciences and/or mathematics. The solution here may be my proposed three-year sixth form (again, fitting in well with a 14 to 19 concept). I cannot see why people should complain about the delay of entry to higher education: other youngsters are having their vocation held back because of the economic situation. Make use of this situation by creating a comprehensive three-year sixth form. The projected AS levels might also solve a problem for students directed to combine curricular depth and breadth. Also, AS levels could be taken in both the compulsory elements, the pastoral and the multi-cultural.

Alienation – a way out

A section in Chapter 9 traced some of the patterns of alienation in comprehensive schools. Scarce resources and falling rolls may also reduce the capacity of many schools to do something for their pupils. But a more serious problem appears to be the straight rejection of schooling by many pupils, whether the schooling in question is good or bad. Part of this problem is in the economic inequality which reduces some families to poverty, and to unemployment and thus more poverty. Social alienation, however, goes a lot deeper than this: it is part of our social heritage. I would not attempt to analyse it further here.

What can schools do about this? No one should blame them for the alienation yet many of them do little to reduce it or combat it. These schools act in ways which confirm existing social hierarchies and divisions. So, the depressing social experience of some pupils is exacerbated by the schools, yet another blow to their status, their self-esteem and their dignity. No wonder many of them rebel in this situation or at least refuse to co-operate.

Some surface reforms would help, such as getting rid of silly rules and regulations which harrass and irritate young people, rules to do with dress and rituals of 'petty deference', as Peter Daunt (1975) described them. Moreover, using official violence against pupils already relieved of other human rights will not establish fond regard for institutions already alien and hostile. What an anachronism this is. Some pupils, in fact, hardly care whether they are belted or not since they expect schools to give them a 'pain up the posterior'. But for more sensitive personalities corporal punishment may remove the last vestiges of respect for an institution which appears to exist for the benefit of others already claiming considerable social advantages.

Bringing in the 16-plus examination (the GCSE) may help to soften the sharp meritocratic edge of the GCE/CSE divide, and although we are well aware that the new grading system retains sheep and goatery at least there can be a little more egalitarian hope in a united system, rather as there was more faith and hope in comprehensive schools compared to tripartite schools. But teachers could do far more with the present examination system and the one to come by making more use of Mode 3 and school-based assessments, reflecting curriculum relevance to individuals and cultures. It is not possible to blame Sir Keith for the relatively poor use of Mode 3.

My answer to alienation would be a school government, organization and curriculum described in this chapter, based on combined meritocratic and egalitarian objectives, with a special responsibility to help communities, which, in turn, can help schools to establish a separate identity in society. This is not an argument for non-accountable schools, which is silly, but for schools which give credit to the special expertise of their teachers (who need to ensure that they have it). Are schools to be no more than lackeys of a socio-economic meritocracy? This is a sad dependence and a powerlessness. A strong political system needs a liberal education system.

The school with wide educational objectives is the self-evaluating and self-developing institution with a curriculum relevant to the pupils it has and what it can do for them and their communities. The school programme, too, must stimulate pupils so that they do not drop off into the boredom and inattention which is the hallmark of too many classrooms. The teaching material must be personal and social, and one of the best ways of achieving this is to make it controversial. Is this beyond the wit of experts in pedagogy, which teachers must aspire to be? Lessons in all curriculum areas must move into crucial socio-political and moral issues. This is the basis for effective learning, backed by a strong tutorial system, in turn backed by a staff development council, staff collaboration and an integrated pastoral/academic organization and by the head teacher.

In short, we should be saying to pupils – and meaning it – that we are interested in them as persons and how they might behave or have behaved in interpersonal situations and in various wider social situations and organizations, including those concerned with vocation; interested in their physical well-being, their special talents and needs, their cultural origins and environments, their ability to communicate and be numerate; interested in how they might fare in future careers, possibly after further or higher education. This is a way out of alienation, as far as schools are concerned anyway. It is a process which requires people of courage in schools in the way that Michael Duane of Risinghill was a courageous man (Berg 1968). The Advisory Centre for Education (ACE 1985) re-read Leila Berg's book in 1985 and found its message as relevant and challenging as it was in 1968.

Bibliography

(Books, chapters and articles marked with an asterisk indicate that they are recommended for further reading on comprehensive schools.)

Advisory Centre for Education (ACE) (1985) 'Risinghill – the unfinished experiment' *ACE Bulletin*, 4, March–April, 4–7.

Allen, Bryan (1968) 'How Head Teachers are Chosen' in Allen, Bryan (ed.) *Headship in the 1970s*, Oxford, Basil Blackwell.

Allison, Ralph and Woods, Robin (1970) 'Points of Disagreement' in Donnison, David (Chairman) *Public Schools Commission. Second Report*, vol. 1, London, HMSO.

Anderson, Digby C. (1982) *Detecting Bad Schools. A Guide for Normal Parents*, London, The Social Affairs Unit.

*Armstrong, Michael and King, Lesley (1977) 'Schools Within Schools: the Countesthorpe "team" system' in Watts, John (ed.) *The Countesthorpe Experience. The First Five Years*, London, George Allen & Unwin.

*Armstrong, Michael (1970) 'The case for small comprehensive schools', *Where*, 50, July, 100–2.

Ashford, Douglas E. (1974) 'The effect of central finance on the British local government system', *British Journal of Political Science*, 4(3), 305–22.

Assistant Masters' Association (AMA) (1974) *Mixed-Ability Teaching*, London, AMA.

Bagnall, Colin (1977) 'Taking the plunge', *Times Educational Supplement (TES)*, 30 September.

Baldwin, R. W. (1979) *Performance at GCE A Level in Maintained Schools*, London, National Council for Educational Standards (NCES).

—— (1980) 'Exam rights and wrongs', *Times Educational Supplement (TES)*, 11 January.

—— (1981) *Secondary Schools, 1965–1979*, London, National Council for Educational Standards (NCES).

*Ball, Stephen, J. (1981) *Beachside Comprehensive. A Case Study of Secondary Schooling*, Cambridge, Cambridge University Press.

*—— (1984) *Comprehensive Schools. A Reader*, London, Falmer Press.

Barker, Bernard (1982) 'Root-based leader or cloud-based manager', *Times Educational Supplement (TES)*, 8 October.

*Barrow, Robin (1977) 'Competence and the Head' in Peters, R. S. (ed.) *The Role of the Head*, London, Routledge & Kegan Paul.

Barton, Len and Tomlinson, Sally (eds) (1982) *Special Education: Policy, Practice and Social Issues*, London, Harper & Row.

Basini, Augustine (1981) 'Urban schools and disruptive pupils: a study of some ILEA support units', *Educational Review*, 33(3) November, 191–206.

*Batley, Richard, O'Brien, Oswald and Parris, Henry (1970) *Going Comprehensive. Educational policy-making in two county boroughs*, London, Routledge & Kegan Paul.

*Bellaby, Paul (1977) *The Sociology of Comprehensive Schooling*, London, Methuen.

Benn, Caroline (1968) *Comprehensive Reorganisation in Britain*, London, Comprehensive Schools Committee for the Campaign for Comprehensive Education.

*—— (1972) *Comprehensive Schools in 1972. Reorganisation Plans to 1975*, London, Comprehensive Schools Committee for the Campaign for Comprehensive Education.

—— (1980) 'Selection still blocks growth of comprehensives', *Where*, 158, May, 8–11.

—— (1982) 'The myth of giftedness', *Forum for the Discussion of New Trends in Education*, 24, 2 and 3, Spring and Summer, 50–2 and 78–84.

Benn, Caroline and Simon, Brian (1970) *Half Way There. Report on the British Comprehensive School Reform*, London, McGraw-Hill.

*—— (1972) *Half Way There. Report on the British Comprehensive School Reform*, Harmondsworth, Penguin.

*Berg, Leila (1968) *Risinghill: Death of a Comprehensive School*, Harmondsworth, Penguin.

Best, Ron (1983) *Education and Care: the study of a school and its pastoral organisation*, London, Heinemann Educational.

Best, Ron, Jarvis, Colin and Ribbins, Peter (eds) (1983) *Perspectives on Pastoral Care*, London, Heinemann Educational.

Beynon, John (1984) *Initial Encounters in a Comprehensive School*, London, Falmer Press.

Blackie, Penny (1977) 'Not quite proper', *Times Educational Supplement (TES)*, 25 November.

—— (1980) 'Glad to be out of it all', *Times Educational Supplement (TES)*, 25 April.

Blyth, W. A. L. and Derricott, R. (1977) *The Social Significance of Middle Schools*, London, Batsford.

Booth, Tony and Statham, June (eds) (1982) *The Nature of Special Education*, London, Croom Helm.

Booth, Tony and Pym, Christopher (1982) 'Some aspects of Special Education in Oxfordshire' in Booth, Tony and Statham, June (eds) *The Nature of Special Education*, London, Croom Helm.

Boyson, Rhodes (1974) *Over-subscribed: Story of Highbury Grove*, London, Ward Lock Educational.

—— (1975) *The Crisis in Education*, London, The Woburn Press.

Briault, Eric and Smith, Frances (1980) *Falling Rolls in Secondary Schools (Part One)*, Slough, National Foundation for Educational Research (NFER).

Briault, Eric (1982) 'A case for change', *Times Educational Supplement (TES)*, 26 February.

Brooks, Caroline St John (1982) 'Loose in the city: the underworld of roaming children', *New Society*, 23 September, 491–4.

Bruner, Jerome, S. (1972) *The Relevance of Education*, London, George Allen & Unwin.

Bullock, Sir Alan (Chairman) (1975) *A Language for Life (Bullock Report)*, London, HMSO.

*Burgess, Robert, C. (1984) *Experiencing Comprehensive Education: a study of Bishop McGregor School*, London, Methuen.

*Burgess, Tyrrell (1970) *Inside Comprehensive Schools*, London, HMSO.

Burgess, Tyrrell and Travers, Tony (1980) *Ten Billion Pounds: Whitehall's takeover of the town halls*, London, Grant McIntyre.

Burghes, Louise (1980) *Living from Hand to Mouth*, London, Child Poverty Action Group.

Burkhardt, Hugh (1982) 'The missing classroom activities', *Times Educational Supplement (TES)*, 22 October.

Burrows, John (1978) *Middle Schools – High Road or Dead End?*, London, The Woburn Press.

Burt, Sir Cyril (1975) *The Gifted Child*, London, Hodder & Stoughton.

Button, Leslie (1980) 'The Skills of Group Tutoring' in Best, R., Jarvis, C. and Ribbins, P. (eds) *Perspectives on Pastoral Care*, London, Heinemann Educational.

Byrne, Eileen, M. (1974) *Planning and Educational Inequality: a study of the rationale of resource-allocation*, Slough, National Foundation for Educational Research (NFER).

Clegg, Sir Alec (1965) 'West Riding of Yorkshire' in Maclure, Stuart (ed.) *Comprehensive Planning. A symposium on the reorganisation of secondary education*, London, Councils and Educational Press.

Clifford, Peter and Heath, Anthony (1984) 'Selection does make a difference', *Oxford Review of Education*, 10(1), 85–97.

Cockcroft, W. H. (Chairman) (1982) *Committee of Inquiry into the Teaching of Mathematics in Primary and Secondary Schools in England and Wales.* Mathematics Counts, London, HMSO.

Cooke, George (1980) 'Too tough at the top', *Times Educational Supplement (TES)*, 1 February.

Cornall, Peter (1983) 'Carisbrooke High School, Isle of Wight. Implementing the Common Curriculum' in Moon, Bob (ed.) *Comprehensive Schools: Challenge and Change*, Slough, NFER–Nelson.

Cottle, Thomas (1978) *Black Testimony*, London, Wildwood House.

Cox, C. B. and Boyson, Rhodes (eds) (1975) *Black Paper 1975. The Fight for Education*, London, Dent.

Cox, C. B. and Dyson, A. E. (1969) *The Fight for Education*, London, The Critical Quarterly Society.

Crosland, Anthony (1962) *The Future of Socialism*, London, Jonathan Cape.

*Daunt, P. E. (1975) *Comprehensive Values*, London, Heinemann Educational.

Davies, Jean (1980) *Attendance at 3 Secondary Schools*, London, Inner London Education Authority (ILEA).

*Dawson, Peter (1981) *Making a Comprehensive Work. The Road from Bomb Alley*, Oxford, Basil Blackwell.

Dawson, R. L. (1980) *Special Provision for Disturbed Pupils: a Survey (Schools Council Research Studies)*, Basingstoke and London, Macmillan Educational.

Dean, J., Bradley, K., Choppin, B. and Vincent, D. (1979) *The Sixth Form and its Alternatives*, Slough, National Foundation for Educational Research (NFER).

*Department of Education and Science (DES) (1965) *The Organisation of Secondary Education (Circular 10/65)*, London, HMSO.

—— (1966) *New Problems in School Design: Middle Schools. Building Bulletin 35*, London, HMSO.

—— (1972) *Education: A Framework for Expansion*, London, HMSO.

—— (1974) *Community Service in Education (Education Survey 20)*, London, HMSO.

—— (1977a) *Curriculum 11 to 16: working papers by HM Inspectorate: a contribution to current debate*, London, DES.

—— (1977b) *Gifted Children in Middle and Comprehensive Secondary Schools: a discussion paper by a working party of Her Majesty's Inspectorate*, London, HMSO.

—— (1977c) *Ten Good Schools: a secondary school inquiry (HMI Series: Matters for Discussion, 1)*, London, HMSO.

—— (1978a) *Mixed-ability Work in Comprehensive Schools: a discussion paper by a working party of Her Majesty's Inspectorate (HMI Series: Matters for Discussion, 6)*, London, HMSO.

*—— (1978b) *Comprehensive Education. Report of a Conference held at the*

invitation of the Secretary of State for Education and Science at the University of York on 16–17 December, 1977, London, HMSO.
—— (1978c) *Behavioural Units: a survey of special units for pupils with behavioural problems*, London, DES.
*—— (1979) *Aspects of Secondary Education in England: a survey by HM Inspectors of Schools*, London, HMSO.
—— (1981a) *Statistics of Schools 1979*, London, HMSO.
—— (1981b) *The Effects on the Education Service of Local Authority Expenditure Policies. Financial Year 1980*, London, HMSO.
—— (1982a) *Bullock Revisited: a discussion paper by HMI*, London, DES.
—— (1982b) *The Effects on the Education Service of Local Authority Expenditure Policies. Financial Year 1981*, London, HMSO.
—— (1982c) *The New Teacher in School: a report by Her Majesty's Inspectors (HMI Series: Matters for Discussion, 15)*, London, HMSO.
—— (1982d) *Education Statistics for the United Kingdom 1980*, London, HMSO.
—— (1983) *9–13 Middle Schools. An illustrative survey*, London, HMSO.
—— (1984) *Parental Influence at School: a new framework for school government in England and Wales*, London, HMSO.
—— (1985a) *Better Schools*, London, HMSO.
—— (1985b) *Education 8–12 in Combined and Middle Schools*, London, HMSO.
Department of Education and Science, Assessment of Performance Unit (APU) (1981) *Mathematical Development. Secondary Survey Report No. 2*, London, HMSO.
Dickson, David (1975) '"Remote" DES condemned for secrecy in OECD report', *Times Higher Educational Supplement (THES)*, 9 May.
Dierenfield, Richard, B. (1982) 'All you need to know about disruption', *Times Educational Supplement (TES)*, 29 January.
Doe, Bob (1983) 'The virtues of necessity', *Times Educational Supplement (TES)*, 18 February.
Donnison, D. V. and Chapman, Valerie (1965) *Social Policy and Administration*, London, George Allen & Unwin.
Donnison, D. V. (1967) 'Education and opinion', *New Society*, 26 October, 583–7.
Donnison, David (1968) *Public Schools Commission. First Report*, London, HMSO.
—— (1970) *Public Schools Commission. Second Report*, vol. 1, London, HMSO.
Doran, Anthony (1981) 'Education writers as whipping boys', *Times Educational Supplement (TES)*, 13 February.
Douglas, J. W. B. (1964) *The Home and the School. A Study of Ability and Attainment in the Primary Schools*, London, Macgibbon & Kee.
Durham, Mike (1983) 'Big is best', *Times Educational Supplement (TES)*, 25 March.

Eggleston, John (1965) 'How comprehensive is the Leicestershire plan?', *New Society*, 25 March, 17.

—— (ed.) (1980) *School-based Curriculum Development in Britain: a collection of case studies*, London, Routledge & Kegan Paul.

—— (1982) *Work Experience in Secondary Schools*, London, Routledge & Kegan Paul.

Evans, Bob (1983) 'Countesthorpe College, Leicester. The Countesthorpe team system: towards the "mini" school' in Moon, Bob (ed.) *Comprehensive Schools: Challenge and Change*, Slough, NFER–Nelson.

Everard, K. B. (1982) *Management in Comprehensive Schools: what can be learnt from industry*, York, Centre for the Study of Comprehensive Schools, University of York.

Exeter University (1982) *Perspectives 1. The Rutter Research*, Exeter, School of Education, University of Exeter.

*Fenwick, I. G. K. (1976) *The Comprehensive School 1944–1970*, London, Methuen.

Field, Frank (ed.) (1977) *Education and the Urban Crisis*, London, Routledge & Kegan Paul.

*Fiske, Dudley (1982) *Reorganisation in Secondary Education in Manchester (Bedford Way Paper 9)*, London, University of London Institute of Education.

Flecknoe, Mervyn (1983) 'The Sutton Centre, Mansfield, Nottinghamshire. A philosophy of assessment' in Moon, Bob (ed.) *Comprehensive Schools: Challenge and Change*, Slough, NFER–Nelson.

Fletcher, Colin (1983) *The Challenge of Community Education: a biography of Sutton Centre 1970 to 1982*, Nottingham, Department of Adult Education, University of Nottingham.

—— (1985) 'Paying the price of democracy', *Times Educational Supplement (TES)*, 8 February.

*Fletcher, C., Caron, M. and Williams, W. (1985) *Schools on Trial: the Trials of Democratic Comprehensives*, Milton Keynes, Open University Press.

Fogelman, Ken (ed.) (1976) *Britain's Sixteen-Year-Olds. Preliminary findings from the third follow-up of the National Child Development Study (1958 cohort)*, London, National Children's Bureau.

*Ford, Julienne (1969) *Social Class and the Comprehensive School*, London, Routledge & Kegan Paul.

Galloway, D., Ball, T., Blomfield, D. and Seyd, R. (1982) *Schools and Disruptive Pupils*, London, Longman.

Galton, Maurice and Willcocks, John (eds) (1983) *Moving from the Primary Classroom*, London, Routledge & Kegan Paul.

Garner, Richard (1983) 'Pay as you learn crisis hits schools', *Times Educational Supplement (TES)*, 6 May.

Gill, C. James (1974) 'The Possibilities of Counselling' in Marland, Michael (ed.) *Pastoral Care*, London, Heinemann Educational.

Goldstein, Harvey (1981) 'Research on comprehensive schools', *Forum for the Discussion of New Trends in Education*, 23(3), Summer, 79–81.

—— (1984) 'The methodology of school comparisons', *Oxford Review of Education*, 10(1), 69–74.

Gooch, Malcolm (1982) 'Out of bounds', *Times Educational Supplement (TES)*, 10 September.

Gray, John and Jones, Ben (1983) 'Disappearing data', *Times Educational Supplement (TES)*, 15 July.

*Gray, J., McPherson, A. F. and Raffe, D. (1983) *Reconstruction in Secondary Education: Theory, Myth and Practice since the War*, London, Routledge & Kegan Paul.

Gray, John, Jensen, David and Jones, Ben (1985) 'The verdict is still not proven', *Times Educational Supplement (TES)*, 26 July.

*Griffiths, A. (1971) *Secondary School Reorganisation in England and Wales*, London, Routledge & Kegan Paul.

Groves, Malcolm (1980) *Community Service and the Secondary School*, Leicester, National Youth Bureau.

Grunsell, Rob (1981) *Beyond Control? Schools and Suspension*, London and Richmond, Writers and Readers and Chameleon.

*Halsall, Elizabeth (ed.) (1970) *Becoming Comprehensive. Case Histories*, Oxford, Pergamon Press.

*—— (1973) *The Comprehensive School. Guidelines for the Reorganisation of Secondary Education*, Oxford, Pergamon Press.

Hargreaves, A. and Tickle, L. (eds) (1980) *Middle Schools: Origins, ideology and practice*, London, Harper & Row.

*Hargreaves, David H. (1982) *The Challenge for the Comprehensive School. Culture, curriculum and community*, London, Routledge & Kegan Paul.

Harvey, Bernard (1980) 'LEA versus community', *Times Educational Supplement (TES)*, 17 October.

Hegarty, Seamus and Pocklington, Keith (1982) *Integration in Action: case studies in the integration of pupils with special needs*, Slough, NFER–Nelson.

*Hill, Christopher, J. (1972) *Transfer at Eleven*, Slough, National Foundation for Educational Research (NFER).

*Himmelweit, Hilde (1970) 'Why we cannot afford to stream', *Comprehensive Education*, 16, 12–13.

Hirst, P. H. and Peters, R. S. (1970) *The Logic of Education*, London, Routledge & Kegan Paul.

Hitchfield, E. M. (1973) *In Search of Promise. A Long-term National Study of Able Children and their Families*, London, Longman.

Hodgson, Ann, Clunies-Ross, Louise and Hegarty, Seamus (1984) *Learning Together. Teaching Pupils with Special Educational Needs in the Ordinary School*, Slough, NFER–Nelson.

Hood, R. H. (1983) 'Proven worth or proven wrong?', *Times Educational Supplement (TES)*, 6 May.

Hughes, Cyril (1965) 'Secondary modern love story: enchantment lends distance', *Times Educational Supplement (TES)*, 19 March.

Inner London Education Authority (ILEA) (1966) *London Comprehensive Schools*, London, ILEA.

—— (1984) *Improving Secondary Schools: report of the Committee on the Curriculum and Organisation of Secondary Schools*, London, ILEA.

Izbicki, John (1979a) 'Too good to die', *Daily Telegraph*, 15 October.

—— (1979b) 'When cuts have to be made', *Daily Telegraph*, 26 November.

Jackson, Brian and Marsden, Dennis (1962) *Education and the Working Class*, London, Routledge & Kegan Paul.

*James, Philip, H. (1980) *The Reorganisation of Secondary Education: A study of local policy making*, Slough, National Foundation for Educational Research (NFER).

Jayne, E. (1980) *Trained for the Job*, London, Inner London Education Authority (ILEA), Research and Statistics Branch.

Jennings, Robert, E. (1977) *Education and Politics: policy-making in local education authorities*, London, Batsford.

Jones, Arfon (1980) 'Sidney Stringer School and Community College' in Fletcher, Colin and Thompson, Neil (eds) *Issues in Community Education*, Lewes, Falmer Press.

—— (1983) 'Sidney Stringer School and Community College, Coventry. A developing relationship between a multi-cultural population and an educationl institution' in Moon, Bob (ed.) *Comprehensive Schools: Challenge and Change*, Slough, NFER–Nelson.

Kerrison, Martin (1985) 'A Leicestershire cluster', *Forum for the Discussion of New Trends in Education*, 27(3), Summer, 83–5.

Kogan, Maurice and Van der Eyken, William (1973) *County Hall: the Role of the Chief Education Officer*, Harmondsworth, Penguin.

Kogan, Maurice (1981) 'Platform', *Times Educational Supplement (TES)*, 30 January.

Lacey, Colin (1984) 'Selective and non-selective schooling: real or mythical comparisons?' in *Oxford Review of Education*, 10(1), 75–84.

Little, Alan, Mabey, Christine and Russell, Jennifer (1972) 'How to skim cream', *Times Educational Supplement (TES)*, 30 June.

Lydiat, Mike (1977) 'Mixed ability teaching gains ground', *Comprehensive Education*, 35, Winter, 12–16.

MacDonald, Barry (1979) 'Hard times: Educational accountability in England', *Educational Analysis*, 1(1), 23–43.

Macfarlane, Eric (1978) *Sixth-form Colleges: the 16–19 comprehensives*, London, Heinemann Educational.

McHugh, Royston (1976) *A Case Study in Management. Sidney Stringer School and Community College*, Milton Keynes, Open University Press.

Makins, Virginia (1983a) 'Exams cause of narrow teaching', *Times Educational Supplement (TES)*, 27 May.

—— (1983b) 'Total curriculum', *Times Educational Supplement (TES)*, 16 December.

—— (1984) 'London's pride', *Times Educational Supplement (TES)*, 30 March.

—— (1985a) 'The pioneer that began to lose its way', *Times Educational Supplement (TES)*, 15 February.

—— (1985b) 'The full course', *Times Educational Supplement (TES)*, 26 July.

*Marland, Michael (1974) *Pastoral Care*, London, Heinemann Educational.

—— (1980) 'The Pastoral Curriculum' in Best, Ron, Jarvis, Colin, and Ribbins, Peter (eds) *Perspectives on Pastoral Care*, London, Heinemann Educational.

Marks, John, Cox, Caroline and Pomian-Srzednicki, Maciej (1983) *Standards in English Schools. An analysis of the examination results of secondary schools in England in 1981*, London, National Council for Educational Standards (NCES).

Marks, John and Pomian-Srzednicki, Maciej (1985) *Standards in English Schools. Second Report*, London, National Council for Educational Standards (NCES).

*Marsden, Dennis (1969) 'Which comprehensive principle?', *Comprehensive Education*, 13, 2–5.

—— (1971) *Politicians, Equality and Comprehensives, Fabian Society Tract 411*, London, Fabian Society.

Marsh, Peter, Rosser, Elizabeth and Harre, Rom (1978) *The Rules of Disorder*, London, Routledge & Kegan Paul.

*Mason, Stewart (1970) *In Our Experience. The changing Schools of Leicestershire*, London, Longman.

*Measor, Lynda and Woods, Peter (1984) *Changing Schools. Pupil Perspectives on Transfer to a Comprehensive*, Milton Keynes, Open University Press.

Miles, Margaret (1968) *Comprehensive Schooling, Problems and Perspectives*, London, Longman.

*Monks, T. G. (1968) *Comprehensive Education in England and Wales*, Slough, National Foundation for Educational Research (NFER).

*—— (ed.) (1970) *Comprehensive Education in Action*, Slough, National Foundation for Educational Research (NFER).

*Moon, Bob (ed.) (1983) *Comprehensive Schools: Challenge and Change*, Slough, NFER–Nelson.

Moore, David (1979) 'A second-generation immigrant's view of society – aims, aspirations and educational needs', *Trends in Education*, Winter, 13–18.

Musgrove, Frank (1971) *Patterns of Power and Authority in English Education*, London, Methuen.

National Union of Teachers (NUT) (1962) *The State of our Schools*, London, NUT.

Naylor, Fred (1975) 'Day of the dogmatists', *Times Educational Supplement (TES)*, 14 February.
—— (1983) 'Proving worth in selective schools', *Times Educational Supplement (TES)*, 29 April.
Neave, Guy, R. (1975) *How They Fared. The Impact of the Comprehensive School upon the University*, London, Routledge & Kegan Paul.
—— (1982) 'On the edge of the abyss: an overview of recent developments in European higher education', *European Journal of Education*, 17(2), 123–44.
Newbold, David (1977) *Ability Grouping and the Banbury Enquiry*, Slough, National Foundation for Educational Research (NFER).
Newell, Peter (ed.) (1972) *A Last Resort? Corporal punishment in schools*, Harmondsworth, Penguin.
Newsom, John (Chairman) (1963) *Half our Future; a report*, London, Ministry of Education.
Nisbet, John, D. and Entwistle, Noel (1966) *The Age of Transfer to Secondary Education*, London, University of London Press.
Norcross, Lawrence (1981) 'Education writers as whipping boys', *Times Educational Supplement (TES)*, 13 February.
O'Connell, P. J. (1970) 'Sir Richard of Chichester School, London' in Halsall, Elizabeth (ed.) *Becoming Comprehensive. Case Histories*, Oxford, Pergamon Press.
O'Connor, Margaret (1982) 'The middle muddle', *The Guardian*, 18 May.
—— (1977) 'Who is liberated now?', *Times Educational Supplement (TES)*, 1 April.
Parkinson, Michael (1970) *The Labour Party and the Organisation of Secondary Education, 1918–1965*, London, Routledge & Kegan Paul.
Passmore, Biddy (1981) 'Mapping the future', *Times Educational Supplement (TES)*, 11 September.
Passmore, Biddy and Durham, Mike (1984) '11-plus plans come under parental fire', *Times Educational Supplement (TES)*, 15 June.
*Pedley, Robin (1963) *The Comprehensive School*, Harmondsworth, Penguin.
*—— (1978) *The Comprehensive School (Third Edition)*, Harmondsworth, Penguin.
Peschek, David and Brand, J. (1966) *Policies and Politics in Secondary Education: Case studies in West Ham and Reading*, London, London School of Economics and Political Science.
Peters, R. S. (1970) *Ethics and Education*, London, George Allen & Unwin.
Poster, Cyril (1981) 'Where will it end?', *Times Educational Supplement (TES)*, 20 March.
—— (1982) 'Pulling together', *Times Educational Supplement (TES)*, 4 June.

Postlethwaite, Keith and Denton, Cliff (1978) *Streams for the Future? The long term effects of early streaming and non-streaming – the final report of the Banbury Grouping enquiry*, Banbury, Pubansco, Banbury School.

Price, Christopher (1973) 'What is wrong with our secondary schools?', *Times Educational Supplement (TES)*, 2 March.

Radical Statistics Education Group (1982) *Reading between the Numbers. A critical guide to educational research*, London, BSSRS Publications.

Raynor, John and Harris, Elizabeth (eds) (1977) *Schooling in the City*, London, Ward Lock Educational.

Ree, Harry (1980) 'A case of arrested development?', *Times Educational Supplement (TES)*, 17 October.

Redpath, Andrew and Ackroyd, Neville (1980) 'Mini-detention centres', *Times Educational Supplement (TES)*, 14 November.

Reid, Ivan (1981) *Social Class Differences in Britain: a Sourcebook*, London, Open Books.

Reid, Margaret, Clunies-Ross, Louise, Goacher, Brian and Vile, Carol (1981) *Mixed-ability Teaching: Problems and possibilities*, Slough, NFER–Nelson.

Richardson, Elizabeth (1975) *Authority and Organisation in the Secondary School*, London and Basingstoke, Macmillan Educational.

Ridley, Frank (1980) 'To do is to understand', *Times Educational Supplement (TES)*, 11 July.

Robertson, T. S. (1977) 'Pupil progress in ten comprehensive schools: a follow-up study', *Comprehensive Education*, 36, Summer, 8–19.

Robbins, Lionel Charles (1st Baron Robbins) (1963) *Higher Education: report of the Commission appointed by the Prime Minister*, London, HMSO.

Robbins, Wayne and Williams, Wyn (1977) 'Community education' in Raynor, John and Harris, Elizabeth (eds) *Schooling in the City*, London, Ward Lock Educational.

Rogers, Rick (1980) 'Case for revival?', *Times Educational Supplement (TES)*, 13 June.

*Ross, J. M. and Chanan, G. (1972) *Comprehensive Schools in Focus*, Slough, National Foundation for Educational Research (NFER).

*Ross, J. M., Bunton, W. J., Evison, P. and Robertson, T. S. (1972) *A Critical Appraisal of Comprehensive Education*, Slough, National Foundation for Educational Research (NFER).

Rowan, Jean (1973) *The Writing on the Blackboard*, London, Tom Stacey.

Rowan, Patricia (1977) 'Co-operation or separation?', *Times Educational Supplement (TES)*, 4 November.

Rowe, Albert (1971) *The School as a Guidance Community*, Hull, Pearson Press.

*Rubinstein, David and Simon, Brian (1973) *The Evolution of the Comprehensive School 1926–1972*, London, Routledge & Kegan Paul.

Rutter, M., Maughan, B., Mortimore, P. and Ouston, J. with Smith A.

(1979) *Fifteen Thousand Hours. Secondary Schools and their Effects on Children*, London, Open Books.

Sands, Margaret and Kerry, Trevor (eds) (1982) *Mixed-ability Teaching*, London, Croom Helm.

Saran, Rene (1973) *Policy-making in Secondary Education: a Case Study*, Oxford, Oxford University Press.

Schools Council (Department of Education and Science) (1967) *Some Further Proposals for Sixth Form Work (Working Paper No. 16)*, London, HMSO.

—— (1970) *Cross'd with Adversity: the education of socially disadvantaged children in secondary schools (Working Paper No. 27)*, London, HMSO.

Scrimshaw, Peter (1981) *Community Service, Social Education and the Curriculum*, London, Hodder & Stoughton.

Shapland, Jeff (1977) 'Individualised Learning in Science and Worksheets – My Changing Attitude Towards Them' in Watts, John (ed.) *The Countesthorpe Experience. The First Five Years*, London, George Allen & Unwin.

*Sharp, John (1973) *Open School. The Experience of 1964–1970 at Wyndham School, Egremont, Cumberland*, London, Dent.

Sharpe, Sue (1976) *'Just like a Girl'. How Girls learn to be women*, Harmondsworth, Penguin.

*Shaw, Beverley (1983) *Comprehensive Schooling. The Impossible Dream?*, Oxford, Basil Blackwell.

Smith, C. H. (1976) *Mode 3 Examinations in the CSE and GCE*, London, Evans for the Schools Council.

Society of Teachers Opposed to Physical Punishment (STOPP) (1978) *Alternatives to Corporal Punishment*, London, STOPP.

Souper, Patrick, C. and Kay, William K. (1982) *The School Assembly in Hampshire*, Southampton, Southampton University Press.

Steedman, Hilary (1982) 'Recent developments in Higher Education in the United Kingdom', *European Journal of Education*, 17(2), 193–203.

*Steedman, Jane (1983) *Examination Results in Selective and Non-selective Schools*, London, National Children's Bureau.

—— (1980) *Progress in Secondary Schools: findings from the National Child Development Study*, London, National Children's Bureau.

Stevens, Auriol (1980) *Clever Children in Comprehensive Schools*, Harmondsworth, Penguin.

Stone, Maureen (1981) *The Education of the Black Child in Britain: the myth of multiracial education*, London, Fontana.

Stradling, Robert (1979) 'Political Education in the 11 to 16 curriculum', *Cambridge Journal of Education*, 8(2 and 3), 98–109.

Stuart-Jervis, Charles (1974) 'The Teacher and the Task of the School' in Marland, Michael (ed.) *Pastoral Care*, London, Heinemann Educational.

*Sullivan, F. B. (1980) *Lord Butler: the 1944 Act in Retrospect*, Milton Keynes, Open University Press.

Taylor, Mervyn and Garson, Yvonne (1982) *Schooling in the Middle Years*, Stoke-on-Trent, Trentham Books.

Taylor, William (1973) *Heading for Change*, London, Routledge & Kegan Paul.

—— (1977) 'The Head as Manager: some criticisms' in Peters, R. S. (ed.) *The Role of the Head*, London, Routledge & Kegan Paul.

—— (1978) 'Values and accountability' in Becher, Tony and Maclure, Stuart (eds) *Accountability in Education*, Slough, National Foundation for Educational Research (NFER).

Thompson, Neil (1983) 'Abraham Moss Centre, Manchester. The experience of continuing education' in Moon, Bob (ed.) *Comprehensive Schools: Challenge and Change*, Slough, NFER–Nelson.

Thornbury, Robert (1978) *The Changing Urban School*, London, Methuen.

Times Educational Supplement (TES) (1982) 'Tough on teachers' (accounts of 11 to 16 schools by various authors, pp. 18–21), *TES*, 26 February.

Tizard, B., Burgess, T., Francis, H., Goldstein, H., Young, M., Hewison, J. and Plewis, I. (1980) *Fifteen Thousand Hours. A Discussion*, London, University of London Institute of Education.

*Toogood, Philip (1984) *The Head's Tale*, Telford, Dialogue Publications.

Trends in Education (1967) 'Community school', April, 28–32.

Turner, Glenn (1983) *The Social World of the Comprehensive School*, London, Croom Helm.

Tyler, Brian (1982) 'Kingswood: what the camera didn't show', *Times Educational Supplement (TES)*, 31 December.

Vaughan, Mark (1975) 'Selection still the norm for one pupil in four' and 'Comprehensive changeover: area by area', *Times Educational Supplement (TES)*, 21 March.

Venning, Philip (1980a) 'Yes, and then again, no, Minister', *Times Educational Supplement (TES)*, 12 December.

—— (1980b) 'A level Absolutes', *Times Educational Supplement (TES)*, 18 January.

—— (1980c) 'Overloading the system', *Times Educational Supplement (TES)*, 31 October.

—— (1980d) 'Parent power props up schools', *Times Educational Supplement (TES)*, 4 July.

—— (1981) 'A giant step to a job', *Times Educational Supplement (TES)*, 3 April.

—— (1983a) 'The walls came crumbling down', *Times Educational Supplement (TES)*, 30 September.

—— (1983b) 'The mystery of the vanishing students', *Times Educational Supplement (TES)*, 25 November.

Vernon, P. (ed.) (1957) *Secondary School Selection. A British Psychological Society Enquiry*, London, Methuen.

Warnock, Mary (Chairman) (1978) *Special Educational Needs: Report of the Enquiry into the Education of Handicapped Children and Young People*, London, HMSO.

Watkins, Peter (1983) *The Sixth Form College in Practice*, London, Edward Arnold.

Watts, A. G. (ed.) (1983) *Work Experience and Schools*, London, Heinemann Educational.

Watts, Janet (1974a) 'Sir, you bastard', *The Guardian*, 3 October.

—— (1974b) 'The gang leader', *The Guardian*, 4 October.

Watts, John (1976) 'Sharing it Out: the role of the Head in Participatory Government' in Peters, R. S. (ed.) *The Role of the Head*, London, Routledge & Kegan Paul.

*—— (ed.) (1977) *The Countesthorpe Experience. The First Five Years*, London, George Allen & Unwin.

Wedge, Peter and Essen, Juliet (1982) *Children in Adversity*, London, Pan for the National Children's Bureau (NCB).

Weeks, Alan (1982) 'The conservative curriculum', *Times Educational Supplement (TES)*, 21 May.

—— (1983) *London Comprehensive Schools in 1982*, unpublished research report, Twickenham, St Mary's College.

—— (1983a) 'Force field', *Times Educational Supplement (TES)*, 20 May.

Whalley, G. E. (1970) 'Guided parental choice', *Trends in Education*, 18 April, 28–34.

Wiener, Martin, J. (1981) *English Culture and the Decline of the Industrial Spirit*, Cambridge, Cambridge University Press.

Wilby, Peter (1981) Letter to the *Times Educational Supplement (TES)*, 20 February.

Wilson, Stewart (1980) 'Eleventh Sessions at Sutton Centre as a Community Involvement' in Fletcher, Colin and Thompson, Neil (eds) *Issues in Community Education*, Lewes, Falmer Press.

Wood, Nick (1983) 'Groomed for the 1980s', *Times Educational Supplement (TES)*, 11 March.

Woods, Peter (1979) *The Divided School*, London, Routledge & Kegan Paul.

Yates, Alfred and Pidgeon, D. A. (1957) *Admission to Grammar Schools: third interim report of the allocation of primary school leavers to courses of secondary education*, Slough, National Foundation for Educational Research (NFER).

Young, D. A. and Brandis, W. (1971) 'Two types of streaming and their probable application in comprehensive schools' in Cosin, B. R., Dale, I. R., Esland, G. M., and Swift, D. F. (eds) *School and Society. A sociological reader*, London, Routledge & Kegan Paul.

Young, Michael (1958) *The Rise of the Meritocracy 1870–2033: an essay on education and equality*, London, Thames & Hudson.

Index